DARK SOULS

Also by Sarah Strudwick

Infidelity Unwrapped – A guide to Online Cheating

A Practical Handbook on Psychopathic Personalities

DARK SOULS

Healing and Recovering from Toxic Relationships

Sarah Strudwick

Second Edition
Date of Publication November 2010
Copyright © by Sarah Strudwick. All rights reserved Worldwide

British Library Cataloguing in Publication Data. A catalogue record for
this book is available from the British Library

Strudwick, Sarah.
Dark souls : healing and recovering from toxic relationships.
1. Strudwick, Sarah. 2. Strudwick, Sarah--Childhood and youth. 3.
Abused women--Biography. 4. Psychopaths--Family relationships. 5.
Personality disorders. 6. Self-analysis (Psychoanalysis) 7. Spiritual
healing. 8. Self-actualization (Psychology) in women.
I. Title
362.8'3'092-dc22
ISBN-13: 9780956645807

Published in the UK 2010 by SS Products
c/o 58a King Street
Kettering
Northants
NN16 8QP
England, UK

www.Noordinarylife.biz
www.Darksouls-thebook.com
email: noordinarylife7@googlemail.com

This book is dedicated to all the lost souls whose lives and spirits have been tainted by Dark Souls and want to find themselves again

CONTENTS

CONTENTS

CONTENTS

CONTENTS

Acknowledgements

I would like thank my children, Laura and Lewis, for putting up with their mother's endless hours spent researching and writing on the PC. They have had to put up with all kinds of hardships as a result of my near *fatal attraction* to Oliver especially when it came to me not being able to pay the bills. It is their strength of character that has inspired me to change, and to teach them how to have proper relationships so that they would not grow up repeating my mistakes, and those of my mother before me. Fortunately they share the same sense of humour and its one of the things that's carried us through as a family. I would also like to thank my ex husband for helping me out both financially and being supportive.

I like to look at the positives and things could have been much worse, my life has improved dramatically since I asked Oliver to leave.

If it wasn't for the help of "everyone" involved in this book including friends and family, this book would have never been published. This is the one time in my life when I swallowed my pride and actually asked for help.

I cannot express how grateful I am to John Nutting for giving me a metaphorical "kick up the arse" and inspiring me to make some changes in myself using voice dialogue. Special thanks go to John, Steve, Yvonne, Michael Gabriel and Melinda Sorensson for help with copy proofing. Its not been the easiest thing writing a book with ADHD without errors. To Dr. Michael Millett, I would like to thank him for all his patience and to my friends, Adam, Angela , Yvonne and Shelly I want to say say thank you for just being there.

Also, a big big thank you to Steve Becker for his inspirational comments, help and his expert knowledge on sociopaths and narcissists. I would also like to thank all of the other wonderful inspiring authors who have been kind enough to give me permission to used their quotes in this book and to Steve Van Aperen for his insightful comments on lying.

My thanks to Eileen Rawson for witnessing the weird esoteric "stuff" that happened after I asked Oliver to leave.

To my mum, I would like to say how proud I am for her understanding me finally. For finding herself after all these years and most importantly for seeing her smile and being genuinely happy for the first time in in many years.

On a final note I would like to thank my younger brother Jonathan Strudwick (AKA Doctor Jon the Magician) for being the good doctor and taking on the "evil role," using his acting and graphic skills and appearing on and designing the book cover, along with PJ, the photographer.

Forward

Written by Sam Vaknin, author of "Malignant Self-love: Narcissism Revisited"

"Dark Soul"! What a wonderful metaphor that captures the very essence of narcissistic psychopaths - although I prefer to think of the darkness that is at the core of pathological narcissism and psychopathy as an absence. It is dark there because these people have no souls at all.

Narcissistic psychopaths like to compare themselves to automata, robots, or machines. In many important respects they are forms of alien and artificial intelligence. They lack the ability to empathize, that quintessence that makes us human in the first place. Consequently, they regard others as mere instruments of gratification to be used, abused, and then contemptuously discarded.

Only a small minority of narcissistic psychopaths are sadistic. The vast majority are cold-blooded, calculated individuals in search of narcissistic supply (attention and adulation) or of material and other benefits. They are possessed of "cold empathy": the ability to instantly and unhesitatingly spot weaknesses and vulnerabilities. Devoid of conscience, they act promptly to leverage these to their advantage. They are not emotionless. On the contrary: they are at the mercy of a strong undercurrent of rage, hatred, and destructive envy. But they project their failings, they blame the world for their self-inflicted defeats, and they are out to grab and ruin and wreak havoc and extract revenge and throughout it all amass possessions, and power, and fame, and sexual conquests, and money, and, generally, have unmitigated fun.

Like all predators in nature, narcissistic psychopaths are great Thespians. They present a well-constructed (though precariously-balanced) façade aimed at charming people and luring them into their dens and webs of deceit. Only when it is too late, when the victim is already in the throes of a "relationship" does the outer shell crumble to reveal the monster. Extracting oneself from the spiralling mayhem that ensues often turns out to be a life-long and maiming quest. Victims are scarred forever, traumatized and adversely transformed. Many of them are unable to trust again.

This book is a painstakingly well-researched tour of the netherlands of such "relationships" with narcissists and psychopaths: the ups and downs, the promise and inevitable disillusionment, the cruelty and mind games and the heartbreak that is the inescapable aftermath. The author's first-hand experience translates into helpful insight both passioned and, where appropriate, impassioned. It is a useful and liberating guide for the perplexed, the disoriented, the sufferer, and the victim. It should be read and studied by both them and mental health practitioners.

Introduction

Dark souls really started off with my intention of finding out as much as I could about psychopathic personalities. I never intended on writing a book or an autobiography on psychopathic personalities. In fact I had actually started writing a book on spirituality before Oliver decided to return. Often these Darks Souls cause us to have an epiphany moment where we wake up spiritually and look at our lives in a different way.

Six months after asking him to leave and with my flat nearly finished, and 2 ½ stone lighter, I celebrate my birthday on July 2010 with a family picnic including my children, my mother, my brother and nephew and my two dogs, happy in the knowledge that my book was finally finished and my journey was over. I now start my new life with new hope and optimism and more importantly a new found wisdom that will stand me in good stead for any future relationships with men.

Although I am not a doctor or writer with professional training or a background in psychiatry, I wanted to explore what made these people tick. I wanted to find out why certain women were attracted to them and whether we were just as some books stated *targets;* or if it was something deeper like our own beliefs that got us into the relationships in the first place. Many books talk about the emotional, financial and physical carnage these people leave behind. However, based on my own experience, and having read many other women's stories and working with clients; the spiritual damage these people do to us is far more long lasting.

Some might compare it to having a *death of the soul* and unless we are able to find some tools to recover some victims remain in that state for years and years being turned into the very Dark Souls that abused us in the first place.

It is a well known fact that children of psychopath/sociopath parents may possibly grow up to be like their own parents however I was not prepared to become one of them and I also wanted to teach my own children how to have a good role model and inspire them not to have the same types of relationships that I had had and my mother before me.

For those of you who may be reading this book you may identity with some of the stories, including my own. If some of the character traits of these Dark Soul personalities ring true with your partner, my hope is that you seek help and that this book inspires you to step out of the victim mentality that keeps us glued to these people. They want us to be victims and by being our true authentic selves we can free ourselves of all the energetic gunk and toxic emotions we are left with from their unowned feelings.

Dark Souls is a handbook for spotting narcissistic psychopaths. It is also a story about a woman's journey to full recovery and healing. In this book you will find tools that you can use to facilitate your own healing journey along with useful insights and carefully researched material to support the pathology of these people. It explores the many ways in which they are likely to manipulate us, the mind games, the lies and more importantly the reason they chose us in the first place. This book places direct responsibility on the victims to look at their own behaviour and ask themselves "why did this happen?" without going into blame and guilt.

I make many generalizations about psychopathic personalities. Probably you will find that some comments are truer than others but at the end of the day we are all unique individuals with unique experiences.

Dark Souls are a complex mix of different psychopathic traits however any type of individual who displays signs of psychopathy or narcissism needs to be diagnosed by a professional healthcare worker.

Although you may decide to apply some of the insights in this book, some of which are immediately beneficial, this book does not replace the need for therapy and counselling for survivors of dysfunctional relationships. Your own journey to recovery is unique and can be as slow or as quick as you make it. However if you do not take time to heal properly there is a small possibility that you may attract another Dark Soul clone again.

I believe that many people can benefit from reading this book, not just victims, from those interested in what drives these people to healthcare professionals who may be able to better understand the affects on their victims. Having spoken to my own clients their immediate reaction was shock and disbelief and then "when can I buy your book".

We all live in a world where things are kept hidden and sometimes when someone speaks up and tells their own story it may shock people but inspires others to speak up too, with the outcome of finally saying No. Its an empowering place when you realise that you can finally put all of your childhood demons behind you and wont be a target for the rest of your life and the little red flashing neon sign that used to be there eventually becomes so insignificant you wonder what all the fuss was about.

As a result of the feedback I received from readers in this newer second edition I have added some additional information on Psychic Self Defence and Stalking which I hope benefits the readers.

I hope that this book gives you some insights into the minds of the Dark Soul and if you have been in a relationship with one, enables you to find the tools to heal and recover and have happy, healthy relationships in the future.

The Man in the Mirror

Well, Gorgeous, looks like you have been found out!

In the hall of mirrors, stands a man.

Looming behind him, dark clouds of darkness descend.

He smiles as he walks into the door of the darkened room,

But is surprised by the luminescent light of this woman in front of him

She shines so brightly;

He feels her warmth.

Radiating a coldness, he wants to get close to the fire

It feeds his empty shell.

Her airy grace of confidence and humble persona radiates warmth,

Her motherly instincts begs him near;

He nuzzles close as she draws him in closer,

The darkness and light such a powerful heady infusion.

Fused, it becomes a hazy shade of mist;

They exchange a kiss, a few words,

The sexual energy they exchange engulfs her

Like a predator about to be eaten alive, he has her hooked under his spell;

He wraps the cloak of darkness around her, slowly drawing each breath from her

She cannot breathe, she is intoxicated.

One slow breath at a time, she will give anything to have her fix

As the vampire drains the last gasp from his victim;

A tiny spark is still aflame in her soulless form.

What has become of the woman in the mirror?

He has taken her soul;

She smashes the mirror and as she does her soul essence is drawn back into her

And there he lies on the floor, the empty shell that was once filled, his lifeless body.

All her energy returned to its rightful place:

"I take back what is mine," she says as she walks away,

"You do not have any part of me anymore."

As she leaves the room the whole room lights up

She smiles, looking back at the darkness

Sooner or later, the light will always expose the darkness.

Sarah Strudwick 2008

1

What is a Dark Soul

"Do I feel bad when I hurt someone? Yeah, sometimes. But mostly it's just like... uh... [laughs]. I mean, how did you feel the last time you squashed a fly?"

The book is entitled Dark Souls and is the name that I came up with when looking at different types of psychopathic personalities after having had a relationship with a narcissistic psychopath. Having spent my adult life having one unhealthy relationship after another until I finally met Oliver who appeared to have all of the personality traits I came up with some other interesting terminology such as Shape Shifters, Energy Vampires and Black Holes because of the energetic damage they do to their victims. Any kind of victim can be damaged by a psychopath however as an Empath often we take on these feelings and end up taking on the unowned feelings these people want to project onto us.

Defining exactly what makes someone a psychopath, or psychopathic, isn't always easy, but one emphasizes, in the assessment, the individual's character traits and, more importantly, his or her impact on his or her victims. And then there is the persisting confusion over whether there's really a meaningful difference between what are called psychopaths versus sociopaths? Many clinicians and researchers use these terms interchangeably; there does not, in the vast literature on the subject, appear to be much, if anything, that meaningfully differentiates them.

So how do we understand or even test these people least of all spot them? There are dozens of psychological tests that are disorder-specific: they aim to diagnose specific personality disorders or relationship problems, for example the Narcissistic Personality Inventory (NPI) which is used to diagnose the Narcissistic Personality Disorder. In the case of psychopathy there is Dr Robert Hares second edition of the PCL-R test, which contains 20 items designed to rate symptoms which are common among psychopaths. The twenty traits assessed by the PCL-R score are: glib and superficial charm; grandiose estimation of self; need for stimulation; pathological lying; cunning and manipulativeness; lack of remorse or guilt; shallow affect (superficial emotional responsiveness); callousness and lack of empathy; parasitic lifestyle; poor behavioural controls; sexual promiscuity; early behaviour problems; lack of realistic long-term goals; impulsivity; irresponsibility; failure to accept responsibility for own actions; many short-term marital relationships; juvenile delinquency; revocation of conditional release; and criminal versatility.

Most tests are either objective or projective. In addition to Hare's PCL-R there are numerous other tests. In projective tests, the responses are not constrained and scoring is done exclusively by humans and involves judgement, which may also include some kind of bias. Clinicians rarely agree on the same interpretation and often use competing methods of scoring, yielding disparate results. In forming a diagnosis the diagnostician's personality becomes a prominent play.

In addition to the DSV diagnostic criteria there is also another diagnostic tool, The Structured Clinical Interview (SCID-II), which was formulated in 1997 by First, Gibbon, Spitzer, Williams, and Benjamin. It closely follows the language of the DSM-IV Axis II Personality Disorders criteria. There are 12 groups of questions corresponding to the 12 personality disorders. The scoring is equally simple. The feature that is unique to the SCID-II is that it can be administered to third parties including spouses and colleagues and still yield a strong diagnostic indication. The test incorporates probes that help verify the presence of certain characteristics and behaviours. There are other versions that can also be self-administered. Most practitioners who administer will use both the self-questionnaire and the self administered test to give a more accurate result.

Whether your partner is a psychopath, a sociopath, a narcissist suffering from NPD or both, or just plain passive aggressive, you cannot diagnose them yourself. It is essential that you get a professional to do it, assuming that you can get them near enough to a professional to evaluate and diagnose them in the first place.

Psychopaths can be found everywhere from the corporate executive at your workplace to your next door neighbour. They're fluent talkers with an uncanny ability to lie. If they change their stories they are able to do it without skipping a heartbeat. Most are totally comfortable in social situations and remain calm and cool under pressure. They are master manipulators and will think nothing of exaggerating or fabricating their credentials or even pretending to be someone else altogether. And when it comes to getting what they want they will say *anything* just to gain your trust. Words such as "I love you" "I am sorry" mean nothing to them, they are just one of the many tools a psychopath can use including the ability to mimic emotions and play on the heartstrings of their victims.

It has been estimated by some that one percent of the general population are psychopaths. As stated, psychopathy is a personality disorder characterized by an abnormal lack of empathy combined with strongly amoral conduct, masked by an ability to *appear outwardly normal*:

"I often torture myself. Wearing new masks and constantly adopting new personas pushes the envelope. My impersonations are increasingly demanding, and I'm often confronted with the limitations of what I can know/do/say. I regularly experience failure trying to pull it off, and I've lost friends and allies because I've either (1) chosen to be the wrong person, (2) given a poor, sloppy performance without studying the part, or (3) locked myself into a role that was too demanding, almost exhausting for the long run, so I had to make a messy 'exit.'"

(From Sociopathworld.com)

The Dark Soul is a combination of any or all of these three personality types.

On a law of averages we are likely to bump into one of these types of people every single day of our lives! So you think you can spot either of them? They blend easily and perfectly into society. They're entertaining and they are the life and soul at parties. They *appear* to be intelligent, fun loving and kind, and are usually very charming. But it is all just an illusion to get you sucked into their game. Will they be sorry for hurting you? Read on.

2

Life is Like an Amusement Ride

In the classic movie *Oliver,* a little boy gets up at the end of the table after dinner and asks very nicely for "more." This is what it feels like to be with a Dark Soul. They are very charming and they will always ask for more. This is why I have dubbed my ex, "Oliver."

My life has been like a ride in an amusement park. And when I went on it, I believed it was real because that's how powerful my mind was. My whole life's journey has been up and down, around and around, with thrills and chills. In some ways, it has also been very loud and brightly coloured. To be honest, it was even fun for a while.

But after a time, I started to ask "Is this real or is this just a ride." Whilst I was on this ride, I met a man by the name of Oliver. He appeared to be a mirror image of myself: a hard-working loving, and kind person. He had everything, including a house and a family, and yet, although everything about this man that appeared to be "real," was, in fact, a lie.

When I finally realised I wanted to get off of this ride because it was neither safe nor fun anymore, he did not want me to. I started to realise my own life was becoming a lie too. He said "I have a lot invested in this ride: look at my big bank account, look at all of my furrows of worry." I started to realise something was wrong.

However, he wanted to stay on the ride because he had convinced himself that his own life was so real and believed his own lies. When I tried to tell him so, he tried to shut me up and wanted to kill me. When I realised it was just a ride and I could change it any time I wanted, and that the demons could no longer hurt me, I finally got off the roller coaster. Even though I had no money, no house, or savings, for the first time in my life, I had a choice: a choice between Fear and Love.

I knew he was a direct reflection of my own darkest demons within me and I had to get off this ride otherwise it would kill me. This was not who I was, and however much this man had hurt me, all that I had believed about myself throughout my whole life had been an illusion.

He, on the other hand, continues to stay on the ride, taking everyone on the roller coaster with him.

This story is about my journey as an intuitive empath, and how we all can get into dysfunctional relationships. How, as a result, I ended up with a narcissistic psychopath. It is about understanding these people and learning how to heal from toxic relationships with them.

As a child, I grew up in a dysfunctional family believing I could fix things; that I could do something special, be someone different, but I wasn't quite sure what. I just wanted to make everyone happy. When I was a small child, most girls dreamed of being hairdressers or air hostesses. Amongst all the million things I had wanted to do, I wanted to be a spy. Little did I know I was to become one of the best detectives on the planet, and for all the wrong reasons. I was to become a few other things too, that I never either wished or dreamed for.

As a child, I remembered the lyrics of a song Doris Day sang, called "Que Sera, Sera:"

"When I was just a little girl, I asked my mother, what will I be? Will I be pretty? Will I be rich?"

If I had known then what I know now, I would have probably pulled the plug right there.

3

Our Beliefs

When we are born, we don't believe we are unlovable, or that we are fat and ugly, or that we deserve nothing better than to be in abusive, controlling relationships. As children, we aren't given the opportunity to choose our beliefs; we just agree with the information passed down to us. As children, we learn to trust in everything that our parents and teachers tell us. If we grow up believing ourselves to be beautiful and intelligent, then that becomes our reality. If we grow up believing we are stupid or lazy, we would equally accept that as our reality.

One of the most eye-opening and simple books I'd ever read (and I believe it should be given to children at an early age) is a book by Don Miguel Ruiz called *The Four Agreements*. He writes about the domestication of children when they are growing up. He refers to a "Book of Law," a collection of rules, and that if you go against it by "breaking the rules" you will feel an odd sensation in your solar plexus. That feeling, I believe, is Fear. To stay in a place where you are following the rules, you will remain safe in your comfort zone.

This is one of the reasons why people find it so hard to break childhood patterns and go on repeating self-sabotaging patterns by having destructive relationships, especially if you have grown up in a family that is dysfunctional and detrimental.

We are all guided by our belief system. I would like you to just let the following wash over you: as a child I used to play in the field and make daisy chains. Inevitably it would lead to picking off the petals one by one and playing "he loves me, he loves me not." As a child, I nearly always got "he loves me not." One day, as an adult, I went into the field and played the game again. I picked up one, two, three, four, up to twenty different daisies, starting off with "he loves me, he loves me not" and each time I got the same answer. I stopped and thought to myself for a moment: did all field daisies have the same number of petals? If that were the case, unless a petal had accidentally fallen off or if a daisy had an uneven number of petals by genetic anomaly, I would *always* get the same answer. I looked it up on the Internet and, sure enough, there are 34 petals on a field daisy, and very occasionally there may be one more or one less. So, unless you were to start off with "he loves me *not*, he loves me" you will nearly always get the same answer. The odds of getting "he loves me" are stacked right against you right from the beginning, because you are taught that the words "he loves me" comes first in the game.

Let's take Father Christmas, for example. I believed, until I was about four, that Father Christmas *did* exist and that he would come into the house down the chimney to bring our presents. One night, when I spied on my mother creeping into the bedroom and putting a full pillow case at the end of the bed, I came to the realisation that he did not exist. My brother, who is about three years older than me, was mortified when I had told him that Father Christmas was not real. Because he had become so upset, I never really forgave myself for telling him the "truth." So, when my own children were born, I made it into a more elaborate story than the one I had been told. I would leave biscuits out and carrots for the reindeer, even to the point of biting chunks off the biscuits until they finally realised it was complete nonsense. Now I can look back and laugh at myself for some of the things we grow up believing about ourselves.

Our beliefs about this life are often unfounded, and when we are willing to question them we are freed from the limitations that hold us back. We are also programmed since birth to believe what others want us to believe. This could be something as simple as how we perceive ourselves or something deeper like whether we should believe in God.

Belief systems are passed down from generation to generation and then selectively filtered out and changed according to the previous generation before us. They are also passed down from family to family, and so forth. We may all like to think that our beliefs come from rational thinking, deep experience and good judgement. However when we start to question we realise that this is not usually true.

It is not until we are adults that we start to understand that most of our beliefs are programmed in during our childhood. I am not just talking about Father Christmas or daisies but deep core beliefs such as believing you are not worth it, that you are fat and ugly, that you are better than everyone else, or that you need to repeat things the same way as your parents did.

We take on our childhood beliefs from our parents, mentors, teachers and siblings or people that played a significant part in our lives, and from society as a whole. Some beliefs we never question because they are entrenched into our consciousness. For example, we all now know that the world is not flat, and yet it took many years before someone proved that the world was round. However, stepping out of the conscious beliefs that we have held our entire lives can be very uncomfortable for many of us.

Often, we have a belief about ourselves that is untrue and we subconsciously try to prove the opposite to ourselves. Here's an example from my life. I was bought up in the sixties when Twiggy was the best thing since sliced bread and people were starting to become body conscious. My father was an overweight child. He was so fat that he could not walk until he was two years old. He carried that weight around for many years for a number of reasons. He was obese until the age of nineteen, when he finally dropped the weight. He became extremely skinny and went off to join the army when he finally left home, and his abusive father and manipulative mother.

Prior to meeting my mother, he became obsessed with being overweight believing that being fat was disgusting and wrong, and would project his beliefs about being overweight on my mother if she started to put on weight. She was normally a healthy size 10-12, and lost all her additional weight after having had children to become a very skinny size 8. As she grew older, she started to gain weight again and slipped up to a size 14. My father obsessed and nagged her about her size. He would make derogatory comments and say she was "disgusting," and made him feel sick.

When I was a teenager I, too, was "plump." In fact, I had been a bit plump most of my life. At twelve years old, I was nearly 5 foot 8 and weighed 11 stone. I was just over a size 12, bordering on a size 14. According to the height/weight charts I should only have been 9 ½ stone. So my father told me I needed to lose weight. First it started with sponsored diets which worked for a while then as I reached puberty I was eating salads most days. Since my natural weight was never going to be 9 ½ stone I was taken to the doctor and given slimming pills: Apisates, Dospans, and diuretic tablets that they would give to old women with heart problems to help them get rid of excess water. I took them for nearly 5 years and my weight never really changed and I ended up in a constant cycle of dieting, with an elusive goal of 9 ½ stone. It was years later when I had discovered the serious negative effects of taking these pills and how they make you feel that I realised what had happened and why as an adult I found it so difficult to lose weight when I did become big. These same pills are now considered dangerous and are banned for health reasons. The long-term side effects have proven to be fatal and are only even rarely used for the morbidly obese. If used inappropriately they are also proven to make people put on more weight when coming off them because their bodes have no idea how to metabolise properly.

I had grown up thinking I was fat and overweight and eventually proved it. And as a result I have struggled with my weight (at my biggest I was a size 24) until recently when I finally got down to a healthier size 16. Because of this one belief alone I have had many medical problems including depression in my early years, body dysmorphia, and bladder problems that continue into adult life.

I was determined to overcome them so I began some meditation work. To do this, I wanted some photographs of myself between the ages of ten and fifteen, so I asked my mother if she could pull some out for me. I could not believe my eyes. I had to show them to my friends to get their opinion and to make sure I was not going mad. In all of the pictures I had seen of me, from age ten until seventeen, I was slim and perfectly normal!

Based on my father's and societal beliefs, I had needlessly spent my teenage years on slimming pills and continued into adulthood believing myself fat and ugly. It's only after years of yo-yo dieting and finally revisiting that one core belief that I was finally able to discover what was true. I may struggle with my weight now but I was not born to be fat.

Now imagine that is just *one* core belief. How many core beliefs have we all been carrying around with us for years? Even positive beliefs can be turned into negatives because of other people's views. I read that a woman used to feel that she was the prettiest girl in the world but felt guilty about it.

Before we are able to change our beliefs, we first need to question them and then to ask ourselves whether or not they are empowering or limiting us. By asking ourselves this question, we can determine not only if they are true or false, but if we can change them and stop allowing them to determine our own actions in the future. We are only able to change or modify our beliefs the instant we receive new information. It's this constant awareness or thinking process that changes our perception of events.

Unlike my case which still took many years to resolve, some are a bit more difficult to identify and are often unconscious. You can just think of it as an illusion of the mind. Our mind is very clever at wrapping up all kinds of stories and beliefs in illusions that are simply not true.

Say you have a fear of starting a new job. You have been given the opportunity for a perfect new job but something is holding you back. You may think that your core belief is that you fear change. When you unwrap the illusion, you find that you have another core belief that goes along with it. For example, you may feel that you don't feel worthy of a new job and feel you are better off staying in the one you are in because you are afraid of change. You may unwrap a little further and find that you really don't want to take the risk of taking on a new job because you think you aren't clever enough. Finally, you may feel like you don't want success because you fear people might not like you. The problem is that unless you unravel the deepest core beliefs that drive you unconsciously, even if you took the job there is a good chance that you will sabotage your position in the future and keep on repeating your old patterns.

These are the same negative beliefs that drive us unconsciously to form negative relationships or relationships of inevitable harm.

So how did my "rule book" or negative beliefs about myself take Sarah Louise Strudwick from being a child that was born with a million and one gifts, like every other woman on the planet, and end up making her believe that she deserved nothing more than to have a relationship with a manipulative, lying Dark Soul?

I realised that most of what I believed about myself was not true. On the surface I appeared to be a strong confident woman and yet, underneath, my whole life was a mess when it came to relationships with men, and I was letting everyone control and manipulate me.

I had been lying to myself all along, I had no self esteem, my finances were in a shambles, and I was unhappy in a relationship with a man who was lying to himself and everyone around him. Yet in a weird way, most of the things I was to find out about him were a "reflection" of the things he was mirroring back to me. In other words, all that I needed to deal with was within me.

4

The Black Hole

Where does one start to write a book about healing from having been in a relationship with what appeared to be Mr Nice and normal but underneath the mask lies a Dark Soul? I have thought long and hard through my healing journey, which involved much soul searching and many tears, and after much research I believe that there is a process you need to go through to really heal. It is a journey, for some taking longer than others. You cannot rush it and if you do not process everything including the reasons why you got into the relationship in the first place you will be back to square one a few years along, entertaining yet another dysfunctional relationship. I believe the universe has a way of *upping the volume* until eventually you start listening.

I've had a number of *not-so-healthy* relationships and, one by one, the universe upped the volume because I just wasn't listening. Eventually it made me hear the inner demons I hadn't been prepared to face and my wakeup call came in the guise of a relationship with the most charming man you could ever wish to meet. Underneath the "mask," Oliver was an amplified clone of one of my closest family members. I ended up with nothing but a conman and an undiagnosed narcissistic psychopath.

Many books talk about the emotional damage a psychopath does to their victims. Some victims are unfortunate enough to have physical damage. While physical abuse might be the most visible sign, other types of abuse, such as emotional abuse also leave deep, long lasting scars. But there is another aspect into which I will delve a bit more deeply. My view is that much is overlooked about the *spiritual damage* they do to your energy field and many books miss out how you can actually heal from these people.

The tears have now gone. During the healing process the bitter taste never quite leaves you and you are left with the feeling that can only be described as aftershock, with nothing quite adding up. You always remain hyper vigilant to some degree, and you are left to clean up what can only be described as a relationship that had no substance, because the person you were with never really existed. Some people find it difficult to move on through the grieving process because it's unlike a normal relationship. However you can heal and there is light at the end of the tunnel. I hope that this book will inspire those of you who have been wounded by these people to pick up the pieces and come out shining, perhaps better than the way you were before you met them.

Although *anyone* is a target to a psychopathic personality, many of the victims who get preyed upon are highly sensitive, empathic and may also have come from previous relationships in childhood where they were abused. They may even on the surface appear to have removed the little "come and get me flag" that sits like a beacon on the top of their head. Psychopaths are extremely intuitive and can hone in on victims however successful and strong they appear on the outside, by looking for subtle clues even down to the way a target walks.

I was watching a video on psychopaths and there were twenty women, one of whom had this unusual kind of walk: a bit "oopsy daisy" and carefree. I too walked like that. The interviewer asked the psychopath which target would he choose and he explained that he always chose the women with the funny walk. It turned out all those women had been sexually abused as a child. In a speed dating experiment they took 50 women and 50 men in a room and told them to mingle together. One man was an abuser and one woman was a previous abuse victim. It took 3 minutes for them to find each other and leave the room together. That's how fast they can spot you. So, yes, a psychopath will use anyone for their needs, but if you're vulnerable, you are going to be spotted far more easily. It's because of this that your emotional warning radar needs to work better than theirs.

This book is partly about my own journey, it is also about spotting these predators in their numerous guises. There are ways in which you can disconnect and heal from the psychopath/narcissist in your life. But the essence of this book is about examining the core values within us that lead these people to finding us in the first place and how to get your emotional radar working one hundred per cent so that it never happens to us again. There are many victim stories and, make no mistake, the victims are out there in their thousands, but the only way to come out of the devastation that Psychopaths bring into our lives is to come out victorious and strong. After all, it was that strength of character in you that attracted them to you in the first place.

For the purposes of research, I have looked at the following types of personality: psychopaths, sociopaths, and those with Narcissistic

Personality Disorder (NPD). I've done so because many of these predators appear to have both sociopathy/psychopathy and/or NPD. There are many kinds of predators, and throughout this book I just call them Dark Souls. Sociopaths appear to be the lesser version of the psychopath, but they, too, are predators despite their everyday persona. There are many sociopaths living in the community and not all of them are locked up in prisons for murder.

Steve Becker, a well known writer who writes for a resource website on sociopaths, called Lovefraud.com wrote in an article entitled The Sociopath's Imperturbability"

> "But the point is, he just doesn't care. The sociopath just doesn't take these laws and interpersonal boundaries seriously, because he doesn't take you, or others, seriously."

So my wish is that what I write in this book is taken seriously enough for those people that have been affected by abusers that they may find some strength and courage in the reality that they can recover from these people. It's not an easy journey, but you can make it as easy or as difficult as you want to. As a small note to my abuser, if by chance he may be reading this book, and who ultimately tried to destroy my life and my sanity: you did not break me, and I am back, fighting and strong, exactly as I was before you met me. It is my humour, my spirit, and my willpower that have kept me strong and helped me to come out of this, although the scars will remain forever. They can try and pinch your money and your possessions, but they cannot steal your soul and spirit. They will try their very best, especially if you are Empathic, but when you finally heal from them, you will come out shining.

I have always been passionate about spiritual energy and the universe and, in my naivety, I wrongly assumed that everyone was good. Of course now I realise that is not true; it was just a fairy tale I wanted to believe in. I was trying to think of the perfect name for these people and I called up a friend of mine, Dr. Michael Millett. He uses hypnosis and EFT, and has a Masters Degree in Metaphysical Science (M. MSC) with the University of Metaphysics, Sedona, Arizona, USA. We were discussing the concept of how psychopathic people such as sociopaths and narcissists had the need to feed off their victims, a bit like energy vampires, and somehow got to talking about quantum singularities, known more commonly as black holes. No one really knows exactly what a black hole is, although it's clear that a black hole sucks everything in; not even light can escape it, which is why it appears black and invisible.

Scientists believe that a black hole occurs when a massive star, much larger than our sun, runs out of fuel. The remaining mass of the star collapses in on itself, causing an enormous vacuum that draws everything around it, including light, into itself.

This is exactly how sociopaths appear to us. Their *real* personalities are invisible to everyone else around them and they spend their lives sucking people in drawing in the light and positive qualities of their victims' personalities, money, or whatever they can get from them. Once you are in a relationship with them it's extremely difficult to get out. Anything or anyone that is sucked in will be eventually depleted until there is nothing left. Once you have been sucked dry emotionally, spiritually, and financially, it's almost impossible to leave, whilst they, on the other hand (especially if they are narcissistic), thrive on your *light* or energy. Perhaps they will be enjoying all the money they have sponged from you. Of course, the minute they have run out of supply, they will move on to the next victim because, like the black hole, they constantly need input to survive.

I must point out, without prejudice, that I am not a psychologist. I have referenced and discussed sociopaths, psychopaths and narcissists throughout the book with the help of colleagues. Although to some degree, all the pathological personalities tend to have vast similarities among them, the little dissimilarities between them make them stand apart. Therefore, it is very important to go through the case history of an individual before labelling him or her as a sociopath, psychopath, or narcissist.

My ex, Oliver, fits into several of these classifications, including the "black hole" category. I wondered if I should bestow Oliver with such a grand title as Black Hole, which, with so much power associated with it, would only inflate his galaxy-sized ego. A black hole conjures up the image of a bottomless void that relentlessly feeds on light. If you think about people and energy, although we all exchange energy amongst ourselves, both sociopaths and narcissists tend to be energy vampires, i.e. only consuming. In the case of a sociopath, I would describe them from an energy point of view, as consciously and intentionally *stealing* your energy for themselves, be it for fun or out of vindictiveness. The narcissists' reality is so distorted and dark they may not even realise that they are doing anything wrong, and their inner darkness is temporarily made brighter by those people that feed their false egos.

I pondered on the concept that actually there is some debate as to whether psychopaths have a soul at all. In the book, *The Mask of Sanity*, Hervey Cleckley speculates that what is really wrong with these people is that perhaps they lack a soul. Whereas Adolf Guggenbuhl-Craig, author of *Emptied Soul*, implies that psychopaths are just lost souls. Eileen Rawson who works as a space clearer and healer suggested that these people have a "walk-in" soul that takes over their bodies. Sam Vaknin suggests in the forward that the narcissistic psychopath has no soul at all.

As the debate goes on, I therefore decided to give Oliver and other predators a lesser title and nicknamed him a Dark Soul. I have also used the same term as a general label for predators and disordered personalities who abuse victims. Why? Because they are all very similar and it implies that they *might* have a soul but that it is a soul that is tainted and perhaps somewhat damaged and that a big chunk of it is missing.

5

The Broken Bed

I begin my description of Oliver with an analogy, a man who, in his quest to destroy me, left me with no option but to put some humour into my tale. My sense of humour was one of the endearing things he found so appealing when he had first decided to prey upon me. Since the only time these people have any sense of humour is when they are hurting us, I hope that by coming out strong and victorious with a little bit of humour thrown in along the way, it will go some way towards restoring the balance.

When you first meet a Dark Soul you have no idea what their motives are and how very difficult they are to discern. When we had first met, Oliver, who came from an excellent family, was charming, well mannered, and sophisticated. He appeared to be the perfect "nice guy." However, eventually, the cracks start to appear. It's a bit like buying a new house that you think is your *perfect* home, only to find that it was built on a shoddy foundation, the structure is crumbling, and there is no insurance policy in place to cover it when it all starts to collapse.

Oliver worked for a company for over 10 months, going to work daily as the sales manager of an eco-friendly company where he was supposedly selling wind turbines. In fact, he had been fired from more than four jobs during the time that I'd known him. Being with a Dark Soul is like uncovering the pieces of a jigsaw puzzle. Five months after telling me he had cancer when a lump was removed from his head, and a second dose of cancer that miraculously re-appeared the following year, but then went into "remission". I would go on to spend nearly five years in a relationship with him. I once called up his firm to learn that he had been fired from his job six months earlier, and, moreover, the so-called wind turbine sales manager job had never even existed. It turned out that Oliver had, in fact, been working for an unethical, environmentally *unfriendly* company (that had been investigated by the press for their unscrupulous sales practices), selling products on a commission only basis at extortionate prices to poor victims, especially to old and infirm customers. When I had contacted a former salesman from that same company, he had chosen to describe the business as being "at the top of the food chain," which, by coincidence, is a fitting description for a Sociopath, too, since he feeds off victims for his own gain and pleasure. So much for his eco-friendly job!

When I finally kicked Oliver out in January 2010, I had sold my house the previous year and lost everything, but I had exposed him for who he really was after having played private detective. The last straw was his "impotency" story with which he had strung me along for about 3 months. I realised that *everything* he had told me about himself was a lie, not the least of which was an interesting double life which included bisexual swinging and being a sperm donor to lesbian women.

I had uncovered a whole can of worms and so I confronted Oliver. At least I was lucky enough to know his real name unlike other victims who don't even discover who their partner is. I remember a couple of times laughing at some of the stupid things I have allowed myself to put up with over the last couple of years, but it's when you can look back and laugh that you know you've really healed. With beds, sex, lies, and impotency on my mind, I dreamed up *an analogy* of a salesman for a company whereby the "product" was actually Oliver himself. Here is what I wrote:

The Crapmatic Salesman

It was about five years ago, when one day I decided to go shopping and buy myself a lovely new "bed." The salesman was lovely, attractive, and well-mannered, and the product appeared to be fantastic. It was unique and "special," unlike any other product I had ever known. It also had all kinds of gadgets and things I had never seen before. Oliver demonstrated the product with great skill and, before long, I was convinced that this was a bed I needed to have. He even suggested that it might benefit my health and well-being and would therefore be a good long-term investment. In my head I knew I couldn't afford it but he played on my emotions so well with such skill and dexterity and made it sound lovely and appealing I could not resist the urge to buy it. Even the option to "buy now, pay later" didn't put me off. I was sure I could have it and pay the instalments as they came due. I had never thought about reading the fine print.

He was such a genuine salesman and I truly believed I was getting a product that was unique and exclusive. I bided my time for a while. Tested it out and it appeared to feel quite comfortable. I sat on it a number of times and although the mattress appeared to be firm, at times it felt a bit uncomfortable. When I questioned the good salesman, he always had a great answer: "No problem! Any problems with the manufacture are guaranteed. I promise this bed will never let you down." He seemed to use the word "promise" a lot, but it helped to convince me that it might be a good idea to invest in this bed after all. With all the claims he had made and all the guarantees I felt I had nothing to lose.

I made my decision. But after a few weeks the bed began to develop a number of faults. I was paying big instalments every single month and the interest was exorbitant. I realised I couldn't afford this bed and finally read the fine print and realised I had made a huge error in the calculations and I would be paying for this bed for the rest of my life. Not only did this bed *not* offer what it claimed but health benefits were nil, contrary to what the salesman had promised. I started to feel very unwell, the bed worsened my health, and I could not sleep. First, it was a few little things like a small tear in the mattress which the manufacturers promised to fix. They did but they came with a staple gun and did a botched up job and then it tore again, even worse than before. Then one of the springs went. I couldn't sleep on the mattress anymore, and demanded a new one. Oliver said, "It's not a problem! It's quite normal for a mattress to be "bumpy." It takes time for it to settle. Just be patient and it will all be fine!" I waited and waited and still I got the same answer every single time.

It was one promise after another and all the time I was paying interest. My debt was accumulating and still I was not sleeping comfortably. Often, I would be awake all night. The bed had all kinds of "interesting" gadgets that Oliver had said were unique to my particular model and could not be found anywhere else on the planet. It had a remote control that allowed the bed to go up and down. However one day the remote control broke completely. He promised to fix it but I realised it was irreparable. I had to console myself with the fact that I was sleeping in a bed that could no longer go up and down any more! I was mortified. How could they sell me such a shoddy bed that didn't work properly and, more importantly, at an overinflated price?

When I finally did some investigation I realised that this bed was not "unique" and "special," and that the same "model" had been sold to number of different women over the years. They had all had the same problems. They had bought the bed in good faith only to find it faulty and useless. Moreover, they had invested a huge amount of cash trying to get the bed fixed, only to find that their investment was, in fact, worthless! I was left feeling I had been well and truly conned...

We all invest in "beds" at some point and some are more expensive than others in terms of health, financial, and emotional costs. We trust the salesman to be telling us the truth.

I realised that the bed I had been sold was really Oliver himself, in an analogy for how he sold himself to people. And that is exactly how these conmen sell their products to their customers. What you see is definitely *not* what you get. I am not one to go down without a fight and my own story is quite shocking. It includes some of the most despicable lies and deceit you could possibly imagine. I guess one of the most painful things is coming out of a relationship with a person you think is your "soul mate" or "twin soul" who had, on the previous day, declared their undying love to you. A man who had said they were "waking up spiritually" and wanted to create a website with me about Twin Flames, after he left his wife. Then, when you confront them with more lies, the following day they are nowhere to be found and you are concerned about their safety, you are literally dumped as if you never existed because they were found out. Then the tables are turned back on you and they are threatening you if you try and expose them.

The irony is that Oliver had worked for one of the biggest companies that were known for conning people out of their hard earned money selling faulty products to vulnerable people like the sick and elderly. Their sales tactics were ruthless: a perfect job for a sociopath. The company had claimed that they crafted their beds with skill and quality, yet they had come under investigation by international trading standards for years for unethical practices. They had become insolvent more than a couple of times as a result, and then suddenly reinvented themselves, just as the sociopath does, under a lovely new name.

You will discover when you have relationships with Dark Souls that they lie consistently, and Oliver, always full of grandiose ideas about himself, lied through his teeth. I remember him telling me one day that MI5 had called him up for an interview and he was so convinced of his own lies he even believed it to be true. He told me he had been head-hunted through an agency. When I had quizzed him about why he wouldn't go for the job after all, he said he didn't want to take it because it would mean him being away from his children too much. Most of their life is a fantasy story that they make up as they go along. On discovering the fact he had been fired from his "eco- friendly" job and remembering the MI5 story, I tried to keep my sense of humour. When he had come home that evening, I had left him a note on his bed saying "I see you have been working 'under cover.'

Being the eternal optimist, I had decided to turn the dodgy bed story around and see it through the Dark Soul's eyes. Although I cannot – and will not – diagnose Oliver, he showed many of these traits. The most common denominators are a lack of Empathy, a feeling of entitlement, and no feelings of guilt or conscience.

If a Dark Soul were to buy themselves a new luxury top-of-the-range bed with a hundred and one gadgets that did the most amazing things, they would probably show it off to all of their friends. Chances are, they would probably find a way of getting it for free. Probably they'd try stealing it or lying on the purchase agreement forms, but, either way, they would do their best to get it for nothing. What do you think would happen if a normal person brought this type of product home? If you were to purchase a wonderful new "toy" like a bed or a TV, and then find out that it no longer works and the warranty is null and void: the only option, if it were a large item, would be to repair it, give it to someone else, or take it to the local skip and dump it.

This is how a Dark Soul sees the object of their desire, i.e. you.

6

Disordered People

So What Exactly Is a Psychopathic Personality?

A psychopathic personality is a class of personality types and behaviours that the American Psychiatric Association (APA) defines as "an enduring pattern of inner experience and behaviour that deviates markedly from the expectations of the culture of the individual who exhibits it."

The APA is the main professional organization of psychiatrists and trainee psychiatrists in the United States, and the most influential worldwide. The association publishes various journals and pamphlets, as well as the Diagnostic and Statistical Manual of Mental Disorders, or DSM.

The onset of these patterns of behaviour can typically be traced back to late adolescence and the beginning of adulthood and, in rare instances, can stem from their childhood. Psychopathy is most strongly related to Anti Social Personality disorder, which according to the American Psychiatric Association's DSM is "a pervasive pattern of disregard for, and violation of, the rights of others that begins in childhood or early adolescence and continues into adulthood."

People having Antisocial Personality Disorder are sometimes referred to as "Sociopaths." There is much debate over the use of the term sociopath or Antisocial Personality Disorder. The sociopath is now described as someone with Antisocial Personality Disorder. The main characteristic of a Sociopath is his or blatant disregard for the rights of others and his or her total lack of Empathy. Sociopaths are also unable to conform to what society defines as normal, although on the surface to other people they usually appear extremely normal.

They are almost certainly unable to hold down a steady job and find it difficult to sustain relationships. One of the major traits of sociopaths is their total indifference to others; this can appear as a disregard for the physical or sexual well being of their victims.

Sociopathy appears to be more common in men than women, although this may be because the male sociopath is more likely to receive a diagnosis. Although my book is aimed at "Dark Souls", in particular men, based on my own experiences, there is no question that women can be equally dangerous. Martha Stout refers to female sociopaths in her excellent book *The Sociopath Next Door*, as do Roy Sheppard and Mary T Cleary, whose book *Venus: The Dark Side* deals entirely with female sociopaths.

Like many other personality disorders, antisocial personality disorder has symptoms that can be explained by the presence of other conditions, and these conditions must be ruled out during diagnosis. Such conditions include manic episodes and schizophrenia, as well as other personality disorders, including: narcissistic personality disorder, histrionic personality disorder, borderline personality disorder, paranoid personality disorder.

Typical personality disorders that might exhibit psychopathic behaviour might include the above but many people diagnosed with Anti Social Personality Disorder or psychopathy patients are also diagnosed with Narcissistic Personality Disorder and/or Borderline Personality.

One final point about the often confusing, interchangeable terminology used to describe the constellation of exploitative personalities. My book will be focused on the psychopathic personality, to be defined more specifically ahead. Although I will be referring to these personalities as psychopaths, I do not see, in the literature, much to differentiate them from so-called sociopaths, although some researchers see differences.

Psychopaths and sociopaths both seem to represent the human being's highest capacity for ongoing exploitation of others. In contrast, individuals diagnosed with Antisocial Personality Disorder may also be psychopathic or sociopathic, but *not* necessarily. The diagnosis antisocial personality disorder has, historically, been very behaviourally and criminally weighted, and thus encompasses a much larger percentage of the population, especially the incarcerated population, than the more specific, nuanced diagnoses of psychopath and sociopath. The latter two diagnoses weed out from the greater pool of rule and law-breakers the truly manipulative, deceptive, unconscionable exploiters.

Psychopaths

Psychopathy is a personality disorder whose hallmark is a lack of Empathy. Psychopaths are glib and superficially charming, and many psychopaths are excellent mimics of normal human emotions; some psychopaths can blend in, undetected, in a variety of surroundings, including corporate environments. There is neither a cure nor any effective treatment for psychopathy; there are no medications or other techniques which can instill empathy, and psychopaths who undergo traditional talk therapy only become more adept at manipulating others. The consensus among researchers is that Psychopathy stems from a specific neurological disorder which is biological in origin and present from birth. It is estimated that as many as one percent of the general population are psychopaths.

To expand of some of the psychopath traits.

Glibness and Superficial Charm, Manipulative and Conning

Psychopaths don't recognize the rights of others and see their self-serving behaviours as permissible. They may appear to be charming, yet are covertly hostile and domineering. Their victim is merely an instrument to be used.

Grandiose Sense of Self;

Psychopaths feel entitled to certain things as "their right." This includes pathological lying. Being expert liars, it is almost impossible for them to be truthful on a consistent basis. They can create, and get caught up in, a complex web of deceit and belief about their own powers and abilities. They are extremely convincing and even able to pass lie detector tests.

Lack of Remorse, Shame or Guilt

Some speculate a deep seated rage, split off and repressed, as lying at the psychopath's core. Psychopaths do not see others around them as people, but only as targets and opportunities. Instead of friends, they have victims and accomplices who end up as victims. The end always justifies the means and they let nothing stand in their way.

Shallow Emotions

When psychopaths express what seems to be warmth, joy, love, and compassion it is a mask and based on feigned, "mimicked" emotions rather than experienced emotions; it always serves an ulterior motive. They may be bored by insignificant matters and outraged at inconveniences, yet remain unmoved and cold in the face of what would upset a normal person. Since they are not genuine, neither are their promises.

Incapacity for Love with a need for Stimulation

Often psychopaths live on the edge with a need for stimulation. Verbal outbursts and physical punishments are normal. Promiscuity, gambling and infidelity are common. Sexual deviancy, sexual abuse, rape and sexual acting out of all sorts is also commonplace.

Callousness and Lack of Empathy

Psychopaths appear unable to empathize with the pain of their victims, having only contempt for others' feelings of distress and readily taking advantage of them.

Poor Behavioural Controls and Prone to Impulsive Nature

Rage and abuse, alternating with small expressions of love and approval produce an *addictive cycle* for abuser and abused, as well as creating hopelessness in the victim. In their grandiosity, psychopaths believe they are all-powerful, all-knowing, with a deep sense of entitlement. They have no sense of personal boundaries, no concern for their impact on others.

Early Behaviour Problems or Juvenile Delinquency

Psychopaths usually have a history of behavioural and academic difficulties, yet they usually "get by" by conning others. Often, you will find their references or qualifications do not add up. They have problems in making and keeping friends, or they may lack friends altogether. There is also a higher incidence in their histories of early cruelty, such as to people or animals.

Irresponsibility and Unreliability

Psychopaths are not concerned about wrecking others' lives and dreams. They are often oblivious or indifferent to the devastation they cause their victims. They will not accept blame themselves, but blame others, even for acts they obviously committed.

Lack of Realistic Life Plan/Parasitic Lifestyle

Psychopaths tend to move around a lot or make all encompassing promises for the future; often, they also exhibit a poor work ethic, although they're inclination and capacity to exploit others remains constant.

Criminal or Entrepreneurial Versatility

Psychopaths may change their image and/or identity, as needed, to avoid detection and perhaps prosecution. They may change their life story readily. They may also have a history of failed jobs and change careers often because of their inability to hold down a job.

Some exploitive combination of the above characteristics separates psychopaths from the rest of the population. This isn't to say that "normal" individuals aren't capable of any of these attitudes and behaviours. Rather, it's to stress that these characteristics are endemic to the psychopath's make-up. They don't just describe the psychopath, they *define* the psychopath.

Narcissists

Mirror, Mirror on the Wall
Who Is the Most Narcissistic Person of All?

The term "Narcissist" is from the Greek word *Narcissus*, meaning "sleep, numbness." In Greek mythology, he was a hero from the territory of Thespiae in Boeotia who was renowned for his beauty. In the various stories, he is exceptionally cruel, in that he disdains those who love him. As divine punishment, he falls in love with a reflection in a pool, not realizing it was his own, and perishes there, not being able to leave the beauty of his own reflection.

Healthy narcissism is formed through a structural truthfulness of the self, achievement of self and object constancy, synchronization between the self and the superego and a balance between libidinal and aggressive drives (the ability to receive gratification from others and the drive for impulse expression). Healthy narcissism forms a constant, realistic self-interest and mature goals and principles and an ability to form deep object relationships. A feature related to healthy narcissism is the feeling of greatness. This is used to avoid feelings of inadequacy or insignificance.

Healthy narcissism exists in all individuals. Freud says that this is an original state from the individual from where to develop the love object. Freud argues that healthy narcissism is an essential part in normal development. The love of the parents for their child and their attitude towards their child could be seen as a revival and reproduction of their own narcissism according to Freud. The child has an omnipotence of thought. The parents stimulate that feeling because in their child they see the things that they have never reached themselves. Compared to neutral observations, the parents tend to overvalue the qualities of their child. When parents act in an extreme opposite style and the child is rejected or inconsistently reinforced depending on the mood of the parent, the self needs of the child are not met.

In pathological narcissism such as the narcissistic personality who has Narcissistic Personality Disorder, the person's libido has been withdrawn from objects in the world and produces megalomania. Some clinical theories see pathological narcissism as a possible outcome in response to unsympathetic and inconsistent early childhood interactions. They suggested that narcissists try to compensate in adult relationships. The pathological condition of narcissism is, as Freud suggested, a magnified, extreme manifestation of healthy narcissism.

Narcissistic Personality Disorder

Although most individuals have some narcissistic traits, high levels of narcissism can manifest themselves as Narcissistic Personality Disorder (NPD), whereby the patient overestimates his or her abilities and has an excessive need for admiration and affirmation. In order for a person to be diagnosed with NPD, they must meet five or more of the following symptoms:

1. Has a grandiose sense of self-importance (e.g. exaggerates achievements and talents, expects to be recognized as superior without commensurate achievements)

2. Is preoccupied with fantasies of unlimited success, power, brilliance, beauty, or ideal love

3. Believes that he or she is "special" and unique and can only be understood by, or should associate with, other special or high-status people (or institutions)

4. Requires excessive admiration

5. Has a sense of entitlement, i.e., they have unreasonable expectations of especially favourable treatment for themselves or automatic compliance with his or her expectations

6. Is interpersonally exploitative, i.e. they take advantage of others to achieve his or her own ends.

7. Lacks empathy and is unwilling to recognize or identify with the feelings and needs of others.

8. Is often envious of others or believes that others are envious of him or her.

9. Shows arrogant, haughty behaviours or attitudes

NPD is considered to result from a person's belief that they are flawed in a way that makes them fundamentally unacceptable to others. This belief is held below the person's conscious awareness. If confronted or questioned, such a person would typically deny thinking such a thing. In order to protect themselves against the intolerably painful rejection and isolation that they imagine would follow if others recognized their supposedly defective nature, such people make strong attempts to control others' view of them and behaviour towards them. They may do this in a number of ways by taking advantage of people, lying and manipulating to achieve their own needs and exploiting people.

Sam Vaknin D, a twice diagnosed narcissist, writes:

"The Narcissist's sense of entitlement encourages his indolence. He firmly believes that he should be spoon-fed and that accomplishments and honours should be handed to him on a silver platter, without any commensurate effort on his part. His mere existence justifies such exceptional treatment. Many Narcissists are under-qualified and lack skills because they can't be bothered with the minutia of obtaining an academic degree, professional training, or exams."

He further writes:

"My name is Sam Vaknin. I'm a Ph.D. My book, Malignant Self Love - Narcissism Revisited, offers a detailed, first-hand account of what it is like to have a Narcissistic Personality Disorder (NPD). It offers new insights and an organized methodological framework using a new psycho dynamic language. I warn you, though, Narcissism is a slippery subject. The Narcissist is an actor in a mono drama, yet forced to remain behind the scenes. The scenes take centre stage, instead. The Narcissist does not cater at all to his own needs. Contrary to his reputation, the Narcissist does not "love" himself in any true sense of the word. He feeds off other people who hurl back at him an image that he projects to them. This is their sole function in his world: to reflect, to admire, to applaud, to detest – in a word, to assure him that he exists. Otherwise, they have no right to tax his time, energy, or emotions – so he feels."

Narcissistic Rage

Narcissistic rage is a term coined by Heinz Kohut in 1972. This article, entitled "Psychoanalytic Study of the Child," pertains to Kohut's use of the concept in Kohut's Self Psychology, a school of thought within the psychodynamic/psychoanalytic theory. Narcissistic rage is a reaction to narcissistic injury, when the narcissist feels degraded by another person.

When the narcissist's grandiose sense of self-worth is perceivably being attacked by another person (typically in the form of criticism), the narcissist's natural reaction is to rage and pull down the self-worth of others (to make the narcissist feel superior to them). It is an attempt by the narcissist to soothe their internal pain and hostility, while at the same time rebuilding their own self-worth. Narcissistic rage should not be confused with anger (although the two are similar), and is not necessarily caused by a situation that would typically provoke anger in an individual. Narcissistic rage also occurs when the narcissist is perceivably being prevented from accomplishing their grandiose fantasies. Narcissistic rage is frequently short-term, and passes when the narcissist rationalizes the shame that they felt. Interestingly enough, rage doesn't last for very long; it's often over in moments but it is explosive. Narcissistic rage can be very explosive or passive aggressive:

Explosive rage - The narcissist erupts and attacks everyone in their immediate vicinity. They may cause damage to objects or people. It is usually verbal and psychologically abusive.

Passive aggressive -The narcissist will say nothing at all. They may sulk or give the silent treatment. However in the background they are plotting their next move on how to punish the perpetrator and put them in their place. These types of Narcissists are far more sneaky and vindictive and often prone to becoming stalkers.

When they go into Rage, they can be extremely dangerous and highly unpredictable. It will happen when you least expect it. They never forget anything. So if you slight them they will have it marked up on the "I hate you scoreboard" to use against you later. A close friend of mine was saying how her narcissistic ex had gone into a complete rage one day because she "stole" his last sweet. Years later she was eating a chocolate and as she was about to eat the nut in the middle he snatched if off her and said "that's for stealing my sweet all those years ago." Often their rage is not always physical and comes out in passive aggressive ways. They will turn up late and then tell you they hadn't arranged to meet you or selectively "forget" to do things. If you ever criticise them you will have your work cut out for you trying to repair the damage. Whenever they criticise you or anyone else they are normally making autobiographic statements about themselves.

Understanding the Narcissist

What is confusing is that when they are "upset" it is in a different way from how normal people are upset. When this happens they can be dangerous. So how does this work?

There is a big difference between insulting a narcissist and a *narcissistic injury.* A narcissist is all about "them," therefore in their mind they "exist." To exist they thrive off narcissistic supply, whether it be giving them adoration or insulting them. You showing that he does not exist in your life by kicking him in the teeth and telling him he is a cretin; with a long letter, explaining how much they have hurt you; or saying they have no credibility or even providing evidence to that effect, is *not* a narcissistic injury. Why? Because doing any of these things shows he must therefore exist. You could even go as far as to humiliate him and tell him he has a small penis or use references from past relationships. They might feel hurt, but to the narcissist this is not a narcissistic injury either. If you are not sure about this paragraph, then re read it again, as this is the core of understanding the narcissist.

In the meantime they might actually do things on purpose and actually expect you to write such a letter, and, if you don't bother, it might make them even more angry, because everything is someone else's fault, and what they want is a reaction to their childlike behaviour. They may react by insulting you or acting up, causing *you* to react. Often this is seen when the marriage of a narcissist is failing and they intentionally go out and cheat.

They have a massive self-destruct button which they can switch on at any moment: getting themselves into the most ridiculous of situations just so they can get caught or even told off. Remember they *need* narcissistic supply and it doesn't matter whether it's good or bad, since any attention is supply. If you react, they may insult you back, or cry, or ask forgiveness, or beg for mercy, but they will do anything to maintain the relationship. They may say and do outrageous things that they know will cause you to respond again, making promises they cannot keep to prolong your connection with them, even if they cause themselves misery. They do not care that their actions makes both you and them miserable; all they actually care about is that there is a *you* and there is *them*.

However, one of the worst things you can do is to ignore a narcissist or become indifferent to them. If you ignore or humiliate them (i.e. an actual narcissistic injury) they will want to kill you. Not all narcissists will kill everyone who injures them. The point is that they are raging. They may never act on it, or they may break a window, or try and attempt suicide.

If you want to have the upper hand with a narcissist, start exposing their secrets or at least threaten them with it. Their biggest fear is others finding out the real truth about them. It is the narcissist's greatest fear and injury, revealing their mask. They will do anything to avoid this including leaving you alone. A warning, however, is you have to be extremely careful when doing this. If you do this you may risk putting yourself and others in danger. Many a narcissist has flipped out and murdered people for this reason.

Devalue and Discard

"The narcissist will only act civilised towards potential Sources of Narcissistic Supply. If, when the relationship is over, he believes you are likely to supply him with adoration or attention then he will not devalue and discard you and will make the separation as courteous as possible. If on the other hand he judges you to be useless as far as future Narcissistic Supply goes, he will likely dump you, discard, devalue and even purposefully hurt you in the process ". As Sam Vaknin puts it,

"That's all there is to it. Narcissists regard other people as you might regard a faucet. As long as it spews forth water, you maintain it. Once it stops, you ignore it without giving it a second thought."

He goes onto say:

"Narcissists sometimes fail to say goodbye because they find it difficult to confront their own failure. It is too painful and threatening. Narcissists are terrified of pain. The False Self – the essence of pathological narcissism – is an elaborate, multi layered reaction to past traumas and their attendant anguish. The Narcissist is conditioned by his torturous past to avoid grief at any cost – even at the cost of self-annihilation and re-invention as a narrative, a piece of fiction. "

It is often difficult for the victims of narcissists to understand what has really happened to them. They believe that the narcissist loved them and cared for them but it was not real, just a confabulated lie based on their false ego. When they end the relationship, they find the narcissist either devalues and discards them, leaving them to question the reality of the relationship, or he ignores them using the silent treatment. If you return to a narcissist they will continue on as if nothing happened especially if they are lacking in Narcissistic Supply. And so the cycle continues.

Sam Vaknin. Goes onto say:

"The narcissist simply discards people when he becomes convinced that they can no longer provide him with Narcissistic Supply. This conviction, subjective and emotionally charged, does not have to be grounded in reality. Suddenly – because of boredom, disagreement, disillusion, a fight, an act, inaction, or a mood – the narcissist wildly swings from idealisation to devaluation.

The narcissist then detaches immediately. He needs all the energy he can muster to obtain new Sources of Narcissistic Supply and would rather not spend these scarce resources over what he regards as human refuse, the waste left after the extraction of Narcissistic Supply."

When you are discarded overnight you are left stunned and confused. It doesn't matter how much time you have spent with them or how much you have given them. The callous speed that they exit your lives and disregard their victims is astounding. Unless you leave them first you you must be prepared for this kind of harsh and sudden betrayal at a time of his choosing, not yours. Why because he has run out of Narcissist Supply.

If on the other hand you continue to give him Narcissistic Supply but have already unmasked him he will still discard you anyway but only when its suits him.

Narcissists and Projection

I had an interesting conversation with an NLP practitioner who said to me once that perception is projection. While this sounds a touch cryptic, it actually means that we are fully in charge of what we perceive from other people. Simply put, what we recognize in others as being arrogant or opinionated or any other charming description, we actually recognize as part of ourselves, otherwise how would we be able to know what it was? So, basically, what we see in others is really ourselves. This is the basis for NLP and mirroring people. Therefore the theory would be that if you are with a narcissist and they are being angry its because you are angry and if they are being controlling its because you are controlling. So does that also mean we are all Dark Souls or narcissists underneath ?

However with the exception of having the same sense of low self worth in relationships, I am actually quite different from Oliver in many ways. I don't get easily angered, I tend not to procrastinate and I stick at things for a long time until they are finished. I tried to be a good parent and work hard at improving myself and being introspective. I try my hardest to be honest at all times and I have empathy. If anything we are polar opposites with regards to most things including taste in music, clothes and so on. The things we had in common were sex and the other things that he "appeared" to have in common with me which of course turned out to be false. The false persona he created was the guise to get me sucked in. These were things like being hard working, being a reasonably good parent, keeping a job, being honest and so on. Having dealt with so many narcissist personalities in the past I wanted to explore why we felt so confused and worthless when we are around narcissists. After having a conversation with a counsellor friend who explained that one of the ways narcissist type personality abuse is us by projecting their feelings onto others. Transference and counter transference occurs in all relationship dynamics and can occur between the patient and their therapist but since I am not a psychotherapist I wont go into psychological jargon. However I will explain how it works in conversation.

What happens is they are hooking you in, usually with xxx tiny hook, projecting their feelings onto you and making you feel like you are at fault. Often a narcissist will accuse you of being something or doing something and then, you will find they have actually been guilty of doing it themselves. Many, people are capable of projecting their feelings, and the following conversations are examples of projection although not necessarily with people suffering from Narcissistic Personality Disorder.

This is a real conversation I had with a person named x "You are a terrible parent, you never do things properly, I am fed up of listening to all of your stuff. You have never grown up and you will you never sort your shit out." What happens is they find one thing in the sentence that is usually true, and the include a lot of other things that are not. For example the one line that was true was "I am fed up of listening to all of your stuff" whereas the rest of the conversation was talking about themselves. If you have been on the receiving end of narcissistic abuse it can be quite unnerving because if a person believes the one hook they end up taking on all of the other things that have been said and owning them.

Here is another example of projecting.. One of my relatives had not finished their work commitments and were behind with their work project because they were busy playing computer games and going to the gym instead of working. They could not afford to buy something but none the less they went out and bought a £100 computer game. They had made a promise to help me out with some leaflets and I had been busy all week working on and helping them out looking after their daughter as well as doing errands like shopping and so on. I had also just come out of hospital. When I asked them if they could help me they got really angry and said "You are taking up my time, I will help you but you are stopping me from doing my work." I offered to back down and then they got even angrier. They replied "Anyway what are you doing on the computer anyway, you spend all your time doing useless things and buying yourself gifts that you cannot afford" I said are you talking about this necklace that I bought myself on Ebay last week for £10 because I am sorry to tell you you are talking about yourself. I have been working all week and the reason you are behind is because you have been down the gym all week and playing computer games and as for buying myself presents I cannot afford, I did not buy myself a computer game" At which point they stormed off in a complete rage and then finally came back an hour or so later and apologised.

Since it is impossible for the narcissist to admit thoughtlessness or error, it must have been someone else who was at fault. The narcissist despises what he perceives to be weakness within himself so instead of owning those weaknesses he projects them onto those closest to him. It is almost impossible to describe the feeling of confusion that the abused feels when they not only have to endure the abuse, but be accused of being the abuser as well. You end up being sucked down the dark black hole of their psyche and end up being a clone of them.

When we come out of the relationship with a narcissist we are still absorbed in their narcissistic reality and still own the narcissistic projection of ourselves, which by this time is usually pretty awful. We may end up viewing ourselves as worthless, inadequate, ugly, stupid and a number of other choice things. We also take on their feelings, which could be feelings of being crazy, or suicidal and so on. It is not because this is who we are but because the narcissist has disowned these things within himself and projected them onto you.

I once remember unknowingly calling Oliver a Robot a couple of years ago and said that he had no emotional response to anything apart from Anger. His response to my comment was total indifference. As Sam Vaknin perfectly describes the narcissistic psychopaths as comparing themselves to automata, robots, or machines. Then one of the easiest ways of dealing with their projected feelings onto you is to imagine that all you are doing is running their corrupt software that they have dumped on you and you need to uninstall it and reboot the computer system to get it working again. Then you can go back to the original software you once had before you met them. This may take time and effort if you have been pre programmed by years and years of narcissistic abuse but it can be done.

Narcissists versus Psychopaths

As opposed to most narcissists, psychopaths are either unable or unwilling to control their impulses or to delay gratification. They use their rage to control people and manipulate them into submission.

The common denominator is that psychopaths, like narcissists, lack empathy but many of them are also sadistic. They literally take pleasure in inflicting pain on their victims or in deceiving them. I believe that when it comes to sex they literally get off sexually on hurting their victims.

Narcissists will always need narcissistic supply to feed their false ego whereas psychopaths are far less able to form interpersonal relationships than narcissists. Psychopaths really do not need other people while narcissists are addicted to narcissistic supply in the form of the admiration, attention, and envy of others.

Both the psychopath and the narcissist have a blatant disregard for society, its conventions, social cues and social treaties. But the psychopath carries this disdain to the extreme and is likely to be a scheming, calculated, ruthless, and callous career criminal. Psychopaths are deliberately and gleefully evil, while narcissists are absent-mindedly and incidentally evil by accident or more often because they have slipped up or been foolish.

Although Sam Vaknin refers to the vast majority of narcissists as "cold-blooded, calculated individuals"

Some narcissists have been known to incorporate moral values into their grandiose sense of superiority, however, most narcissists are simply indifferent and careless in their conduct and in their treatment of others. Their abusive conduct is off-handed and absent-minded and less calculating and premeditated like the psychopath's. When the two personalities are **combined** and a Dark Soul emerges who has both NPD and psychopathy, the lack of Empathy and extreme sense of superiority of the narcissist, *combined* with the impulsiveness, deceitfulness, and criminal tendencies of the antisocial psychopath or sociopath results in a devastating cocktail. The result is an individual who seeks the gratification of selfish impulses through "any means" they can whatsoever without Empathy or remorse.

Sounds like a lovely cocktail. If I were to offer you a glass with the label "poison" on it, would you drink it? Well, the answer lies in the disguise. You would likely drink it if you didn't know what was in the bottle. Both personalities are masters of illusion and they can con anyone. So when you meet a Dark Soul, what you see on the outside label, or the bottle, is NOT what is inside. It's only when you drink it that you find out its poison.

One of my colleagues, a well known psychotherapist (who shall remain nameless) was convinced of my ex's genuineness. It was not until the end of the relationship, when all the lies came out, that he realised I was the one actually telling the truth and even to this day he sits on the fence as to whether Oliver really is dangerous. Why? Dark Souls are very charming and manipulative; in fact, I had to spend many months arguing with my family about gut feelings that I had been having. At one point, my own brother told me he thought I had been exaggerating and making it all up.

Dark Souls are able to con and manipulate people at the drop a hat and many a good psychologist or psychotherapist has been taken in by a narcissist, sociopath or even a borderline personality because of the *veneer* of their charm. It can take many months to diagnose them and many do go undiagnosed. Those that are unlikely to have psychotic tendencies will probably not admit to their failings. They are not likely to put that they are a psychopath on their CV. They are also very adept at playing games with the therapist and will often use them as a way of narcissistic supply, or perhaps if they are a psychopath may use it to learn how to manipulate people better.

In an article entitled 'Games Sociopaths Play in Psychotherapy' by Steve Becker on *Lovefraud.com* , he writes :

"Finally, for now, we have sociopaths who play the **dedication to their spiritual development** game. These are typically well-educated sociopaths with a *polished psychological rap*, who posture as *committed spiritual seekers*. Some of these sociopaths may go so far as to make a sort of cult—a *seeming life mission*—of their alleged spiritual development, raising irony and farce to new levels.

This category of sociopaths validates another principle that applies to sociopaths in general: While they are absolutely *in*capable of genuinely pursuing their personal and spiritual growth, yet smoother, more glib sociopaths can be *highly capable* of *un*genuinely, *in*sincerely, *manipulatively* pursuing their so-called personal growth.

Think of the predatory trollers (and rollers) at AA and NA meetings, and all other sociopaths, who *posture one way or another* as honest, open books seeking to confront their trauma responsibly and seriously.

Summoning guises like *Mr. Sensitive, Mr. Wounded, Mr. Relationship Builder, Mr. I'm In Touch With Vulnerability, Mr. I'm In Recovery From Co-Dependence*, and countless other *pseudo-evolved* raps, these sociopaths can be magnets—and they know it—for genuinely vulnerable women seeking sensitive, emotionally available, vulnerable men with whom to partner in their own recovery. "

Oliver played all of those games. He was definitely able to play the *Mr Wounded* with his "poor me" sob stories that seemed so incredible he could not have possibly made them up. Oliver would often do spiritual workshops if his wife twisted his arm and claimed he had trained in Reiki and studying The *Course of Miracles.* Yet he was enraged that his mother in law was a light worker and would ridicule the church groups she belonged to. When push came to shove and he finally saw a therapist who had suggested that it might be *him* that has a problem and it could take more than just a few sessions to sort out his behaviour problems, he was nowhere to be seen. Off he vanished into the horizon with a trail of devastation behind him and I never heard from him again. I believe that although I am not knowledgeable enough about Psychopathy to have a fixed opinion, I tend to lean toward the view of the increasing number of those who see no real difference between these disorders and that Narcissistic Personality Disorder is just a milder form of psychopathy.

Every kind of con artist, predatory priest, rapist, serial killer, wife beater, child abuser, animal abuser, bully, dictator, or cult leader is a primary narcissist doing his thing in different ways. All of them have sadism in common. Because these people have so many things in common, perhaps the western theorists have got it all wrong by labelling these people into *separate* categories and misleading us.

The Darker Side of Narcissistic Personality Disorder

Narcissists are pathological liars and are often able to pass lie detector
tests so does that make them even more dangerous than the psychopath? Is
calling NPD a "milder" form of psychopathy just a cop out because of the number of people that would be deemed to be termed criminally insane? Known narcissists such as OJ Simpson seem perfectly capable of murder. In a documentary broadcast by Channel 4, entitled *Egomania*, different levels of narcissism are discussed. Interestingly enough, Sam Vaknin, a well known narcissist appeared in the film. It became increasingly interesting to watch when Sam Vaknin appears because it shows it from a narcissists point of view as well as from a victim point of view. Sam has also appeared in *I Psychopath*.

Throughout the film there are a number of different cases including a cult leader named David Berg. The cult leader is a perfect example of the narcissistic personality. He typically has seven or eight traits, the most dominant ones being excessive need for admiration, and exploitation of others. Berg developed a term called "flirty fishing" in which Jesus tells two fishermen that he will make them "fishers of men." David Berg had set up a church called "The Children of God" which still runs a website today. He extrapolated from this that women in his movement should be "flirty fishers" (also called "bait" or "fisher women"). The targeted men were called "fish." The cult published several documents with precise instructions. Flirty Fishing was defined as using sex appeal for proselytizing. If masturbation, oral, or penetrative sex ensued, this was termed as "loving sexually" and also counted as a "deep witness", meaning that the "bait" earned more brownie points within the group than by mere flirting. The financial benefit of Flirty Fishing soon led to a further degeneration of the practice from mere flirting into "loving sexually" to escort servicing described as "making Flirty Fishing pay" by Berg. In this, female cult members would work as regular call girls for escort agencies or just freelance, and merely "witness" to their clients when the occasion offered itself.

In the documentary they discuss how thousands of victims of his "church" were abused whilst in his care. Berg was involved in all kinds of sexual deviancy and glorified his behaviour. He completely removed the age limit for sexual partners and even two and three years old were taught how to have sex with graphic hands-on classes. For those poor children born into Berg's cult, they had no choice but to follow into his ideals. This man managed to lead the church for a total of 25 years. Many of his "followers" (or victims) went on to commit suicide.

The film goes on to talk about Brian Blackwell who created a web of lies about his life, by claiming he was a professional tennis player. He even hired his own girlfriend and signed over a cheque for her salary despite having nothing in the bank. He applied for credit cards in his father's name and finally killed his parents after they became suspicious about his increasingly lavish lifestyle and began asking him questions about it. He beat both with a claw hammer and stabbed them repeatedly. Immediately after the killings, he took his girlfriend on holiday to New York, where he spent nearly £30,000 using his fathers credit cards. The attacks on his parents were so severe that investigators initially thought the couple had been shot. Blackwell was charged with murder and was due to stand trial; after he pleaded guilty to the lesser charge of manslaughter on the grounds of diminished responsibility, experts diagnosed him to have Narcissistic Personality Disorder. It appears he had an episode of severe Narcissistic Rage which can occur when the narcissist is perceivably being prevented from accomplishing their grandiose fantasies. This was the first case in an English court where Narcissistic Personality Disorder has been found to be a defence to murder and he is also one of the youngest people to have been diagnosed with it.

On a positive note, Sam Vaknin, one of the most prolific writers and speakers on Narcissist Personality Disorder, talks about the *self aware Narcissist* by saying:

"Sometimes, when the narcissist first learns about the

Narcissistic Personality Disorder (NPD), he really believes he could change (usually, following a period of violent rejection of the "charges" against him). He fervently wants to. This is especially true when his whole world is in shambles. Time in prison, a divorce, a bankruptcy, a death of a major source of narcissistic supply - are all transforming life crises. The narcissist admits to a problem only when abandoned, destitute, and devastated. He feels that he doesn't want any more of this. He wants to change. And there often are signs that he IS changing. And then it fades. He reverts to old form. The "progress" he had made evaporates virtually overnight. Many narcissists report the same process of progression followed by recidivist remission and many therapists refuse to treat narcissists because of the Sisyphean frustration involved. "

"I never said that narcissists cannot CHANGE - only that they cannot HEAL. There is a huge difference between behaviour modification and a permanent alteration of the psycho dynamic landscape. Narcissistic behaviour CAN be modified using a cocktail of talk therapy, conditioning, and medication. I have yet to encounter a healed narcissist."

"The emphasis in therapy is thus more on accommodating the needs of those nearest and dearest to the narcissist - spouse, children, colleagues, friends - than on "treating" the narcissist. If the narcissist's abrasiveness, rage, mood swings, reckless and impulsive behaviours are modified - those around him benefit most. This, as far as I am concerned, is a form of social engineering."

However, unlike Sam Vaknin who is a self aware narcissist, and bearing in mind that Berg (the flirty fishing cult leader) had only seven of the full nine traits of full blown Narcissistic Personality Disorder, I go back the the previous question. Who is more dangerous: a narcissist or a psychopath? I'll leave that to you, my dear reader, to decide.

In all of the confusing data I have found; whether your partner is actually a narcissist, psychopath/sociopath (or both) I came across a very interesting article by Steve Becker in which he talks about a new breed of psychopathic personality "The Narcissiopath" which can also be found on the Lovefraud.com website. This is a person that shows both signs of sociopathy and NPD.

Although Steve doesn't necessarily discuss the spiritual

energetic energy that these people take from us which I have outlined in the Dark Soul check list, their personalities are very strikingly similar and is one of the reasons why I wrote this book.

An Alternative View on Psychopathic Personalities

I trained as a TCM acupuncturist some 10 years ago. There are a number of different theories around Chinese acupuncture. The most common teaching in the UK when it first arrived here was the Five Elements Theory of acupuncture. Although I hardly ever use Five Elements acupuncture now, it is believed that certain mental illness is a result of possession by the body. You treat the person with a series of ghost points that release the entity or possession from the host.

During the time that I was with Oliver, something very strange happened. We were in my bedroom one day making a home movie. At the time everything was wonderful. I was happy, I had lost weight, and my ex had just started to really make plans for the first time in ages. Both of us couldn't have been happier. There was something that showed through on the camera. One day, when I was playing the video back, I noticed a large orb of light which appeared to come through the window from the left upper corner and moved down diagonally onto the floor. I showed it a couple of years later to a few friends to see if it had not been a figment of my imagination, as it was very clear on the film. It appeared as a golf ball size white light that came whizzing through the window and into the room at reasonably high speed, which is why I had missed it earlier when watching the playback on the tape.

A few months after the light incident, Oliver, who'd had a large lump the size of a two pence piece on his head since childhood that looked like a flat mole, complained that it had started to become irritated. I lifted his hair and noticed it had been bleeding. My gut feeling was to send Oliver to hospital. A month later I was told he needed to see a specialist. The lump on his head had started to change and the mole had become malignant. They removed the mole and Oliver spent a few weeks in recovery with severe headaches which he had never had before. He doesn't remember the headaches, but I remember one day sending him to the hospital because he was acting strangely and was suffering from what appeared to be a migraine. After the operation and healing occurred, things started to change dramatically. Oliver's behaviour wasn't the same as it was before and he started to be a different person.

Oliver had promised that he was going to leave his wife prior to the operation but once he'd had it done, he would always come up with excuses as to why he could not leave. His job situation had also started to deteriorate. He got fired for not doing his job properly and was asked to leave. He became angry and defensive and we would fight for weeks at a time. Often he would complain that I didn't understand how he felt or that I wasn't being patient enough. Oliver took a job working at home being self employed, which lasted a couple of months, and then had a few different jobs. His overheads were quite hefty, with a high maintenance wife and private school fees to pay, so finding a well-paid job was essential for him before he could leave. Three or four jobs later, and I was delighted when Oliver finally found himself a job with a local firm that appeared to be permanent.

What I noticed throughout this time was a rapid deterioration in his character which would be classic diagnosis of the way a Psychopathic personality would act because his "mask" had slipped. However, being an Empath (i.e. a person that can feel other people's feelings), I noticed a rapid decline in my own energy field since the time that the light orb event happened. I went for some healing and was told I had a thought form attached to me, which left but would have a habit of reattaching itself periodically. Often the feelings I would feel about myself were not even my feelings at all, this is because many of the feelings are a projection of their own feelings.

Empaths appear to be interconnected with those they have relationships with so I started to look at the theory behind the acupuncture theory of possession and also other views in the professional field about spirit attachment or demonic possession. Could it be that the route of the changes in behaviour were as a result of entity attachment or a thought form rather than being a Dark Soul? And were the feelings I was picking up about him as a result of them trying to attach themselves onto me via the connection we had. Although having experienced psychic attacks and entity attachments I wasn't sure whether the "mainstream" experts would agree with some of my theories. I actually use spirit release therapy myself. I am not a trained psychologist, and so I researched and found that a small number of psychologists believe in spirit release therapy, too. This corroborated with the Five Elements Theory I had been trained in, many years ago. So I decided to investigate a bit further.

Michael Crichton who wrote the film *Jurassic Park*, was originally a Harvard-trained physician who went onto become an acclaimed writer and movie director. In his autobiography, *Travels* (2002), he describes in great detail four dark spirit attachments. Also, the movie *The Exorcist* was based on a true story about a boy who is supposedly still alive. Michael attempts to rationally explain those phenomenon that dwell in the irrational entities, other dimensional realms and the underrated "sixth" sense that we've come to know as intuition. His proposition is that, fundamentally, just because certain phenomena cannot be explained "rationally," doesn't mean they don't exist.

Most mental health care professionals don't acknowledge the existence of spirit; at least when it comes to their work directly. Freud, and his followers, did their best to separate science from religion. According to western medicine the most common causes of mental illness, that are put forth by most mental health care professionals, are, either abusive input from surrounding individuals, or Chemical imbalance. Of course I am not questioning that these are primary causes of mental illness but could it be that we should start looking outside of the box and beyond its surface. Many hypnotherapists acknowledging the existence of spirit in the cause of mental illness by looking at past lives and so on and there are now a limited number of psychiatrists or psychologists who recognize dark spirit attachments as the primary cause of mental illness.

Psychiatrist Shakuntala Modi's book, *Remarkable Healings: A Psychiatrist Discovers Unsuspected Roots of Mental and Physical Illness*, is one of the best books on this subject. She is part of a new generation of medical people who are changing their outlook on illness. With some people, Modi uses hypnosis to have them look inside themselves for the cause of their ailments, and with others, she uses other techniques. Some people spontaneously regress to other lives or can see the spirits inside. Modi then converses with those spirits through the patient, this is where all the information comes from. Modi herself does not form an opinion about the existence of past lives or spiritual entities. For her, it is more important that the method works, and her patients get better quickly. Some spirits are really malevolent; they are usually called dark or evil spirits, demons, and devils. She further goes on to discuss in her book that dark entities feed and stimulate negative emotions in us. We have a choice to react on a situation with increased anger, hate, etc., or not. One who lets his negative emotions run free, attracts a lot of dark entities.

Interestingly enough, *Remarkable Healings* is not based on Modi's own religious or spiritual beliefs, but is pieced together entirely from the reports of her patients, who discover under hypnosis that their psychological and physiological problems stem from supernatural causes such as trauma in a past life or the interference of a discarnate entity. The picture that emerges is an odd mixture of Christian motifs involving God, Satan, and hell, combined with other ideas such as karma and reincarnation. Modi is the first to suggest that this milieu may simply be a construction of her patients' subconscious, but stresses that treatment based on this system has a much higher success rate than conventional pharmaceutical and talk therapy. And there are a growing number of mental healthcare professionals who come to the same conclusion as Ms. Modi and use spirit release attachment as part of their treatment protocol.

I once treated a patient who suffered from severe depression. In fact, when he first arrived on my doorstep, I was quite afraid of him. He first came for acupuncture and then, ten years later, he turned up to see me again, this time suffering from a frozen shoulder. I asked him how he was and he said he had been much better since I last saw him all those years ago. He had managed to find himself a job for the first time in many years and was starting to be much happier. However I noticed darkness about him. His eyes had no spark and they appeared lifeless. On discussion, I agreed to do a cord cutting with him, however was surprised to find that he actually had a spirit attached to him.

It was two days later after the lost spirit followed me around the house for two days I realised this spirit had a childlike quality to it. It was trying to find a new host and playing tricks on me such as moving bits of cutlery around and opening and banging doors in a playful type way. When he returned he actually looked like a different man. I asked him about the spirit that had been following me around for a couple of days and he then told me that his young daughter had been killed many years ago. He said he didn't want to let her go and that he had subconsciously been carrying her around for over 30 years. Once we agreed to let her go into the light she never returned.

I would often pick up energies but I realised quite early on in the relationship with Oliver that I was energetically picking up his unowned feelings including hate and anger. Empaths tend to pick up on other people's feelings and take them on as their own, especially those people whom they are close to. I was reading through Rose Rosetree's *Empowered by Empathy*, in which she suggests that Empaths must do more than just spot narcissists. She writes

"Here's the big problem with Empaths: spotting Narcissists, and having to deal with a Narcissist enabling."

'Enabling' is often used in the context of alcoholics, rather than dealing with Narcissists. Say that you live with "Pat," who is an alcoholic. Even a non-Empath may be tempted to make excuses for him/her. By hiding Pat's problem, an enabler unintentionally keeps Pat from hitting bottom. Often, hitting bottom is what alcoholics need to do before they can become motivated to change.

Well, what if Pat is a Narcissist rather than an alcoholic? (Okay, some "lucky" people are both.) Maybe you spot that Pat is a Narcissist, and maybe you don't. Either way, if you are an Empath, perhaps an unskilled Empath, you are likely to act as an enabler to every Narcissist in your life. You see, it's so easy for Empaths to experience another person's point of view, or pain, or even physical discomforts (depending on what your gifts actually are as a born Empath). Unskilled Empaths tend to give. And give. And give. Narcissists, of course, love to take. And take. And take. Sounds like a match made in Hell, doesn't it? So, what do you do?

Cut the cords of attachment to every Narcissist in your life, present or past. Until you cut that cord, you're going to have that Narcissist's *stuff* playing inside your subconscious mind 24/7. It's a very toxic kind of stinking thinking."

And believe me, Rose couldn't be more right. Having grown up in a family where narcissism was rife, I was perfect prey to my ex and at that point in time I was an "untrained" Empath. Their thinking is warped and very toxic, but being in love with one was a whole different story. I have since learned how to control my empathy and switch it off.

It left me wondering if I had been trying to carry these negative energies around with me to take away his pain so he wouldn't have to deal with it or whether it had been attached to both of us. It left me wondering whether my theory of him being a Dark Soul was just my way of covering up and enabling him, since he was an undiagnosed narcissistic psychopath. Was I just a fantasist and did I merely want to believe in fairy tales in the hopes that they would find some kind of "cure" for what can only be described as madness and pure evil? This leaves me with the opinion of whether or not a person is ill because they cannot help themselves, as though they have a choice? People will never be cured of anything unless, of course, they want to change. It's also a known fact that psychotic personalities will not acknowledge they even have anything wrong with them. They are happy in their messed up, twisted reality. Call me cynical, but the proof of the pudding is in the eating. And, although I like to consider myself spiritual, I also consider all the facts and have to look at hard evidence. The hard evidence in Oliver's case was that things actually just got worse and worse. Last time I had heard of him, he had gone AWOL with a trail of debts behind him. No one had heard from him for months. I have no idea whether Oliver even has a job any more.

So did my Dark Soul, Oliver, fulfil his promises of going and seeking alternative means to heal himself? Not as far as I am aware. Having had free counselling before and stopped it after a couple of months. He then paid for one session with a professional psychotherapist and healer and the minute they suggested that he may need to do a bit more work on himself than just a couple of sessions he stopped seeing them, exactly as he had done in the past. He has probably slipped into a bottomless pit of misery, choosing to do the same old crap he has been doing for years, never to be seen again.

7

Dark Souls

A Big Chunk of Them is Missing: a Part of Their Soul

There is much written on the Internet and in books about how sociopaths lack empathy. However, how do we define empathy? Empathy is the capability to share another being's emotions and feelings. Many other personality disorders have a similar lack of empathy, for example NPD and Borderline personality. Without empathy, we are not able to be in another person's shoes, and if we hurt someone, we are unable to see the effect of our actions on them.

I prefer to look at the deeper issues that are missing in their make-up: whether or not they have a soul and the fact that they are unable to give. People without a conscience are incapable of Empathy and will lie, manipulate, and deceive to get what they want. I mentioned earlier in the book that often, the rest of us will be seen as targets or victims. If the person is more narcissistic, they may be more inclined to see the person they are in a relationship with as a mirror of how they wish to see themselves, idealising you at first, prior to having a narcissistic injury. Fundamentally, what is common in all the Dark Soul personalities I have mentioned is that they are incapable of loving and caring about others. The bottom line is that anyone who chooses to engage in hurtful, selfish behaviour has less conscience than most people, if any at all, is devoid of Empathy, and is not evolved spiritually compared to the average person who does not suffer from a personality disorder.

Many people believe that a narcissist or sociopath has an inflated sense of ego, so whilst doing my research I thought I would clarify a few things. First, let's look at sociopaths. There are three types:

1. **Primary**, an emotional shell

2. **Secondary**, often becomes a criminal

3. **Dissociate**, made anti-social by the environment, i.e. terrorism, child abuse, etc.

What they all have in common is that they lack a conscience. So what exactly is the conscience?

Conscience tends to be defined as that feeling which may make us believe that certain actions or failures of actions are inherently wrong. When we ignore these feelings, we feel guilt or remorse. Philosophers, religious leaders, psychologists and a variety of others have over the centuries tried to determine the source of it, and many have arrived at different answers. Some people believe a conscience to be "the little voice," i.e. something that makes us feel with extraordinary conviction that an action committed (or not) may be wrong. The little voice may nag, complain, or harass us when we act in a way we don't consider right. This leads quite naturally to early psychological explanation of *consciousness.*

To psychologists like Sigmund Freud, the voice within is the "superego," the set of rigid moral precepts that helped to control the *want* and *take* aspects of the id. Superego is the sum of things learned early in life about right and wrong, which impose themselves on the id to allow the ego (i.e. self) to function within the bounds of a particular society. A person with poor superego control is considered id-driven. What appears to be common in sociopaths is that they all lack a super ego, the part of our conscience that tells us right from wrong within the boundaries of society.

Narcissists, on the other hand, are somewhat more complex and many people who are diagnosed with sociopathic personality may also have NPD. Sam Vaknin, a narcissist who has also been tested for psychopathy explains that in the narcissist the ego is dormant and nonexistent. He has a fake, nonexistent substitute ego. He writes in "Malignant Self-love: Narcissism Revisited":

"The ego in healthy people preserves some sense of continuity and consistency and serves as a point of reference. It relates events of the past to past actions at present to plan for the future. It incorporates memory, anticipation, imagination and intellect. It defines where the individual ends and the world begins. Though not coextensive with the body or with the personality, it is a close approximation. In the narcissistic condition, all these functions are relegated to the False Ego. Its halo of confabulation rubs off on all of them. The narcissist is bound to develop false memories, conjure up false fantasies, anticipate the unrealistic and work his intellect to justify them. The falsity of the False Self is dual: not only is it not "the real thing" – it also operates on false premises. Moreover, the narcissist cannot be consistent or coherent. His False Self is preoccupied with the pursuit of Narcissistic Supply. The narcissist has no boundaries because his Ego is not sufficiently defined or fully differentiated. The only constancy is the narcissist's feelings of diffusion or annulment. This is especially true in life crises, when the False Ego ceases to function. The child's pursuit of mastery of his environment is compulsive. He is obsessed with securing gratification."

He also goes on to say:

"Moreover, many narcissists don't feel responsible for their actions. They believe that they are victims of injustice, bias, prejudice, and discrimination. This is because they are shape-shifters and actors. The narcissist is not one person - but two. The True Self is as good as dead and buried. The False Self changes so often in reaction to life's circumstances that the narcissist has no sense of personal continuity."

As normal spiritual beings, our spirits are housed in physical bodies. Most of us have what some believe to be a *higher self* and *lower self*, and we are constantly striving to overcome our biological limitations to live by higher ideals. Often, we categorise people who spend their lives searching for ways in which they can transcend their lower states by doing as much good as possible, as spiritually enlightened beings. We refer to those that have no conscience or soul as evil or sociopathic. I believe most people have a choice. They know what the difference is between right and wrong. We may stumble and fall sometimes: it's part of our human make-up. However the difference between the pathological personalities, in particular narcissists and sociopaths, is in their inability to look *inside themselves* at that aspect of their higher self. The higher self *is* the soul. It is that part of us which allows us to self reflect, and to have insight and intuition. When we are in an awakened state of consciousness, our higher self comes through during reflection and is the voice of conscience. Since it is rooted in our bodies, it is an intrinsic part of us. It's the part that guides us to step out of danger when we are placed in a difficult situation, and to trust that we are looked after when things are down. It is the voice of the higher self that stops us from acting selfishly towards others. It urges us to be kind, to do the right thing, and try to become better people. Sociopaths, psychopaths, and narcissists appear to lack a higher self. They lack impulse control and only possess a limited ability to see the difference between right and wrong, hence the expression: "no remorse, no conscience."

So does this mean that a sociopath, or a psychopath or narcissist has no soul because they have no ego to control them? I believe that they are wired differently, whether it's from birth or as a result of childhood circumstance. I do believe they lack a soul, or if they do indeed have a soul, it is *unlike* that of a normal person. Their ability to function and be attuned to a higher self is quite different. Take an extreme version of a sociopath a psychopath, for example. Has there ever been a case where anyone has shown remorse for their actions? They may put on a good display for manipulative purposes but hardly ever will you find them saying "sorry" unless they get caught out in a lie. A real apology is a process: you experience regret/remorse/ guilt/empathy and apologise; you examine what you did wrong, and often you find out what you can do to fix things; and you don't repeat the same mistake again. All of these are important parts of the process of a real apology: remorse, empathy, and perhaps even reconciliation. Most of all, we are acknowledging one's part in the process i.e. admitting guilt. Ultimately, the sincerest apology is to not repeat the same transgression. If someone apologises and then repeats the same transgression, that deems the apology null and void. But how do you know if someone is sincere until you give them another chance? If you're the kind of person that forgives completely, and not with condition (that the same mistakes are not to be repeated) then you're a perfect victim for the Dark Soul.

Narcissists rarely apologise. They can do some of the cruellest things to hurt someone and won't think anything of it. They will openly apologise to you only if it makes them look good, if they think it will somehow make you praise them for being so "sincere," or, as I had mentioned earlier, if they're caught in a lie. It's all an act to get you to trust and let your guard down. I read on a web post once that one woman said her boyfriend was a narcissist and did not even know how to apologise. She went onto explain

"He boasted that he never apologised to anyone for anything.

It was a real point of pride for him. But one day, he was asked to apologise to someone by another person who he was completely dependent on. So he called me for help because he didn't know how. I explained to him that to apologise, he needed to acknowledge that he hurt the other person's feelings and to assure them that it would not happen again. I told him to say these words, 'I'm sorry that I hurt you and I want to be a better friend to you in the future than I was in the past.' He could not get the words straight so I had him write them on an index card and read them to the person he was apologizing to. Afterwards, I had asked him how it went and he told me that he took out the card and tried to read it but that he messed up a 'little bit.' He couldn't even read a simple apology off an index card!"

I'd spent many months and years trying to understand Oliver's condition trying to make him "get it," to understand the consequences of his actions, not only to me, but to his wife and children, and other people he hurt. I asked him to say sorry once for hurting me and mentioned that I noticed he never really said sorry. He acknowledged that he had never said sorry before and then after that his favourite word became Sorry but he would say it like he was saying "Hello". It never meant anything.

He appeared to love having discussions about this deep spiritual bond we had together and how no one ever made him feel like I did. As a spiritual person I even rationalised that I had shared some kind of weird Karmic link with him in past lives (through regression) and that perhaps it was my job to be more understanding to his behaviour as a result of some karmic ties and that eventually he would *wake up*.

Yet, when their actions and promises do not match their words and you try and reason with a Dark Soul, you are wasting your time. It is not possible for them to "get it" because there is something missing in the first place: a big chunk of their soul. They are not spiritual beings at all. If their souls exist, their souls are not the same as those of normal people. The only difference is that a psychopath will hurt people deliberately, whereas a narcissist can switch his conscience off and on like a tap and hurts people "accidentally, on purpose." Does it make either one less dangerous? I do not believe so. Are they equally dangerous to people both emotionally and spiritually? Yes.

As a spiritual coach I believe we are energetic beings and we are here to exchange energy with one another. It is through the healthy transfer of energy that I have learned that the exchange between two people must be reciprocal, meaning giving and taking. I am not implying that you should not give of your energy sometimes for free, as in taking care of your children or donating to charity, where you would not expect anything in return. However, in adult relationships, there should be a healthy exchange, in both personal and business relationships. It can be love, care, support, resources, friendship or money. If there is no give and take in relationships and you are the one who is always giving, you open yourself up to becoming vulnerable and depleting yourself. You are also clearly announcing that your wellbeing doesn't matter and that people can walk all over you.

Whatever their diagnosis, a Dark Soul, has no interest in giving you *anything*. Their only interest is getting something from the person with whom they are in relationship.

The Sadistic Dark Soul

The Sadistic Personality Disorder is no longer part of the DSM III-TR and was removed from the DSM IV and from its text revision, the DSM IV-TR. Some scholars, notably Theodore Millon, regard its removal as a mistake and lobby for its reinstatement in future editions of the DSM. The Sadistic Personality disorder is characterized by a pattern of gratuitous cruelty, aggression, and demeaning behaviours which indicate the existence of deep-seated contempt for other people and an utter lack of empathy.

This disorder was dropped from DSM-IV for two reasons:

- because of scientific concerns, such as the relatively low prevalence rate of the disorder in many settings

- for political reasons - sadistic personalities are most often male and it was felt that any such diagnosis might have the paradoxical effect of legally excusing cruel behaviour.

The definition of *Sadism* is deriving of sexual gratification or the tendency to derive sexual gratification from inflicting pain or emotional abuse on others. *Sadism* and *masochism* describe psychiatric disorders characterized by obtaining feelings of pleasure or gratification when *inflicting* suffering (sadism) or having suffering *inflicted* upon the self (masochism). Such pleasure is often sexual, but *not* exclusively so.

Both psychopaths and narcissists can be equally sadistic , however a narcissist is both a sadist *and* a masochist which makes for a lethal cocktail if you are in relationship with a Dark Soul.

Any kind of sadist likes to inflict pain because they find suffering psychologically amusing. They torture animals and/or people both physically and emotionally because they find it hilarious and extremely pleasurable. Whether or not they "get off" sexually by inflicting hurt on others is incidental to the pain they cause to their victims. Either way they may go to extremes, by lying, deceiving, and committing crimes just so they can enjoy the cathartic moments of witnessing someone else's misery.

Most sadists are have a fascination for horror, gore, violence and sexual S and M. There are a number of reasons commonly given for why a sadomasochist finds the practice of S&M enjoyable, and the answer is largely dependent on the individual. For some, taking on a role of compliance or helplessness offers a form of therapeutic escape; from the stresses of life, from responsibility, or from guilt. For others, being under the power of a strong, controlling presence may evoke the feelings of safety and protection associated with childhood. The DSM-IV asserts that *"The fantasies, sexual urges, or behaviours"* must *"cause clinically significant distress or impairment in social, occupational, or other important areas of functioning"* in order for sexual sadism or masochism to be considered a disorder. The manuals' latest edition (DSM-IV-TR) requires that the activity must be the *sole means* of sexual gratification for a period of six months, and either cause "clinically significant distress or impairment in social, occupational, or other important areas of functioning" or involve a violation of consent to be diagnosed as a paraphilia (A paraphilia is a condition involving sex fetishes where a person's sexual arousal and gratification depend on fantasizing about, and engaging in, sexual behaviour that is atypical and extreme)

Not all sadists are psychopaths or serial killers and not all sadism is sexual. However there is strong evidence to suggest that any kind of sadism has some sexual overtones.

Those who are more likely to channel their homicidal urges are more likely to do it in *socially acceptable ways* by "studying" and admiring historical figures such as serial killers or people like Hitler. They love guns and other weapons, are are usually fascinated by death, torture, and martial arts in all their forms.

Most sadists like to feel omnipotent. Power plays are important to them and they are likely to treat people under their control or entrusted to their care harshly. Partners, children, co workers, patients, prisoners and so on are expected to fall in line with their exacting standards. They may also enjoy the emotional mind games by playing the guru and saying things like "I am only trying to help you" and "its in your best interests" or even suggest that you the victim are actually enjoying it!

Sam Vaknin has written extensively on the sadistic narcissist, He writes :

"A narcissist on the other hand would tend to display the sadistic aspect of his personality in one of two cases:

1. That the very acts of sadism generate Narcissistic Supply to be consumed by the narcissist ("I inflict pain, therefore I am superior and omnipotent"), or

2. That the victims of his sadism are still his only or major Sources of Narcissistic Supply but are perceived by him to be intentionally frustrating and withholding. Sadistic acts are his way of punishing them for not being docile, obedient, admiring and adoring as he expects them to be in view of his uniqueness, cosmic significance, and special entitlement.

The narcissist is not a full-fledged sadist, masochist, or paranoiac. But, he *does* enjoy punishing himself when it provides him with a sense of relief, exoneration and validation. This is his masochistic streak.

Because of his lack of empathy and his rigid personality, he often inflicts great (physical or mental) pain on meaningful others in his life and he enjoys their writhing and suffering. In this restricted sense he is a sadist.

The narcissist is as much an *artist of pain* as any sadist. The difference between them lies in their motivation. The narcissist tortures and abuses as a means to punish and to reassert superiority, omnipotence, and grandiosity. The sadist does it for pure (usually, sexually-tinged) pleasure. But both are adept at finding the chinks in people's armours. Both are ruthless and venomous in the pursuit of their prey. Both are unable to empathise with their victims, self-centred, and rigid.

If one had to distil the quotidian existence of the narcissist in two pithy sentences, one would say:

The narcissist loves to be hated and hates to be loved.

Hate is the complement of fear and narcissists like being feared. It imbues them with an intoxicating sensation of omnipotence. Many of them are veritably inebriated by the looks of horror or repulsion on people's faces: "They know that I am capable of anything."

It is a perpetual background noise of devilish, demeaning scorn. His inner voices "say" to him: "You are a fraud", "You are a zero", "You deserve nothing", "If only they knew how worthless you are".

The narcissist attempts to silence these tormenting voices not by fighting them but by agreeing with them. Unconsciously – sometimes consciously – he "responds" to them: "I do agree with you. I am bad and worthless and deserving of the most severe punishment for my rotten character, bad habits, addiction and the constant fakery that is my life. I will go out and seek my doom. Now that I have complied – will you leave me alone? Will you let me be?"

Of course, they never do."

Sam finally goes on to say:

"I find it difficult to accept that I am irredeemably evil, that I ecstatically, almost *orgasmically enjoy* hurting people and that I actively seek to inflict pain on others. It runs so contrary to my long-cultivated and tenderly nurtured self-image as a benefactor, a sensitive intellectual, and a harmless hermit. In truth, my sadism meshes well and synergetically with two other behaviour patterns: my relentless pursuit of narcissistic supply and my self-destructive, self-defeating, and, therefore, masochistic streak.

The process of torturing, humiliating, and offending people provides proof of my omnipotence, nourishes my grandiose fantasies, and buttresses my False Self. The victims' distress and dismay constitute narcissistic supply of the purest grade. It also alienates them and turns them into hostile witnesses or even enemies and stalkers."

So Why is a Dark Soul So Dangerous?

To the outside observer, although the symptoms as described in the previous chapters may all be present, they may not always be apparent to the person they are in contact with. Dark Souls are usually extremely charming, often attractive and intelligent. They may, on the surface, appear friendly, cooperative, and considerate, but these attributes are typically *superficial*. The Dark Soul uses this superficiality as a way of misguiding victims and hiding their own personal agendas, as well as their real character. They use a number of different methods, including manipulation, lies and gaslighting of their victims, but there is always a *hidden agenda* behind any of their relationships.

On the surface, they may appear to be the perfect catch, perhaps with a nice job they have told you about or they may seem to come from a good family. They will nearly always *appear as what you want them to appear.* They use mirroring as a way of catching their victims. For example, if you tell them that you had been a victim of sexual abuse, they may use the connection tactic by suggesting they too had been sexually abused when they were younger as a way of bonding with you. They may have no interest in anything you do but will find things with which they can have a common interest.

Many cyber predators have been known to find common interests on forums so that they can create a bond with their victims. For example joining the same charities and so on so that they have something in common to discuss with their soon to be victim. Depending on your needs or those of the abuser, you may have met them thinking you were going to have a casual relationship, only to find yourself having sex with them. To a psychopath it's all about control and sex is one of the ways they control their victims. Any woman who has sex with a man knows that if you start looking for just sex, eventually you will form an emotional bond. As another example, if you start off as friends with someone, you may end up developing an emotional bond with them and then reinforcing it by having sex.

There is something known as the limbic bond. Whenever a person is sexually involved with another person, neurochemical changes occur in both their brains that encourage limbic, i.e. emotional bonding. Yet, limbic bonding is the reason casual sex doesn't really work for most people on a whole mind and body level. Two people may decide to have sex "just for the fun of it," yet something else is occurring on another level they might not have decided on at all; sex is enhancing an emotional bond between them, whether they want it or not. One person, often the woman, is bound to form an attachment and will get hurt when the affair ends. The reason is that the size of a female's limbic system, in comparison to the rest of her brain, is larger than it is for a man. Consequently, she is more likely to get limbically connected. Psychopaths know this and that is why they use sex as a way of forming an early emotional limbic bond with their victims. Many women who have been victims of sociopaths talk about this amazing love/sex connection they've had with their abusers, citing comments like "it felt like no other connection I have had with anyone else before" or "he knew how to connect with me on a very deep level."

When you form a deep limbic bond you want to go back for more. And the psychopaths are experts because they, are usually highly sexed. Narcissists on the other hand may have little interest in sex depending on what type of narcissist they are. The psychopath will wear their victims down, bit by bit, until they have formed such a strong bond with their victims it can be confused with love. Conversely, in a pathological individual, some theorists go so far as to claim that sexual sadists are born with their neural pathways wired all wrong – that their limbic system is faulty. When sexually aroused, they argue, these people receive messages from their brains to attack or devour.

I remember saying to Oliver after I had made love the first time, "I am a grown up and you don't need to tell me you love me to get into my knickers." He had come to know my background and pretty much everything about me during a year of friendship before he finally pounced. He knew that what I really wanted was a deep emotional connection, and since the sex with Dark Souls is usually highly charged and very fulfilling, most women will not stay in a relationship for too long if it's only about sex. They will need and want that emotional attachment. Within a month, he was telling me that he was madly in love with me and going to leave his wife for me. By this time I had let my guard down and was hooked. Although I use the word "victim," perhaps the more appropriate word is "target," because to a Dark Soul you are just that: a target. They are unable to show any empathy, and when they hurt people, they lack the ability to show regret for their actions. To you, they are just a victim of their own sick games, whether their agenda is money, sex, or power. To them, it is all about power, control, and winning. In Martha Stout's book, *The Sociopath Next Door,* she draws the conclusion that sociopaths only want to win. However, I agree with some of the interpretations given by the writer of *TranSociopathica.com*, who calls a sociopath another name: a "Demonic Sociopathic Entity" They suggest that a sociopath is not human, but is in fact a non-human entity incarnated in human form:

"What they really want is the emotional energy released by the victims they have defeated. This is what they are really after. Sociopaths/Psychopaths feed on their victim's emotions, all of them. Not just the emotional carnage and misery they leave in their wake, but also the prior feelings of love and affection they have extracted from their victims. They need this energy, too."

I believe that the energy that they take from a victim is not merely emotional. It comes in the form of psychically feeding off their victims, which is one of the reasons I first used the term Dark Souls. By the time I had ended the relationship, I was left drawn and haggard, a shadow of my former self. The minute I got my spark back, he was back on the scene, playing the "poor me, pity me" tactic, or trying to find some other excuse to draw me back into the game. What I noticed was that by the time the relationship was over, he was full of energy and I was not. As soon as I was back on my feet again, he would be back again for another "feed," literally sucking the life source out of me because he had no one else to prey on. I had noticed a difference in his eyes: they were soulless and lacking in life, which helped him to play on my therapist background. Yet he would get the "spark" back whenever he was with me. And there I was thinking it was because he was in love or was spiritually waking up.

It was a long time before I had figured out that he was not only draining me emotionally, but quite literally sucking the life force out of me. On an energetic level, we allow these people to draw our own life force out of us. We become the Dark Souls that they are and they end up being the light. This can be highly dangerous for us both emotionally and spiritually. They lack the ability to have that energy in themselves and look to others to gain it from whatever supply may be available.

To a Dark Soul, you are just a source of entertainment, energy, sex, or income. Once they have used up all your resources, they will move on to the next target. I can only describe it as a game that they play very well. A psychopath wants you to believe you are stupid and that they are the clever ones, and will use all kinds of devious tricks to undermine even the brightest of victims. I remember once telling my ex that I had an IQ of 146 (which is reasonably high) and being told that his was 178. He will always have to be smarter, and the last thing a psychopath wants is an intelligent victim undermining his confidence.

If you imagine a spider and you have it helpless in front of you, a normal person would either kill it because they are afraid, put it outside, or perhaps just ignore it. A psychopath, however, being a predator, might not kill the spider (although he knows he can at any time he chooses) but instead decides to pull the legs off, one by one, until the spider can no longer walk and becomes immobilized. They do it because they can, just to see what happens. The psychopath likewise enjoys the pain they cause their victims, to just observe what happens. They want to break the victim down a bit before engaging in more direct attacks, so that the victim is weakened and will be less likely to understand and protect themselves. Once they have pulled all their targets legs off "metaphorically speaking" then the psychopath will need a new victim afterwards.

I remember once having sex with Oliver and it just felt *weird* and very frightening. We weren't doing anything strange but I really felt at one point like I was making love to the devil himself. I felt very uncomfortable and slightly sick and could not understand why I felt that way.

It took me a long time to figure out that psychopaths like Ted Bundy and Charles Manson were just brutal killers, but a *Socialised Psychopath* can just blend in with the crowd. Also because of my background as a spiritual energy worker it took me even longer to understand the term "lacking in empathy." As a moral person, I always try to weigh the pros and cons of my actions upon another person and the impact they might have. I also wanted to believe everyone had a conscience and a higher self.

Oliver, was married when he first met me, although he did finally leave his wife before the end of the relationship (or perhaps she was smart enough to kick him out). It's all part of the "unfinished business" you are left with when you end a relationship with a Dark Soul. In a *normal* relationship, one grieves and is eventually left with some positive feelings. With a Dark Soul, you are left coming to terms with the fact that you were not an object of love but a source of narcissistic supply. Any nostalgic memories and tender memories of affection you have for them are corrupted by their hidden agenda and lies. Everything about the relationship shifts into the stark, clinical light of the DSM IV manual as you realise they are disordered. Despite the fact that you are totally relieved that they are out of your life, you always retain some unresolved grief, perhaps wondering "Who are they hurting now?" or "Will they ever come into my life again?". Unlike a normal relationship, you are just left with a *hole,*

One time, when his wife started to see the cracks and flaws in his personality, she had issued Oliver with a letter from her solicitor advising that she felt threatened by his actions and his behaviour. She believed he was a threat to her children and wanted only supervised access arrangements. She decided to take the children away for a couple of weeks and he became absolutely livid. He told me that she had removed the children from him. In his rage he drove up the motorway at 100 mph texting me on the way. I had no idea at the time what had been happening, and when he finally showed up, there was almost steam coming out of his eyes. He said he had been fantasising about killing her and had explained that if he could get away with it, he would murder her.

There is much evidence to believe that the only reason a psychopath would not kill you is because going to prison would simply interfere in their daily routine. How inconvenient for them to have to go to prison and do time for something they could do at a drop of a hat! They know how to kill you and if they think they can get away with it, they would not hesitate. For them, there is no moral recourse because they do not have a conscience. A rational, normal person might possibly fantasise about killing their spouse perhaps because they are so angry, but they will quickly reconsider their decision based on the impact it would have on the children. A psychopath will not.

This was not the first time I knew something was *very* wrong with Oliver. Once, I had caught him at what appeared to be a white lie and said I'd had enough. He became very defensive and started to get angry. I told him I was fed up with his anger at me and that if he did not stop shouting at me and telling lies I would tell his wife about our affair. It was then that he hung up. A few minutes later, he called and said "I want to kill you." I laughed, thinking he was not serious, and he replied "No. When you mentioned telling my wife, I meant it. I really want to kill you. You are a threat to my children." I replied that I am not a threat and that I had no plans to tell his wife. Later, when he had calmed down, I asked him about his wife. When I had questioned his threat to me, he replied "I was deadly serious." In response to his wife hypothetically leaving him long before he had left her, and taking the children away, he retorted "I would kill her as well." Years later, when I had confronted Oliver again on his outrageous plans to kill his wife, his response was "She is a threat to my children." More likely this is merely a projection of his own craziness. Of course, from what I understand now, *he* was the real threat to the children, not her.

When you end a relationship with a Dark Soul, they may try to be amicable and suggest that you can still remain friends. In my case, Oliver would say he "could not imagine [his] life without me in it." He even suggested once that his life was not worth living without me and if we parted ways, he would never have sex with another woman again. He even implied once that he might commit suicide if I left him.

Some people believe that psychopaths will never commit suicide. However, there is some evidence against this. Since their ultimate aim is power and control, what better way to inflict pain on a victim than to threaten to kill themselves if they can't keep you in the relationship? On the other hand, if they do follow through, it is more likely to be their way of saying that *no one can control them* and therefore they will take control of their own life (and *death*, in this case).

If they are trying to be amicable and leave on friendly terms then it would only be to appease you and to leave the door open for a possible chance to come back into your life. That would, of course, be to further manipulate you or to re-establish a narcissistic supply when they do come back. There may be something "endearing" about you that they can use as a ploy at some later date (when they have messed up) or they may play upon your sense of pity if they want to come back. It could be anything that attracts them: your money, your status, your mind, or even an appealing part of your anatomy that they desire for their own pleasure (most usually your sex organ). If they have sex with you its not because they love you or because you are attractive, intelligent, kind, sexy and so on. Its a basic need to gain narcissistic supply. Its like a drug to them. They could be having sex with anyone! You are just *an object* to them – a form of gratification for their distorted ego. They do not, have not, and never will have feelings for you. They never had any to begin with. Everything about them is merely a façade, like a cardboard cut-out character. Probably the hardest thing you will have to come to terms with is the fact that you had never meant anything to them, maybe even harder than losing money or possessions. It may even be harder than the emotional or physical abuse you had suffered with them. Why is it? Because it is very difficult for many to believe the relationship never really existed in the first place.

In retrospect, I can see the cracks and flaws of the "crapomatic bed" I had been sold i.e. Oliver, even before we began our relationship. I realise now that I was nothing more than a sex object and the feelings I had had about not wanting to go near him had been there for a reason! Looking back at when I first started with my "pitiable" Dark Soul, he was in a deeply unhappy relationship with a bullying wife. Of course now, in hindsight, I realize that he was describing himself. It was all merely projection. His wife was truly the poor victim, deeply unhappy and he was the bully.

At the beginning of the relationship when we first started dating we had already been friends for a year. He had built up the *image* of a trusted friend as I had been dating someone else at the time. When I had ended my relationship and started seeing Oliver officially, he had led me to believe that he had not had sex in over a year with his wife. We had met for lunch and were discussing how we would pursue our relationship and to figure out how he was going to leave his wife. As we were sitting there, he asked "How can I find a way of introducing you to my wife so that she doesn't know we are having an affair?" At the time I didn't think anything about it, and replied that he could say he was seeing me for acupuncture. He replied "But then my wife would want to come too." I mused that it wouldn't be the first time I had treated a husband and wife, but that I felt it was probably not a good idea, anyway. With a sadistic glint in his eye, he added "Yes, but I bet you weren't shagging the husband." He seemed titillated at the thought that his wife suspected and could find out at literally any moment and was also fearless and arrogant and said she "hasn't got a clue". When he went to his regular jujitsu classes during the first part of the affair, everyone in the room knew his wife. Although he wanted to hide the affair he considered it fine for me to bring my son to classes and talk to him openly. He also took my son to weekend courses. He would often wink at me whilst doing manoeuvres on the mats. Yet everyone knew we were more than just friends (despite my silence) and he yet he had the nerve to think that his wife would never find out even though she worked at the same centre.

Steve Becker of *Lovefraud.com* wrote a powerful article entitled "The Shameless Audacity of the Sociopathy"

> *"All* sociopaths, I think we can agree, are *exploitative personalities.* But exploitativeness *alone* insufficiently captures sociopathy. Something more is needed. That *extra something,* I suggest—which really captures the sociopath's style—operative style, is his or her *shameless audacity.*
>
> When the *non*sociopath commits an exploitative behaviour, he or she is likely, on some level, to feel uncomfortable. The *audacity* of the act (*unless* it has earned sub-cultural acceptance, as in certain cut-throat business or gang cultures), will produce feelings of discomfort, shame.
>
> I want to be clear: people commit *shamelessly audacious* acts all the time who are not at all sociopathic. Exhibitionistic personalities, among others, can attest to this. We see audacious personalities doing all sorts of edgy things that make us think, "What is that person *thinking?*" And such individuals may commit these acts without any shame at all. That is fine, and often entirely *non*sociopathic.
>
> But here's the caveat: So long as *no one is being exploited in the process.*

The *exploitation* element radically changes the equation"

Dark souls also have a distinct lack of accountability and with a lack of accountability comes a lack of shame. They justify their behaviour and when caught out they may say things like "I don't understand what I did wrong" or "I don't know."

My ex was not ashamed of the fact that he was having an affair; in fact, he clearly relished the thought. Occasionally he would say he felt guilty for hurting me and not treating me right then go back to the same selfish behaviour again. Yet he had no problem exploiting others including myself, bosses, and family members. When his very wealthy grandmother was dying he was immediately at her bedside. After the funeral he even asked me if I would put any inheritance money in a separate bank account so his wife wouldn't find out. Oliver was very disappointed after all the care and attention he had given her, to find out after she died that she had left nothing to him in her will but a few hundred quid. When it came to work when his boss sacked him for negligent work practice he tried to sue him using the "cancer" story and claiming he had been wrongly dismissed and not understanding enough. It made me wonder whether the first cancer story was ever true at all.

At one point during the relationship Oliver planned to open a therapy business and became friends with a man whom he knew had some money to invest. This man became his new found "best friend" and Oliver would often go round and offer to help him out playing the role of the perfect gentleman. Nothing appeared to be too much trouble for Oliver. The man even entrusted him with the keys to his house. However, the potential investor was about to retire and investing in something at his age, if not managed properly, could have caused him to loose his pension and life savings. When I questioned Oliver's motives for not wanting to invest in the business himself, since he appeared to be so passionate about it and suggested he mortgage his own house or raise some finance, his reply was "Why use my own money when I can use someone else's". Interestingly enough the minute the man refused, Oliver never really paid much attention to him again.

So now a picture of a person who is flawed and damaged like the "crapomatic bed" I described in Chapter 4 is starting to emerge. Dark Souls wander around the planet looking to prey on victims. Interestingly, the more powerful and successful you are, the more attractive you are to them. Psychopaths literally "get off" by breaking their victims. There is no fun in destroying a pathetic victim that has no self esteem, money, or sex appeal, and it's far more interesting to find a victim who presents a challenge and yet we have so many traits that these psychopathic personalities find so endearing and easy to manipulate.

In *'Women Who Love Psychopaths'*, Sandra L. Brown discusses some of the traits of the victims of psychopaths have. She describes them as "*Super Traits*" which include:

1. High empathy "He's this way because he's been hurt."

2. Low impulsiveness "I'm not going to just run away."

3. High sentimentality "He can be sweet—like when he ..."

4. High attachment "I love him like I've never loved anyone else—I feel so connected to him."

5. High relationship investment "I've poured my soul in this relationship. I know we can make it work."

6. High regard "I want him to think well of me. What am I doing wrong?"

7. High harm avoidance "Would I ever find anyone else if I left him?"

8. Low harm avoidance "He's not that bad. I'm sure he can turn this around."

9. High resourcefulness "I could find a counselor for him and we could get couples counseling."

Sandra further writes:

"There is much to tolerate in these relationships. The psychopath gets a "feel" for her level of tolerance by starting out with small boundary violations and working up to full fledged relationship transgressions. What is tolerated is then pushed as a limit. Her ability to endure the hardship and pain keeps her telling herself that it isn't that bad. His ability to get her to tolerate more unbelievable behaviour from him feeds his sense of entitlement and dominance over her and also power to get her to tolerate even more the next time from him."

What makes the Dark Soul so scary and dangerous is the fact that, on the surface at least, they appear so normal. You never imagine for a moment they have a dark side to them. A Dark Soul will push all of your boundaries and stretch them until you break. Many victims have done things they would never normally have done, its a bit like mental brain washing. Remember the Dark Soul wants you to feel like them and become like them. I have always been very open minded about sexuality and also extremely tolerant, however there are limits to what I find I can tolerant and what I find totally distasteful.

I had a friend who was a transvestite. He worked as a sex worker and is now in the process of going through having the entire transgender operation. In his journey to discovering his sexuality, he was what some people might consider quite deviant in his desires and said that many of the clients that met him were straight married males. This was further corroborated when I was doing the research for my first book, *Infidelity Unwrapped*, about online cheating and married men. I found thousands of married straight single men were placing themselves on bisexual swinging sites in the hope of doing something *different*.

My friend the transvestite loved to be cuckolded and had a penchant for eating "cream pies," and I don't mean of the Mr. Kipling variety! I remember at the time not saying anything to him because I frankly found it quite disgusting, but in talking to my ex about it, he replied "Oh god, I would never do anything like that!"

During my healing period, I would often have vivid dreams and nightmares. I'd had a dream about being seduced by a very disgusting doctor who clearly wanted to have sex with me. He had a bisexual male partner who was a chef. The doctor had invited me to a restaurant to eat, and for dinner we were served rice with a side dish of male ejaculate, mixed with public hairs, and the chef invited me to eat it. He was absolutely repulsive, too, and although neither of them told me what was on my dinner plate, I knew! I had wanted to vomit when I awoke. However, upon waking from the *dream* I realised that both characters in the dream were clearly obvious to spot and were not hiding their sexually deviant interests from me, whereas my ex had hidden everything from me (including his interest in "cream pies"). Oliver was quite a different story. On the surface, he was the picture of a perfect gentleman. He came from a good family background. He was polite and genteel, and appeared to be the perfect family guy. From a relationship point of view, even while he was with his wife he made a promise to be committed sexually only to me. He claimed that he wanted me to be monogamous although he would confide that if I wanted to find myself a girlfriend it would be okay. However, when the truth finally revealed itself, I found Oliver on a lesbian sperm donors' site, where he was offering to plant his narcissistic seed into any woman that would care to have it. Worst of all, he was on numerous sex sites, listed as a bisexual male who wanted to play with males, females, or transvestites and listed his favourite hobby as "eating cream pies" and having unprotected sex!

Interestingly, we appeared to have a very open relationship. We would talk freely about sex and our interests and I genuinely thought he was being open and honest with me. However, not only had he put me at risk, because I was seemingly the only person he was having sex with, since his wife was *supposedly celibate* (which I later found out to be another lie), but he was jeopardising his own family and his wife's health, too. Sociopaths have no fear when it comes to catching anything; they have the sheer audacity to believe they can literally get away with murder and catching things such as sexually transmitted diseases would never enter their thinking. Besides which, they like risky, dangerous behaviour.

So how did I find out all of this lovely information? I went on the Internet one day and decided to type in his name: "Mr. Crapomatic". Of course that wasn't really his name. I had scrolled down a page or two to find Oliver wearing a kilt, and there were two pictures of him with his small children on a modelling site. It said that he was available to do photo shoots, commercials, and "walk on Prince Charlie parts." Talk about a Charlie, and being an idiot, one of the pictures was taken from his honeymoon. What nerve I thought to myself when I found the profile. When I first confronted Oliver about it he denied it absolutely, claiming "it was all my imagination." When I showed him evidence, he even suggested that perhaps his wife or mother had put him on there as a joke. Because he was so defensive, I contacted the modelling agency and asked them if they would ever put anyone on their site without their permission, and the owner of the website told me that copies of applicants' birth certificate were required. I then confronted Oliver after finding his Facebook account. Even though he knew I had one, he denied it, even though I had sent him a "friend request." Yet he had a number of different women on there and so the rest of the story unfolds in one lovely big heap. What was most interesting was that he used his real name on all these sites. Oliver didn't even try and hide himself. It was either because he didn't care or because of his super inflated ego he thought he would be able to get away with anything.

When the relationship is finally over and you clean up after all of the mess they have left you with, you look back at the relationship and realise that you had literally been conned. You were gaslighted to the point of oblivion. You are left anxious, confused, and less able to trust your own memory and perception. You may have lost all sense of reality and you may feel like you have literally been in a trance for the whole time you were with them. The grim reality of the relationship manifests and you are left with the aftermath of bankruptcy, sexual diseases, or worse. You look back at the Dark Soul and wonder what did you ever see in them? You may even ask yourself "What was I Smoking?". The superficial façade that they portrayed to suck you into his game falls away, and you are left with the image of a cardboard cut-out, without any substance whatsoever. You are left wondering who was this person I fell in love with? And you look in their eyes and see nothing but a person lacking in spirit being carried around in an empty shell: a Dark Soul.

When my father was asked once why he had multiple affairs (dozens, actually), my father responded "Because I could!" and yet whenever confronted with a lie he would say "I don't know what your talking about, its all your imagination". He has never appeared to show any guilt or remorse for all the women he has exploited over the years. This reinforces the sheer audacity of a Dark Soul, who, as Steve Becker writes, can literally get away with anything if given the opportunity.

A word of warning:

Whatever label you want to give these people I prefer to give them my own label: Dark Souls. What exactly constitutes a Dark Soul? They are *in essence* a narcissistic psychopath or *variations thereof* with a strong emphasis on them being Energy Vampires and Shape Shifters. In the following chapters (with the exception of narcissists) I use the words sociopath/psychopath interchangeably. This is done only because one particular person has referred to them as a sociopath; whereas another has referred to them as a psychopath. So please consider *any* references as just part of the Dark Soul personality trait.

I hope to also give you the tools to spot these abusive predators, controllers, and energy vampires. To help the reader decide what kinds of traits they have I decided to produce a checklist for the Dark Soul Personality.

Although the following list is absolutely NOT a diagnostic tool a Dark Soul may exhibit many of the traits above. If they have more than 15 they may have a Personality Disorder which would need to be diagnosed by a professional. If they display more than 20 then I suggest you run for the hills picking up whatever pieces of your life you have left and leave as quickly as possible.

Checklist for Dark Souls

- Acts out in passive aggressive ways
- Are controlling and emotionally exploitative
- Are Energy Vampires
- Believes they are special and unique
- Claims to be have a special unique relationship and that only you understand them and vice versa
- Despite their confident persona they have little if any friends
- Disregard for the rights of others, including law enforcement agencies
- Easily bored. Starts something then never finishes it
- Easily exploits people such as family members and getting into wills etc. or receiving gifts
- Enjoys hurting people in sadistic way
- Exaggerates their achievements and qualifications (Do a Background check)
- Extremely Narcissistic using lots of poor me sob stories and gaining sympathy to make you feel sorry for them
- Gaslights their victims
- Has a deep underlying anger that can come out as rage
- Has a piercing gaze and yet when thinking up a scam their eyes may move rapidly back and forth
- Has an invisible self destruct button or masochistic streak
- Has fantasies about being someone else
- Has feelings of entitlement
- Has no conscience
- Has shallow emotional response
- Has the ability to shape-shift and mould their persona into whatever they want their victims to see
- History of short term or failed relationships that always end badly where is always the other persons fault
- Irresponsible and unreliable
- Is able to energetically attack their victims, either consciously or unconsciously
- Is envious of others
- Is glib and superficial
- Is highly sexual and is likely to have multiple partners. Their interests may include bi-sexuality and anything out of the norm

- Is incapable of changing at their core
- Is unable to love others
- Is unable to take responsibility for their feelings or actions
- Is unlikely to recall their dreams during sleep
- Lack of realistic long-term goals or failure to plan ahead
- Lacks empathy, guilt, or remorse
- Lacks shame
- Lacks the concept of time, is often late, has missing time lines in their past where they do not remember anything
- May *appear* to be charming, likeable, successful, fun loving, and very spiritual
- May be highly competitive
- May claim to love their children more than anything but shows lack of interest in them
- May dislike animals and children
- May have come from an unhappy childhood or may play on the "my terrible childhood" story which turns out not to be true
- May have had a history of juvenile behaviour problems
- May need far less sleep than most people. Sometimes less than 5 hours a day
- May or may not be violent but is likely to have fantasies about violence
- May regularly change employment status, moves around
- Pathological liars
- Places blame on others
- Prefers to receive from others although they will give gifts if they can get something from their victims
- Projects their feelings onto their victims
- Prone to impulsive behaviour
- Prone to using overt flattery when they want something
- Rarely says sorry or uses it inappropriately
- Requires excessive admiration
- Wants to to know all about *you* whereas their own life history is vague and elusive

A Note on the Checklist

I would like to add when reading the Checklist for Dark Souls they can either have NPD and/or Psychopathy. Either way if they have of many traits above it's likely they fall into the 'extreme' end of the disorded personality rather than being your every day run of the mill narcissist. Its also worth mentonting, that whilst most narcisists are not that covert they tend to be less predatory and are more easy to spot. They are so self-absorbed, they don't actually care what you think which is why so many people avoid them after seeing through their charm and veneer.

However the psychopath's modus operandi is to **intentionally** set out to victimise and exploit others right from the very start with the sold intention of PREYING on victims which is one of the things that victims find so difficult to accept.

Using a combination of the two pathologies along with the spiritual damage they are capable of doing, is what helped me to form the basis of the Dark Souls Checklist.

8

Warning Red Flag Alert

So how do we spot these Dark Souls, whatever their diagnosis and why do we choose to ignore the red flags?

I remember talking to one of my patients one day and she appeared to be very angry. I was determined to get to the bottom of her anger as it helps with healing on an energetic level. So I tried to break the ice, asking her if there had been any bereavement recently. She appeared to be very defensive initially and on her guard, replying that nothing of any note had happened to her. I continued to question her and then asked her about her job as a psychologist. I said it must be an interesting job and told her I was writing a book about sociopaths. She laughed and quipped "Been there, done that, and got the tee shirt!" On further investigation, she too had been the victim of a very Dark Soul who had left her penniless. I posed the question: "Why do you think we as women choose to ignore the red flags? In hindsight, once we are out of the relationship, these flags appear to be very obvious." She replied "Because the green ones are far more appealing."

I believe now that because these people are masters at deception and manipulation, it leaves us vulnerable to not seeing what is clearly in front of our eyes. Once we are hooked or under their *dark spell*, it could take a sledge hammer for some of us to finally see through all the lies and deception. Even personalities such as Borderlines which can accompany psychopathic personalities are masters of deception. A Borderline male, for example, will initially suck you in with the "poor me" sob stories as well as the masterful manipulations of the narcissist and the sociopath. So taking all of the labels aside, let us look at all of the red flags that are likely to warn you about a relationship of inevitable harm.

He's Too Good to Be True

In the beginning if a man seems to good be true, he probably is. There's a reason for this old adage. When you meet a Dark Soul, he appears to be your knight in shining armour. He sweeps you off your feet and is incredibly charming. You are in disbelief that this man possesses all the qualities you have been looking for in a mate. Listen to your gut and trust it. Never ignore it!

The very first day I met Oliver, my gut feeling said to me "do not touch this man with a bargepole." I didn't listen, and for a year, we were friends whilst I was dating someone else because I thought it was *harmless*. The trust had been established and then he jumped in for the kill.

Often, they will want to know everything about you, which may seem very flattering in the beginning, but their own stories are peppered with inconsistencies. When I first met my ex, I was dating someone else and he already knew what type of man I liked. As Oliver and I become "best friends" sadly I had revealed a lot about myself. He knew I had come from a background of childhood abuse and so often abusers will find something with which to bond with you. In his case, he told me he had also been abused as a child and it formed an emotional bond between us where I felt he understood me better. As a side note: don't believe everything he tells you. All Dark Souls have an uncanny ability to figure out what you want in them and then project this ideal image back to you in order to win you over. They are brilliant actors and that is exactly what they are doing when they are courting you: acting. They know who you would like them to be and they play that part perfectly. In the beginning of the relationship, you may come away thinking "how on earth did I deserve this man?" He is the best thing since sliced bread and he may lavish affection on you. He may even lead you to believe that you're his "soul mate" and that no one understands him like you do. Not only does that make you feel special, but it increases his feeling of omnipotence.

Sometimes, they may only talk about themselves, although this is usually only as a means to impress you. Perhaps they may use family and friends as a way of gaining trust or tell you impressive stories about jobs they have had. My ex once told me that he had dated Princess Anne's daughter but that he had found her boring. One of the first things he did was to tell me about his rich and successful parents. I found it a bit odd in the beginning and he even told me what radio stations they were on. This is all about him having an extreme sense of narcissistic supply from others because underneath he has nothing to offer, so uses other people to boost his self esteem. For this reason, he may inflate stories about himself to impress. He would also exaggerate how much money he was earning, and yet he turned out to be one of the stingiest men on the planet earning far less than he had told me. Later in the relationship, when it came to buying things, he never appeared to have money on him and always found an excuse to leave his wallet at home when it came to going out for lunch.

If they do talk about themselves, Dark Souls may often refer to themselves in the third person. You may notice that they are likely to get bored easily. Unless the focus of attention is on them, whether it's giving them sex or making them feel good about themselves, often a glazed look will come over their eyes when others are talking, but suddenly they'll light up when they get to talk or the focus returns to them. One of the easiest ways to spot an abuser is to see how they react when you need them or you are sick. Most abusers will run for the hills or at best put on a display of empathy for the relatives. They are usually terrible parents. Perhaps if their children are sick they may appear to show interest whilst painting their partners as bad parents. This is nearly always projection on their part because they are unable to admit that they are not good parents and will always find a reason to find excuses to run down their partner.

If you ask them what they need to do to improve themselves, they may say that they are already doing some kind of "self help" improvement programme, but the key is whether they are changing. Most therapists know that people with narcissistic tendencies usually revert back to old habits within a couple of weeks or months. Since they believe they are perfect, they may tell you that they have nothing to change about themselves.

Question what their relationship is like. Oliver was always saying how his wife was terrible and an abuser and how she treated him badly. I could never understand why anyone would want to stay with someone so nasty and abusive. It was much later on during the relationship, when he would have a narcissistic injury that I realised that he was actually talking about himself.

When it comes to lying, beware of the defensive liar. Dark Souls are abusers who are very often defensive and may respond with great hostility and perhaps even rage if you disagree with them or suggest that they are lying. They may even suggest you are guilty of something and it is then that you will get a glimpse of their true colours. They also love to lie by omission.

Years ago I was briefly married to a man named Alex whom I had met in my youth in India. Believing in the old *fairytale* that a leopard can change its spots, the man in question had cheated on me and I had gone onto marry another man and stayed with him for nearly 17 years before we finally split up amicably. When I met up with Alex years later, I had decided to give him a second chance. We were married and I found him cheating again. Although I had no proof apart from the fact that a woman had answered the telephone when I called his apartment, his immediate reaction was that of complete rage. Alex came up with the most ridiculous story about how someone may have gone into his room to rob him and answered his telephone. When I pursued it more he turned the tables on me and accused me of cheating on him with my ex husband. Abusers are masters at projecting things back at their victims.

Healthy relationships take time to build. Pathological people have agendas regarding their relationships; they appear intense and deep very quickly. They move fast, getting serious quickly to mask their hidden agenda and your ability to respond to these red flags. They are very quick to tell you they are in love with you or want to move in with you. Women can be particularly vulnerable to these types of men as they spawn intense relationships, in which they are soon seeing each other constantly, not having an outside life, and have the sensation of being breathless and swept off their feet.

If your partner never invites you over or always has excuses not to be there. If he is single and quick to suggest coming over to your place but never you coming to his, be warned. This could clearly be a sign of concealment and should definitely be considered a red flag.

Beware of a person who talks too freely about past relationships or ex partners in general, especially if it's *all* negative. You may possibly be dealing with a heavy load of unresolved anger from their past relationship. Many abusers will blame all of their relationships issues on their partners and not take any responsibility for it ever being their fault. Always ask them about their job. It's one of the things I had never questioned properly. If your partner always has "trouble" at work; they cannot hold steady employment or change jobs frequently; if they rationalize that they are always the victim in employment setbacks; or if they blame their boss or believe that other people are "out to get them," this is a *huge* red flag.

Perhaps your partner is very concerned about their "public image." They may show a different *persona* in public and then become someone else behind closed doors. They may brag about you or your accomplishments to others, but rarely if ever pay you a compliment in person. Perhaps they may do or say hurtful things and then completely deny it's ever happened.

One of the most common signs of an abuser is when they keep saying "I'm sorry" but then continue to repeat the same hurtful behaviour.

The final red flag is the gift of patience. A Dark Soul personality has what appears to be the patience of a saint. The reason is that they are focussed on *you*, their target. They wait and are absolutely adept at staying calm, cool, and collected, even if you are armed with evidence like phone and hotel bills, with the most plausible excuses under the sun. They will not always get angry, and you can find yourself in bed with them by the end of the evening wondering what the hell you were thinking for having accused them in the first place.

Nothing Adds Up When 2 + 2 = 7

As a child, I grew up with a father in whose life nothing really added up. I did not understand what the word sociopath meant until many years later.

My mother had been for counselling years before and was told that my father was an undiagnosed sociopath, and that he was moulded that way from his childhood. She was also told that he would never change and yet she spent nearly 35 years trying to make him "get it" and being abused in the process.

It was when I had met Oliver that I started to learn about sociopaths and NPD. What I had noticed through observing my father's actions as a compulsive womaniser was that he had similar characteristics to my ex. He could lie at the drop of a hat without batting an eyelid. When he was caught in a lie, he would "appear" remorseful. However, he would soon go back to the same behaviour within a matter of weeks or months. During the time he was married to my mother, he admitted to having had 12 affairs of whom at least were with 6 of her friends. What was interesting was he had no problem introducing them to all of us children. On the plus side my father is very likeable and appears to be generous and easy going. As a family we have all suffered emotionally and to this day, with two children out of three that no longer speak to him, he still remarks "I don't understand what I did wrong."

Often you would see a Dark Soul "appearing" to show emotions but the mismatch between the body language and the actions is always apparent. When you are faced with information that doesn't quite add up, it creates cognitive dissonance. Cognitive dissonance is an uncomfortable feeling caused by holding two contradictory ideas simultaneously. The theory of cognitive dissonance proposes that people have a motivational drive to reduce dissonance by changing their attitudes, beliefs, and behaviours, or by justifying or rationalizing them. It is one of the most influential and extensively studied theories in social psychology. Dissonance occurs when a person perceives a logical inconsistency in their beliefs, when one idea implies the opposite of another. The dissonance might be experienced as guilt, anger, frustration, or even embarrassment. This is the feeling of uncomfortable tension which comes from holding two conflicting thoughts in the mind at the same time.

To give you an example, we all have intuition. Some people's intuition is more attuned than others. So, for instance, your partner may come home and you may ask them where they have been. Their body language is odd, they smell of perfume, and yet they have what appears to be a perfectly rational explanation for their behaviour. The discomfort often feels like a tension between the two opposing thoughts. To release the tension we can take one of three actions:

- Change our behaviour.
- Justify our behaviour by changing the conflicting cognition.
- Justify our behaviour by adding new cognitions.

My mother told me a story once about one night when my father stayed out all night. It turned out many years later he had been out with a woman and couldn't get home. In those days there were no mobile phones to call her so he came back in the morning looking dishevelled and in a desperate attempt to come up with a convincing lie he told her that he had been out drinking with friends and there had been a riot. This was during a time when there had been a number of riots in London. During the riot, he said, he had been caught up in the furore and was one of many people arrested overnight. It was such a ludicrous story, and he told it with such conviction that he had diverted my mother from the fact that he had been out all night having sex with another woman. My mother had been so concerned that my father was safe that she never once questioned his truthfulness.

This is a common theme amongst people who lie, using diversionary tactics to keep people off track. Interestingly enough, in my book *Infidelity Unwrapped*, there is a chapter about the different ways in which men and women lie. Men tend to lie by exaggeration. If a man comes home with a very long-winded story about something, there is a good chance he has made it up. Men normally tend to come out with short answers. Women usually have long explanations about things and therefore the opposite is true of them. If your partner is a woman and she normally spends an hour telling you what she has done, and then gives you a very short answer to your question about her day, you can be pretty sure she is lying. Years later, when I spoke to my mother about the story, she admitted she'd had a feeling in the pit of her stomach of something not being quite right.

I, too, had a similar experience. I had been dating Oliver for about five months and had known him as a friend for about a year prior to that. Because we had been married when we first met, Oliver had made all kinds of promises to keep the relationship going, like declaring his undying love for me, telling me that his relationship with his wife was broken and irreparable, and that he was only there for his children. However, this story had started to not sit well with me. I decided to meet Oliver and arranged to give him a letter explaining that I thought it was best that we finished on good terms. Knowing something "didn't quite add up" on his side, he had taken the opportunity to plan his script. On the day I was supposed to end the relationship I was given a massive shock. Before I could give him the letter, he said he had been unwell and had gone to see a doctor about a sore throat. He told me that the diagnosis was throat cancer.

They say that Dark Souls actually get off sexually on the perverse power that they have on knowing they are conning their victims. If anything, at that time our sex life was great considering he had "cancer." Now it just makes me sick to think about it. All I can say is thank goodness for Google, the Internet, and for the gift of intuition!

Many women stay with Dark Souls far longer than they should because they want to believe their outrageous stories and make up for the cognitive dissonance that doesn't match in their heart. In my own case, I kept trying to rationalise why anyone would want to lie about having cancer. It wasn't until much later after his had gone into "remission" and he *miraculously* recovered that I realised why things did not add up. I realised if he could lie about cancer, he could lie about nearly anything. I have since found that the old "I have cancer" story is being used by a few other people and is common practice amongst Dark Souls or compulsive liars. I recently spoke to a friend who said she was concerned for her daughters safety. Her daughter was dating a drug user and he had asked her for money for treatment for cancer. When the mother confronted one if his family members she was told. "Oh he is up that to that old trick again is he".

Mesmerised by Their Charm

As a trained acupuncturist, I learned about the concept of a person's spirit, or *Shen*. According to the Five Elements Principle, when someone's' spirit is missing or is taken (perhaps because they have an entity attached to them) they appear to be devoid of *Shen*. It is often seen as a darkness or lack of spark in their eyes.

Interestingly, many people report that their psychopath partners had hypnotic eyes. It is known as the "sociopathic stare", whereby they will stare almost unblinkingly into another person's eyes because they watch people's reactions far more closely than most people. Normal people are much better at reading each others' emotions, and at sensing what emotion is present. A psychopath, however, is literally reading you and "acting." You may see tearful displays although often they are excessive or unrealistic because the tone of voice or choice of words may be incongruous with the emotion being portrayed. Often, psychopaths display a sadistic glint of glee as they think about their depraved behaviour and subject their victims to excruciating pain.

Once, I was having lunch with Oliver and as I had started to talk to him, his eyes started to glaze over. He then firmly fixed his gaze on me. As we continued to talk, I noticed him intermittently using hand gestures and words that were dichotomous with what he was saying. I felt myself slipping into a trance. I ended up agreeing to carry on seeing him even though I had originally met him for lunch with the intention of breaking off as friends. This was not the first time this had happened and I could not understand why I had felt like this. A couple of years later, while studying Neuro Linguistic Programming (NLP) and hypnosis as part of my coaching practice, I realised he had been anchoring me and using NLP techniques on me to get me to change my mind. In '*Women Who Love Psychopaths*,' Sandra M Brown talks in great detail about the victim's ability to be put into a trance-like state. From my own experience I am easily hypnotised and can slip into trance at will.

Often I would feel like I was in a trance whilst having sex, so I decided to do some further research. According to one study they scanned women's brains whilst having intercourse. During sexual activity, the parts of the female brain responsible for processing fear, anxiety and emotion start to relax and reduce in activity. This reaches a peak at orgasm, when the female brain's emotion centres are effectively closed down to produce an almost trance-like state. When a person is in a trance like state they are highly susceptible to suggestion. The trance state is a dissociative state one enters in which memory and perception are altered.

The dissociative effects of the trance state can also be induced by other conditions such as physical or mental exhaustion, terror, repetitive chanting, hypnotism, rituals, or drugs. Not all individuals are equally susceptible to trance or to dissociation. However research has shown that those people who show a high degree of susceptibility to hypnosis are likely to also possess some apparently biological predisposition to it. They are also more likely to have been victims of abuse as children.

Therefore, for individuals, like myself, who are highly susceptible to hypnotic suggestion it makes them gullible targets to a sex obsessed Psychopath.

My brother Jonathan, who practices stage hypnotism, suggested he can spot a highly suggestible person within minutes when he does his magic routines. Bearing in mind that sociopaths have uncanny ability to "tune in" to victims weaknesses, it made me wonder whether the sociopath had the ability to tune in and spot victims who were prone to being in a trance like state more easily that others.

As a result of my experience with Oliver, I actually chose to study hypnosis and NLP to learn more about it. I had selectively forgotten that Oliver was a practitioner of NLP, hence the incongruence in his actions. While researching on the Internet, I found many cases of men who used NLP technique to chat up women and there are a host of sites focussing on "pick up techniques." My brother is a trained magician and went onto explain in greater detail after my healing that PUA (Pick Up Artists) model their behaviour on a variety of techniques including NLP and hypnosis to get women into bed. I wanted to understand how NLP was used by predators to pick up women. Some of the random techniques I found on numerous websites included learning skills like PUA Routines are field tested techniques you could use to *attract* and *seduce women.*

Growing up with a father who was extremely charming, my brother Jonathan, believes that sociopathy and the charisma that comes with it does so "naturally." However, both of us agree, having trained in NLP, that in the hands of a psychopath some of these techniques are going to be far more dangerous.

Psychopaths appear to be supreme psychological mind readers and many of their victims appear to be mesmerised by them. Often then will even wonder why they felt drawn to them when they leave the relationship totally., although when they are in the abandonment phase of the relationship they may want the psychopath or narcissist back in their lives. Victims feel a unique *bonding* experience with their abusers.

Sandra L. Brown further corroborates this by saying in her book '*Women who Love Psychopaths*'

"Repeatedly women told me about the unusual bonding experience they had with psychopaths. I found it curious that many of the women had identical stories of a 'mystical-type' union they described that was electrified by a vibe-like intensity. Identified as some of the reasons she felt gorilla-glued to the psychopath and why he was hard to leave included the extraordinary sex, the deep bond, 'intense' attachment, and a soul-mate experience of being completely 'known' by him. It led me to investigate the nature of attachment in these love relationships and to explore how these pathological relationships might indeed be different." — Sandra L. Brown, M.A."

Psychopaths are adept at lying but is it also possible that we are now breeding a new generation of people to be con artists and act as sexual predators who are not even psychopaths?

PUA techniques used to be for the *elite* few, but seduction and PUA techniques can now be learned easily and are all over the internet. They can be found in book stores, online videos and forums teaching men how to bed women. They range from how to pick a woman up to giving them a good orgasm. There are numerous seminars giving advice on proven PUA techniques. PUAs are discouraged to use flattery and suggest using "negs" (i.e. negatives) on women. They believe that physical looks are less important to women in selection of a partner than they are to men, as evidenced by top gurus who rated poorly with their looks on a "Hot or Not" style website. Pick Up Artists primary objective is to get women into bed.

Many members of the seduction community work on their "game" (seduction skills) by improving their understanding of female psychology, their confidence and self-esteem (termed "inner game"), and their social skills and physical appearance (physical fitness, fashion sense, grooming) ("outer game"). Many members of the community believe that one's "game" is refined through regular practice, with the idea that the abilities needed to interact with women can be honed.

Some people find lying difficult but it seems to me that as a society we are teaching more and more people to lie and cheat. We all sometimes feel like we have been *played* when it comes to dating, but what if we are dating a psychopath and they wanted another tool to help them. Armed with their ability to lie without batting an eyelid, and their need for sexual gratification, just imagine how dangerous it would be if the psychopath were learning these additional "pick up techniques" to practice on you and all their other victims?

More Tools for their Toolbox

When we are not enabling the psychopath or colluding with their lies its pretty easy since they are so difficult to spot. With regards to covering up the truth there are so many "tools" they can use to help them.

I think in part we are mesmerised by their charm but we are also blinded by their lies. It becomes increasingly difficult to spot lying in psychopathic types. They can often cheat lie detectors. But what if they are caught hands down in a lie and need some evidence to get them out of a difficult situation?

When I researched my book about online cheating I even found a website which is supposedly *secret* that teaches men how to cheat on your wife. You email them, (the book is free) and it tells in in great detail exactly how to lie and cheat on your wife with a few minor warnings about what you are likely to catch as a cheater if you have unprotected sex. Its actually a very well researched book. The book includes sometimes humorous (and often very sinister tips) on how to lie and cheat on your partner and get out of difficult situations. Some of the more sinister ones include medicating your partner by persuading them they are depressed or mentally ill and putting them on Prozac, much like my father had done to my mother.

In addition to this "helpful" manual there are multiple sites that specialise in providing back stories, evidence and excuses for spouses who want to stray from home. These services include anything from sending a phony email to providing a full blown virtual office service. One of the most creative services one website provides is a *rescue service.* It allows the cheater to wriggle out of an uncomfortable situation by receiving a call with a call back number that has an operator on the end of the phone. They even provide a virtual travel agency that will send fake tickets and a virtual business/office service with Toll-free phone numbers and live operator support . What a lovely new tool for a psychopath to use in the already bulging toolbox.

Inside the Mind of the Abuser

"Emotional abuse is a devastating, debilitating heart and soul mutilation. The deepest lasting wound in any abuse is the emotional wound" Robert Burney

First of all I would like to point out not all abusers are Dark Souls or psychopaths. Abuse comes in many disguises. Abuse is *any* kind of behaviour that the abuser can use to gain control, subjugate and coerce the victim through the use of violence, humiliation and degradation, fear, verbal assaults, blackmail, gaslighting, emotional dependence, intimidation, manipulation, physical violence and so on.

Dark Souls are controllers and they will use anything they can to gain your trust If you possess a sense of responsibility, integrity, or consciousness, these are qualities the Dark Soul lacks. When they meet a person who has them, it is a profound reminder of something they do not have. An abuser will constantly be on the lookout for qualities in people they couldn't possibly have in themselves and they will use this as a way to dominate, control, and ultimately destroy you. This is why they were attracted to you in the first place. Being highly envious they hate being reminded of what they do not have and one of their aims is to win at all costs.

Many abusers have been abused themselves. Just as addictions pass down through generations, abusers often leave their families for a family of choice - then repeat the abusive cycle from the other side. The abused becomes the abuser, and vice versa, and so continues the cycle.

Traits that are common in abusers include: uncontrolled rage, jealousy, fear of abandonment, low self esteem, co-dependence, drug/alcohol dependence, and a need for power. In *addition* to the above traits the psychopath abuser may also have an any number of the following traits : uncontrollable temper, be envious, have an inability to respect or compulsion to violate boundaries, be out of control or emotionally volatile, and has a need for power and control.

The abuser thinks of himself as omnipotent with an inflated sense of self image. When anyone says or does anything that doesn't fit into their glorified image of themselves the abuser may take this as an insult. This type of personality is rarely capable of true intimacy and may well feel threatened by the prospects of being open and vulnerable. They often expect their victims to *mind read* and know what they want. They may suffer from *vague thinking* which allows the abuser to avoid responsibility. It is not uncommon for abusers to separate out their abuse. For example: they may beat up members of their own household but may be nice and polite to strangers. Many abusers suffer from this type of fragmented thinking. I remember when I was dating my ex, he would tell me that he hated his wife and couldn't wait to leave. I had started to suspect that he was abusive to her at home rather than the other way round. He would compartmentalise his life into the good bits and the bad stuff, with comments like "I consider my kids and you to be the happy parts of my life and my wife to be the bitch." There was no in-between and yet he went onto abuse me.

Often men and women who have been abused will find that after contacting the previous partners of the abuser where the abuser has accused *them* of being the perpetrator it is usually the other way round.

On the surface, they may appear to be an upstanding person in the community, attending church at weekends with their family, yet could easily batter someone from the same meeting the following day. The abuser does his best to keep his abusive behaviour separate from the rest of their life. They may beat their spouse and/or verbally abuse their kids on a regular basis, but seldom physically attack anyone outside of their home. They also separate their lives psychologically because they suffer from black and white thinking. Abusers see this fragmented, black and white, thought process as acceptable and normal behaviour, and feel it is justified. Yet, ironically, if they hear a report that someone else has abused, such as their loved ones, they are the first to condemn them.

The type of person who is most likely to put up with any kind of abuse is a person who has low self esteem. Equally they may have had a background of sexual, physical or emotional abuse. If they have difficulty setting boundaries or saying no they are more likely to attract an abuser. They may believe that things will change and "If I only I just try harder" things will work out. Their intense need for love and affection or a strong need for a relationships to validate them may be as a result of "love addiction" and likely to attract an abusive type relationship. The victim may have difficulty expressing anger and tend to internalise it. If they are depressed their loyalty to their abuser may take precedence over their own emotional needs or physical safety or they may feel suicidal. Victims may spend their lives attracting different types of abusers with different characteristics. If for example their father was a violent man they may go on to have emotionally abusive relationships. If they had sexual abuse they might have relationships with violent men. For the victim its a distinct lack of power in saying No to whatever abuse comes to them. They may have relationships with abusers throughout their life.

For most people the first thing that comes to mind is physical or sexual abuse. However abuse can be both physical, emotional, psychological, and can include threats, intimidation and isolation of the victim. An abusive relationship means far more than just being punched and beaten and many victims especially those that have suffered severe emotional and psychological abuse come away with a feeling that they have been abused but they are not sure how or why.

Emotional abuse is like brain washing and it systematically wears away at the victims self confidence and sense of self worth, trust in their own perceptions and self-concept.

Any kind of relationship abuse is used to maintain power and control over the partner. Abuse tends to escalate over time and when the abuser eventually uses violence against a partner it is usually part of a larger pattern of longer term abuse or as a last resort to gain control over her/him. For the abuser to be successful they need the victim to be emotionally and physically dependent upon him. Contrary to popular belief, both the abused and the abuser may suffer from low self-esteem and a lack of self-confidence.

Since most psychopaths and narcissists lack a healthy ego, they tend to prey on victims who may have issues about their own self esteem such as co-dependants or Empaths who may try to overcompensate by trying to understand them.

In my own case coupled with my history of abuse and my inability to say no or express my anger; I was far more likely to attract an abuser than most other people. If we feel contempt for ourselves or lack confidence in relationships, we are more likely to choose people who will reflect this image back to us.

Abusers are often very clever and highly charismatic, using manipulative tactics such as lying, denial, blackmail, projecting blame onto others and having a Jekyll and Hyde type personality that makes their victims question their own sanity. Psychopaths prefer to look for traits in their victims where they can break their victims down slowly. They have lots of patience so even if it takes time they will be far happier finding victims who *appear* to be self confident but may have other issues about self esteem in different areas of their life. They delight at slowly turning their victims into mush. Most psychopaths are cold-blooded, calculated individuals with strong undercurrent of rage, hatred, and destructive envy and so they have no problems using manipulative exploitative techniques to undermine their victims in the hope of eventually transforming them into their warped twisted reality.

Abusers may have trouble experiencing intimate relationships but conversely enjoy the drama and excitement that the dynamics of an abusive relationship entails. Abusive people find it exciting to watch others become angry and getting into fights. They are usually prone to hiding their own personal details and that includes their feelings. Often abusers are possessive and believe that anything they want should be *owned* and that as a result even the people they are with can be used and abused and done with as they wish. By seeing people as possessions it justifies in their mind their controlling and physically abusive behaviour. The abuser will often not take responsibility for their actions by minimising their actions and saying things like "I did not hit you hard enough to give you a black eye".

Since the abuser is emotionally dependant on their victims they act in controlling ways to exert power and deny their own weakness. Often they are extremely jealous of their spouse and may attribute certain stereotypical roles to their partners. For example they may consider their wives should be homebodies and not career women and if the wife becomes successful the abuser may start to escalate the abuse.

The abuser will nearly always use blame and *shift the responsibility* for their actions onto others. This allows the abuser to be angry with other people for causing the behaviour. It also applies to other areas of their life, for example, they may have fantasies of being rich and famous or having a successful career if only other people weren't holding them back. By using this tactic they can justify their behaviour when it comes to getting back at their victims. Instead of accepting responsibility for their own feelings, thoughts and actions they will always justify their behaviour by saying things like "you don't understand, I had a bad day at the office and that's why I lost my temper" or "I couldn't just stand by listening to him shouting at me which is why I punched him in the face"

When it comes to violence, abusive and manipulative men have a knack of blaming others for their own deficiencies. Although women can be guilty of violence too. Over a period of time many women, who are hit by men buy into the belief that they themselves are somehow at fault and as a result try harder and harder to change their own behaviours in order to prevent another violent episode. Men on the other hand are often too ashamed to admit that their female partners have been hitting them, in the case of say a borderline woman.

A batterer, for example, may be more likely to dominate women and expect it as their right and privilege. If they are the "macho" type they may tend to associate some feminine qualities with weakness and fear intimacy as a way of making them feel vulnerable. Most batterers suffered from low self esteem. Only a small minority of abusers are likely to turn violent. A batterer is more likely to have higher levels of hostility and their range of emotions tend to be reduced to anger in an attempt to regain their power because they have not lived up to the feminine stereotype by being the perfect man. Often their communication skills are lacking and appear alternatively as passive or aggressive in nature. They are more likely to resolve problems and emotions through violence based on their own view of the male stereotype. Batterers also have a high incidence of drug or alcohol abuse.

With regards to other forms of abuse such as verbal, emotional or psychological abuse, narcissists, in particular, would be more likely to target a co-dependent personality whereas a psychopath could target *anyone*. In fact the more confident the victim, the more likely they are to want to abuse them. Since narcissistic abusers and psychopaths are masters of projection and consider the victims to be an extension of themselves, they may use abuse as a last ditch effort to exert control over the latter, as though punishing her for being a *separate entity*.

In his comprehensive essay, "Understanding the Batterer in Custody and Visitation Disputes," Lundy Bancroft observes:

> "Because of the distorted perceptions that the abuser has of rights and responsibilities in relationships, he considers himself to be the victim. Acts of self-defence on the part of the battered woman or the children, or efforts they make to stand up for their rights, he defines as aggression against him. He is often highly skilled at twisting his descriptions of events to create the convincing impression that he has been victimized. He thus accumulates grievances over the course of the relationship to the same extent that the victim does, which can lead professionals to decide that the members of the couple 'abuse each other,' and that the relationship has been 'mutually hurtful...' He is manipulative; he misleads people inside and outside of the family about his abusiveness, he twists arguments around to make other people feel at fault, and he turns into a sweet, sensitive person for extended periods of time when he feels that it is in his best interest to do so. His public image usually contrasts sharply with the private reality."

Abusers have a tendency to feel they are unique and special and shouldn't have to live under the same rules as everyone else. Many people wrongly believe that people who are verbal and psychological abusers are loud and nasty. It's quite the opposite. Like many psychopathic abusers, Oliver was very polite a lot of the time apart from the occasional bouts of anger when caught out in a lie. Most of the time, his abuse came in the form of passive aggressive behaviour, gaslighting, emotional blackmail, manipulation, creating confusion, lying and fear.

When it comes to abuse, the best way to recognize an *unhealthy* relationship is to know what a healthy relationship looks like. Things like respect, understanding, forgiveness, acceptance, love, affection, and trustworthiness with the ability to connect deeply with someone; yet have the freedom to be oneself within healthy boundaries. If, like myself, you never really knew what a healthy relationship looked like; I had to do things the hard way, and learn from back to front by having one unhealthy relationship after another until I had the most unhealthy relationship on the planet. By knowing what an unhealthy relationship is I have learnt how to have healthy relationships and include that in all areas of my life.

The following describes the types of manipulation tactics an abusers is likely to use on victims.

Emotional abuse is done in the form of intimidation, and many come under a number of lovely guises such as what may appear to be genuine guidance, or helpful advice. The results are all similar, the victim eventually loses all sense of self and their own personal value. Emotional abuse cuts to the very cores of the person and the scars may be far more deeper and more lasting than physical abuse. The victim may become so beaten down emotionally by insults, insinuations and criticism that they are incapable of judging themselves realistically. They may become so convinced by their abusers comments that they wont believe that anyone else could possibly want them. They often choose to stay in abusive relationships because they fear being alone. Coupled with the sexual dynamics that form the psychopathic bond the abusive relationship thrives easily.

Children of alcoholics, for example, are nearly always emotionally abused. Some of the things they end up feeling about themselves may include not being able to accept compliments, expecting others to just know what they want, being extremely loyal even when their loyalty is undeserved, having trouble having fun because their childhood was stolen. Or judging themselves without mercy.

Some of the types of emotional abuse are listed below.

Assuming - Abusers often assume they know better even down to what the other person is thinking or feeling. This allows them to justify their behaviour. They may say something like "I knew you would get p**ed and angry at me for being home late from work, so I decided to go to pub with my mates for a drink after, I figured I might as well enjoy myself anyway"

Blaming - They are experts at playing the blame game and tend to shift responsibility for their actions to their victims. They can become angry because their victim caused them to behave inappropriately. The abuser might claim, "If you hadn't talked back to me, I wouldn't have had to hit you." They may also say things like "Well, I didn't start this relationship; you were the one who seduced me in the first place." They seldom take responsibility for their actions, but try to justify their behaviour by constantly making excuses. They may blame the abuse on a difficult childhood or a hard day at the office. Their mindset tells them that they are never to blame for any negative behaviour. There is always a plausible rationale in the abuser's mind for their actions.

Creating Constant Chaos and Confusion - The abuser may deliberately start arguments with you on purpose, or create situations where they know you may get upset. This allows them to use any number of other techniques on you such as emotional blackmail, invalidation and so on. An example for this is saying they have arranged to meet you then when they have not turned up saying they it was *your* fault because you never reminded them in the first place. Often the abuser will use this when it comes to sex constantly demanding more and more. If the victim doesn't oblige the victim may be constantly criticized and berated because they are unable to fulfil the abuser's demands. Conversely, as a punishment, the abuser will withhold sex altogether. They do this as a way of gaining control over their partner and keeping you in a state of constant confusion.

Denial - This is where the abuser denies all knowledge of ever having said anything for example "I don't know what you are taking about" or "I never said that." They may disallow or overrule any viewpoints which differ from their own experience, denying your perceptions, memory and very sanity. Denying is done with the intent of hurting, punishing and humiliating their victims. The abuser also wants the victim to lose their confidence and in time, probably their mind.

Demeaning - Abusers are like spoilt children, acting out if they don't get their way. They will centre their victim out in front of family and friends by taking small personality flaws and embellishing them to the extreme. They make snide remarks and use sarcasm to erode the victim's sense of self-worth and self confidence. Making the victim look bad in front of others is an attempt to isolate the victim and keep them at their mercy.

Dominating and Controlling - This has the effect of controlling a persons actions. For example "You mustn't do things like this". The abuser may tell the victim that they are not allowed to go and meet one of their friends or control what kinds of clothes they wear. This can be overt or very subtle and eventually the victim loses all sense of self respect for themselves and may lose their identity. When you are having a conversation sometimes the verbal abuser will cut off a discussion in mid-sentence before she/he can even finish her thought. The abuser may try to control all of the victims time and physical environment and suppress their old behaviour. As the abuser instils more and more powerlessness and dependency in their victim along with that comes fear. Verbal and emotional abuse has the effect of amplifying these feelings and as they become stronger over time the victim becomes helpless.

Emotional Blackmail - Because the abuser wants you to feel fear, guilt or compassion they may tap into your empathy buttons to get what they want from you. This could include threats of suicide, abandonment or saying "but if only you loved me." Emotional blackmail may also come in the form of lies to gain your sympathy, like telling you they have no money or they are sick with a life-threatening illness.

Gaining Sympathy – Abusers are experts are gaining sympathy, using sob stories to play on the emotional bond they have with their understanding victims. Feigning illness or saying how badly their previous partner treated them will likely elicit your sympathies. Believe it or not, abusers are actually emotionally dependent on their victim, especially narcissists, who thrive on narcissistic supply. Lacking the supply causes an inner rage that encourages the abuser to lash out. Because he is so dependent, he takes control of his victim's life. This is the way they deny their weaknesses, to make themselves feel powerful. Gaining sympathy allows the abuser to continue to have narcissistic supply from their victims.

Gaslighting – This type of abuse is an increasing frequency of systematically withholding factual information from, and/or providing false information to the victim thus having the gradual effect of making them anxious, confused, and less able to trust their own memory and perception.

Invalidation and Minimalising - Invalidating occurs when the abuser refuses or fails to acknowledge reality. For example you may say that you felt hurt by what they did and they will response with "I think you are being overly sensitive" When minimizing, the abuser may not necessarily deny that a particular event occurred, but they will make the victim question their own emotional experience or reaction to an event by saying things "I think you are blowing this whole thing out of proportion".

Lying - This is the abusers most manipulative tool by lying to control information. They may also be doing it to keep their victim off balance psychologically. Lying can come under a number of disguises from blatant out and out lies to gaslighting, selectively forgetting and so forth.

Overly Demanding - This is where the abuser places unreasonable demands on you and wants you to put a hold on everything else to tend to their own needs. Often the more you give the more they will demand. It doesn't matter how much you give them it will never be enough. If you refuse they may resort to criticising the victim for not fulfilling their needs.

Ridiculing and making jokes - Often abusers like to take cheap shots at their victims by using sarcasm or making snide comments. They may single you out in front of family members or say things like "You don't look as fat as you did a few months ago."

Selective Amnesia - Selective Amnesia includes *selectively* forgetting events and conversations that have happened. Some abusers consistently forget about the promises they have made which are most important to their partners. These include things like birthdays, anniversary's and so on. When it comes to conversations they may say things like "I don't ever remember saying that I think you have you're wires crossed" or "did I really say that". If it comes to birthday presents they may choose not to buy you a present but go pull all the stops out when it comes to celebrating their childrens/friends/parents birthdays.

Silent Treatment - The silent treatment is a quiet form of anger that says "you do not exist." Abusers use this as a form of punishment. Steve Becker writes on his website:

> "The silent treatment is not only silent, but can be deadly. Deadly, that is, to relationships. Deadly, more specifically, to the trust, love, safety, communication and intimacy that preserve and nourish relationships. ....The silent treatment is a statement of contempt, relating, "You aren't worth the energy it would take me to acknowledge your existence, let alone your feelings or needs." ...The silent treatment tactically communicates, You have done something wrong, seriously wrong — wrong enough to warrant my repudiation of your existence. ..The silent treatment is a technique of torture. This may sound hyperbolic, but human beings need (on the most basic level) recognition of their existence. The withholding of this recognition, especially if protracted, can have soul-warping consequences on personality."

Unpredictability – This type of abuse comes in the form of drastic mood changes or emotional outbursts. Often the the abuser may say one thing one day then something completely different the next. The victim feels on edge because they never know where they stand and the goalposts are constantly shifting. They always remain hyper vigilant wondering when the other person is likely to have an outburst or change of mood. As a result the victim may start to feel frightened and unsettled. Other tactics might include keeping the victim unaware of what is going on and what changes are taking place. For example, they may make plans for you and then cancel them or talk about you behind your back with the intention of isolating you from others. This type of abuse is done with the intention of keeping the victim in a constant state of anxiety and confusion.

Verbal Assaults - In the from of name calling, accusing, blaming and/or threatening intimidating behaviour.

Mind Blasting – These are comments or mind numbing techniques that just don't always make sense and or fit into any of the other categories. They may include conversations or actions that divert from the original argument or put blame back on the victim but often they are very ambiguous. The abuser says comments that will put you off guard and make you think your going crazy and almost certainly unable to give a response to. Often these types of comments are irrational and are used to make the victim feel confused, off guard or doubt their reality. You can find some examples in the Chapter On Gaslighting

If you are left feeling confused and crazy by their gaslighting behaviour, their verbal assaults and emotional demands and strange conversations, stop! This is exactly how they want you to feel. The minute you become aware of what they are doing and the fact that they are actually *manipulating* you, sometime miraculous happens.

You start writing down what they are saying and see that much of the conversations you have with them are confusing and make no sense at all. We are left with the feeling that we have been living in the "Twilight Zone."

Sex, Power, and Control

At their core, every abuser is monumentally self-centred. They have egos that need fuelling like the black hole described in Chapter 4. Everything and everyone revolves around them. They are also very much about Sex, Power, and Control.

Narcissists, in particular, have the need to control others which is why they are perfect for jobs where they have lots of followers, like the Flirty Fishing "god-like" cult hero who used his followers of the opposite sex to attract even more followers. We see it all the time in the media:

hyped-up celebrities who actually do not care about criticism and will do anything they can to gain attention. When a very well-known narcissistic couple, the wife half of which had appeared on some reality TV shows had split up, she was in the papers blaming him. She claimed the marriage failure was all his fault, and was determined to destroy his character as well as writing stories about how terrible he was in the bedroom, etc. This is the classic pathology of adulation and disregard: the minute a pathological person has no use for you, you are dirt, and within days along will come a replacement to fill your boots!

In their warped, twisted reality, the Dark Soul cannot possibly look inside himself. He perceives everything outward through an empty shell and failure to worship them will result in your devastation. If you look at the extreme end of the egotistical personality (where people like Adolf Hitler represent the ultimate in egomania), you will usually find them feeling entitled to dominate others. Sam Vaknin writes much about this in his book, "Malignant Self-love: Narcissism Revisited". Anyone who questions the validity of his statements will feel the full wrath of his narcissistic rage.

Usually a Dark Soul will suggest that their victims are the ones that control them, especially if they are the type that want to play on others' sympathies. If you speak to their victims, however, you will find a whole other story. The motive for these Dark Souls always remains control, whether it is sex, money, or power.

Politicians, for example, would never be able to do the job as well were it not for their need to overtly control. If the world was made up of politicians who were empathic and wanted to serve its people, we would have neither wars nor power struggles.

If you the victim question a Dark Soul about their reality, they will lie to your face. After all *they* actually believe it. It is only when you give them hard evidence that they will have to admit that they are wrong, and even then, they will come up with an excuse. Then they will move on and return to their false image of themselves again until they get caught again. At one point in our relationship, Oliver worked as a salesman for a company. In his mind, he was the country's best salesman, an expert in his field. In his mind, he earned the best commissions for the company until he was finally sacked. When he was about to get fired, he blamed the company, spreading rumours about them failing financially. Oliver started saying they never paid their employees and that they owed large sums to their suppliers. When he left, he had been caught with massive telephone bills he had run up at the company's expense, because he had been doing two jobs on company time. As well, although he had been filing false reports on site visits, he had maintained that the company had treated him unfairly because he had claimed to be receiving cancer therapy. The cancer was nonexistent and, supposedly, his therapist was me! Despite unsuccessfully trying to have me corroborate his fabricated story, he still tried to sue them for wrongful dismissal.

The problem with these Dark Souls is that everything is a mask, "an illusion," and they cannot keep the mask up for very long. After a while it starts to slip. When one lives a complete lie, it's very difficult to keep up, since lying takes a lot of energy. A normal person feels guilt and shame at lying, and usually ends up spilling the beans because he cannot hold onto the lies any longer. Failing that, he gets caught and admits everything. Dark Souls, however, have no qualms about lying, and feel no shame. Unless there is hard evidence Dark Souls may often completely deny it using the gaslighting techniques described in a previous chapter and make out its all your imagination.

When observing Dark Souls pay close attention to their facial expressions to those people they like and dislike. Often they will categorise people into black and white or talk about people as if they love them, hate them or own them. They will usually only say good things about people that they believe admire them and have disdainful feelings towards those people they do not like. These are the people who have failed in their eyes to live up to and pander to their feelings of specialness. They always convey a feeling of themselves as being superior to others. If its something as significant as your IQ theirs will be higher than yours. If you went to a certain school, theirs will have been better. If you dated someone famous they will have dated a celebrity. Chances are most of the things they have told you are lies and they usually tell you these things to undermine you and make you feel inferior.

One of the common mistakes that people make when they are being charmed by a Dark Soul is that, unlike a normal person, where it feels healthy and normal to want to please them, you feel like you are being *compelled* or forced to do it. It's very subtle and feels like you are in a trance. Often, victims remark how they cannot believe they ever did some things they would never do under normal circumstances and about how they felt "powerless or paralysed." I found a post on a support forum where one woman wrote about her experience with a Dark Soul "with the eyes and voice of a snake charmer — mesmerising from head to toe." She goes onto write about an "unnatural, nauseating 'bonding' to this man." Unless you have actually had a relationship with a Dark Soul, it's very difficult to describe just how convincing and manipulative they are.

As for power, control and sex, all humans are different. So, if a Dark Soul is obsessed by power, they are more likely to be in a job that involves working in politics or large multinational companies. There are numerous books about sociopaths in the workplace, nearly all describe the sociopath's unique ability to "blend in."

Dark Souls might also be more inclined to be motivated by sex. These are the types, like Oliver, that have affairs, appear on sex sites, swing, have multiple partners, and experiment with prostitutes, bondage, and submission. I am not suggesting that all people who do these things are psychopathic, however, the psychopathic personality is more likely to go and find "victims" on these sites. They are more likely to be dishonest and use people for their gain.

Another part of control is often sex. Many people who have had relationships with these Dark Souls make comments about how wonderful the sex is especially at the beginning of the relationship. I know with my ex it was probably an 11/10 if that's possible. He had a way of hitting all the right buttons and mutually we made each other feel wonderful in the bedroom. However the cracks will always appear. Oliver started off as what can only be described as a "submissive" wanting to please me.

However as time went on Oliver became far more aggressive in the bedroom. The submissive role he took where "I" came first was soon a thing of the past. He started to withhold sex and it became much more about me pleasing him. He became very interested in rougher sex and wanted to have anal sex more and more. Sometimes, he was extremely aggressive and the gentle man I first men in the bedroom soon became an animal. Other times, he would use excuses that he was tired or he didn't have any energy. The marathon lovemaking sessions started to tail off and I would end up having to ask for sex. Many other women have described being in a place where they literally had to "beg" for sex. Towards the latter end of the relationship, I found Oliver on sex sites as he obviously had interests elsewhere. We'd had sex only once in two years. Fortunately, I wasn't stupid enough to have sex with him again and he'd actually had the audacity to claim "impotence," saying he couldn't have sex any more because he felt so guilty and ashamed for what he had done.

Thinking about it now actually makes me laugh that he would stoop so low as to feign impotency but it was one of the kindest things he did because at least I didn't risk catching any STD from him. I believe in Oliver's mind it was all about control. Oliver knew how much I loved sex, so what he would do is kiss me and get me to the point where I would be extremely excited then fall asleep. Otherwise, he would tell me that it wasn't me, but he really didn't feel much like having sex because "it" didn't work properly any more. Oliver even went so far as to "play out the story" by going to the doctors and saying that they had checked him out physically and there was nothing wrong with him. Regardless, it would take months for him to "recover" and there would have to be some time before we could have sex again. A previous ex boyfriend had used the same ploy and I finally found out that it was not because they were "impotent," it was actually because they wanted to control the amount of sex they had with their partners. They know that their partners want sex so they use it as a means of control. I have read other women's stories that where they said their love lives went from a healthy 10/10 to a 1/1, often finding out that their partners had been having an affair or worse. Some even mention that their partners feigned the impotence story as a way of controlling their "understanding" partners.

It's a common tactic for Dark Souls to use sex as a weapon in their relationships. Both women and men do it. Men, however, know that no matter how much their female partners desire sex, she is unlikely to seek it outside of the relationship. It has a way of making her feel simultaneously responsible and guilty for her own desires by using manipulation techniques. By using excuses such as "impotence," "a hard day at work," or feigning "illness" as an excuse, he knows his victim is unlikely to challenge him. At the same time, knowing they have control of their victim's loyalty, they are now in the position to work her sexual longing by timing its gratification. It is common for victims to find that their partners interest in sex diminishes and for the victim to end up blaming themselves or losing her own sex drive when, in fact, her partner is busy having sex with someone else.

Even if your Dark Soul appears to be soft and yielding in the bedroom it could be that they are repressing their angry urges. One commentator wrote about a patient who had an unusual impotence problem. He had no problems making love on his back, but when he was lying on top of a woman, he'd get a permanent hard-on and could not ejaculate. "He was harbouring so much anger toward his mother that he basically turned his penis into a .45-calibre gun. He actually had dreams about it. As long as he was underneath, he wasn't responsible for what happened. In the dominant position, though, to come meant pulling the trigger." Often these types of men are trapped into infancy, trying to please but actually wanting to kill. There is so much anger inside them that to express it becomes unthinkable.

Many victims will say things like "But he must have loved me." Sadly no, in a warped kind of logic all the things that they "loved" about you, they actually despise because they see it as a weakness.

Oliver, the man with so many faces that wanted to kill his wife had another persona too. One of a very subservient person who would do *anything* to service a woman and or a man, or anyone for that matter ! One of the many adverts I found for Oliver was as follows. To fully understand the ad, "TV" stands for transvestite, "TS" is transsexual, and

"CD" is for cross dressers. I have changed some of the wording for privacy and legal reasons, but I had found more than 30 adverts with his details, his star sign, age, and location. He even mentioned that his hobbies including martial arts and that his favourite type of food (of which I wasn't aware) were "cream pies," and not the kind that come with strawberries!

Horny guy loves cream pie

Hi I love cream pie, I love to give and play with sloppy seconds.
I would love to meet up for some fun. Get in touch xxx

I am looking to hear from Female and Couples and Groups and CD / TV / TS members

Gender: Male

Age: 37

Sexuality: Bi

[Town name]xxxxxxxxx

Will travel

Safe Sex: I will tell you later!

I also found a few other interesting ones. Which said "Hi My Motto is I am *extremely adventurous"* and even went so far as to list his star sign and hobbies! Not to mention his *other* interests such as appearing in porn films and cleaning up sloppy seconds which I believe is the same thing as eating cream pies.

As you can see from the adverts I am sure his wife would have been far from delighted if she had found Oliver on these websites. Fortunately, she had been intelligent enough to have kicked him out. I hope, like myself, that she was lucky not to have caught anything.

Oliver is no exception there are thousands of stories of people who have found their partners doing the most unspeakable things and it's scary how much of a double life these people can really lead without batting an eyelid.

Gaslighting Their Victims

According to Wikipedia, gaslighting is a form of intimidation or psychological abuse in which false information is presented to the victim, making them doubt their own memory and perception. The classic example of gaslighting is to change things in a person's environment without their knowledge, and to explain that they "must be imagining things" when they challenge these changes. Gaslighting is a common tactic/symptom of some mental disorders such as Borderline Personality Disorder (BPD) and Narcissistic Personality Disorder (NPD), and other Personality Disorders. People having BPD will use gaslighting (consciously or unconsciously) along with a wide variety of psychologically manipulative/abusive tactics to fend-off criticism of their own actions that they deem too painful to accept responsibility for. The term derives from the 1940 film *Gaslight*. In the film, a wife's concerns about the dimming of her house's gas lights are dismissed by her husband as the work of her imagination, when he is actually fully aware of the reason for their dimming. This is part of a wider pattern of deception in which the husband manipulates small elements of his wife's environment, and insists that she is mistaken or misremembering when she challenges them.

One psychological definition of gaslighting is "an increasing frequency of systematically withholding factual information from, and/or providing false information to the victim thus having the gradual effect of making them anxious, confused, and less able to trust their own memory and perception." For those of us who have never experienced gaslighting, it's something that abusers do to their victims to make them think that they are the ones losing their minds. Used in conjunction with *Mind Blasting*, it breaks the victim's boundaries down bit by bit until they no longer know what is true anymore.

Gaslighting is an abuser's favourite choice of psychological weapon. It is used to ensure the victim is in a constant state of uncertainty and anxiety. The gaslighter will make plans and promises only to break them at whim and often blatantly deny that they made any plans or promises in the first place.

In the movie, *Gaslight*, the main character is a woman who has a wonderful career and falls in love with a man suddenly. Within two weeks, he wants to take her away from her career and marry her. Even at the beginning of the relationship, she has doubts about him and decides to take a break before deciding on a committed relationship but he relentlessly pursues her. The man portrays the classic psychopath personality. Without giving the whole plot away, during the film he gives her a present in the form of a cameo and then makes a point of telling her she has a habit of losing things to which she replies "do I?" Later in the movie, after strategically placing the cameo in her purse, he takes her out to a museum. On pulling out her handkerchief, she finds that the cameo is missing, not realising that her husband has removed it, in a deliberate effort to make her believe she is absent minded and forgetful.

One time, I had let Oliver use my computer to pay for something on line. I would always leave my switch card next to the keyboard, and the following day it was missing. I called him up to ask him if he had inadvertently picked it up as I needed it, knowing that I would never leave the card anywhere else apart from my handbag. Oliver said something very strange: "Perhaps you have put it somewhere silly like the refrigerator." A week later, still not having found the card, I had ordered a new one. That's when I found the card hidden under a bottle of vinegar in the kitchen. When I told Oliver where I had found it, he laughed and said "how strange."

In *Gaslight*, the man continues to play mind games with his wife. He would keep adjusting the gas to dim the lights, causing her to believe her mind was starting to play tricks on her, hence the term "gaslighting." He shows classic signs of Narcissistic rage throughout the movie when questioned about his motives for doing things and projects his feelings back at his victim. There is one particularly uncomfortable scene in the movie where he has stolen a painting from the wall and tries to imply his wife has perhaps removed it. In humiliating his wife, he summons all the servants and makes them swear they haven't taken the painting. The wife, who knows in her own heart, that neither she nor her servants have taken the painting, is tempted to admit to having taken it merely to keep the peace. He humiliates and degrades her by making her search for the picture. She finds it behind a statue where it had been lost before. This is a common tactic used by psychopaths to throw their victims off guard. Another well known tactic for psychopaths is to move things around and try and make their victims appear to have gone insane. Apparently, Charles Manson, in his series of "Creepy Crawler" burglaries in the 1960s, would break into victims' properties during the night and take nothing, but, instead, move all the garden furniture around while the residents were asleep just to confuse them. If they would have tried explaining that to the police, they would have been thought to be insane. This technique can be very bewildering and frightening.

Abusers also use techniques which I have called "Mind Blasting" to avoid truth. These methods act like a sort of "mental confusion," to ensure the original subject disappears and diverts the attention from the original topic. The abuser may also use delay tactics as a subtle means through which to buy time, whereby they can think up new lies and excuses. These are comments or mind numbing techniques that just don't add up at all nor really fit into any of the other emotional abuse categories. They may are diversionary, intentionally ambiguous, put you off balance and are often totally irrational. You may be left wondering how can you respond without arguing further. Some examples are below:

- "So you're implying that I am f**ked up. I am not the one who went for counselling."

- "It's pointless having a discussion with you. Nothing I ever do or say will ever convince you that I am telling the truth. You are always so emotional."

- "What was it your ex-boyfriend use to say about you when you got upset?"

- "We already had this argument just before you decided to go to the doctor when you were feeling down and got put on the sleeping pills. Your probably tired."

- "Honestly! You can't *really* expect me to believe that? Why would anyone do anything so ridiculous?"

- "Just because you feel things like that doesn't mean I have the same feelings as you. I just don't feel things in the same way as you do."

- "I think the fact that you are really angry is stopping you from seeing things clearly. Let's talk about this another time."

- "That's the most ridiculous thing I have ever heard. Why would I do such a thing? I wasn't going to tell you, but only yesterday, I went out and bought you that present you wanted"

- "How is the way you are talking to me so completely differently from the way you speak to your ex husband?"

- "So where were we? You have been talking for so long, I have a headache now."

- "Look, if you are going to cry every time we have a conversation, how can I answer you? You're not really in a fit state to listen properly. Here, have a tissue and let's talk about something else instead"

- "I really don't see any point in discussing this further until you have all your facts straight."

- "It's probably best that this question you have come up with. I am not prepared to discuss it, to be honest. Why because you have been picking a fight with me for ages. I think it's best we finish for a couple of weeks to give you a chance to calm down, then we will discuss it another time"

- "That's interesting."

- "I am astonished you would even think that!"

- "How would you feel if I asked you a similar question?"

- "For someone that is supposed to be so spiritual, you seem to be lacking somewhat in your ability to understand how I am feeling."

- "That's a cruel thing to say! I thought you were a nice person."

- "See, what I told you? You are acting all crazy again!"

- "What would your friends think of you now if they could see you arguing like this?"

- "If you would actually listen for once, you would have heard what I said the first time when I said that...."

- "Have you finally finished? It's obvious you just want to argue."

- "There is no point in having this discussion now. When you have calmed down, I will talk to you."

- "Its all your imagination. Isn't it about time you went back on the anti depressants darling. Here let me make you a cup of tea."

9

Masters of Illusion

What if I were to ask you, halfway into reading this book and armed with the knowledge you already have, what kind of man you would look for in a relationship? You might decide you would write everything down in a list. Perhaps you are looking for a super hero, a good guy, or a great lover, or perhaps just someone who is kind. I am sure by this time you will be writing that you would like someone honest. You might write, "I am looking for a man who is honest, kind, attractive, likes children" and so on.

Unfortunately, the Dark Soul is a Master of Illusion and will change his behaviour according to whatever he feels or whatever makes him look good. He will *appear* initially to be everything on your wish list.

If you go to a shop and buy a tin of paint, you would at least expect it to do whatever it says on the label. When looking for a relationship with a Dark Soul, we automatically assume he is genuine and it wouldn't be unreasonable to expect the label to match up to the contents. Unfortunately, he is the ultimate *Shape Shifter*. He is a magician when it comes to creating an illusion, literally pulling anything out of the hat by lying. He is able to alter and tailor his appearance to deceive others.

Many of their victims are Empaths. Any type of person can be drawn to a Dark Soul usually because they are charismatic, charming and manipulative. However often their victims are Empaths. Why is this? Because they are able to mimic feelings and emotions that for us is genuine, but for them is a tool. And because they "*appear*" to be much like us, we think that they are also Empaths. Sadly nothing could be further from the truth!

Shape Shifters

To describe a Shape Shifter:

> "He's like a artist with a blank canvas, waiting for direction,
> who can mould and shape himself at will. He will appear
> to be *anything* you want him to be. He watches and waits
> for you to give him subtle clues, and direction before he
> picks up the brush and then he'll paint the perfect scene."

Its only when you actually realise that the painting is a façade and that there is a blank canvas underneath that you realise anything is wrong.

One of the biggest red flags when dealing with an abuser is the "pity play" ploy. Once you have worked through your negative beliefs in the "Healing" section of this book, you will be able to spot them. As a child growing up with a not-so-healthy family, I had no idea what the words narcissist, borderline, or sociopath meant, and, least of all, a new word I had made up: "Dark Soul." To me, people were just people and I would treat everyone the same way. However, what I discovered was a little red flashing neon sign over the top of my head to all abusive men saying: "Come and get me!"

To a Dark Soul, you are "special and only *you* really understand them." This is a way of drawing on you emotionally and making you feel unique. They may tell you are the best lover they have ever had. Despite the likelihood they may be sleeping with a dozen other people. While you are the object of their attention you will feel elevated and worshipped. You need to notice how quickly they make you feel special. Relationships with Dark Souls move rapidly – far quicker than a normal relationship. Often, you will find yourself having sex with them within a matter of days. I have read of cases where women have ended up in bed the same night. They will tell you they love you, often within weeks, and make all kinds of promises they can never fulfil, just to keep you ensnared in their game.

They may, in the initial stages, buy you gifts, but beware! Oliver gave me a car once. I was so gobsmacked when he gave me it thinking it was the most lovely gesture - until he kept "forgetting" to give me the log book. Little did I know that the log book was tucked away in a pile of papers and it was only when I finally asked him to leave and put the "lost" log book in front of him to sign that he reluctantly signed it over. I believe that he had given me the car to cover up for all the things he had been hiding from his wife when she asked him to leave his house, hoping I wouldn't say anything because I would be distracted and impressed by this lovely new gift. Which to my surprise was actually the only real gift I ever got from him.

A woman who had lived with narcissists for much of her life suggested, wrote on a web post, that you be very suspicious when they do something really "nice" for you because it can be an indicator that they are about to do something really *nasty,* especially when it comes out of the blue. The car that Oliver gave me reminded me of a time when my own father had just returned back from America from a lovely family holiday only to want to move over there and take my mother with him leaving my teenage brother behind. He spend 6 weeks frantically doing all the jobs in the house he had never done in 10 years. When my mother refused to go there with him thinking something did not add up, he went to the states without her. It turned out he had had an affair whilst on the family holiday a few weeks earlier. The reason he had done all the work he had avoided for so long was to appease my mother in the hope it would distract her from his ulterior motive. He actually wanted to move my mother over to the states in the hope that he could keep both relationships going. This was the final straw, and my mother finally left and filed for a divorce after 35 years.

Oliver would often *shape shift.* At the beginning of the relationship, he would bend over backwards to offer to help me. It was a like a dream come true. He wasn't particularly generous but he had *appeared* to be generous with his time. However, the time he spent wanting to do nothing more than enjoy my company as a friend soon turned into spending hours having marathon sex sessions. When the minute came that he had to return home, he couldn't have left quicker. When I needed him to help me for anything, he was always busy or had the perfect excuse not to be there. Often, he would use his children as the reason, claiming his son was sick. Being a working mother myself, he knew I would never question it, so eventually I would feel guilty for even asking him. I had a couple of operations over the years we knew each other, and he would never be able to visit me in hospital. His jujitsu or his children were always more important. These shape shifters are extremely clever at finding the things that make us tick, such as high moral or family values, and then turning them around and using them to their advantage.

Another ploy Oliver liked to use was pity play. He would portray a downtrodden husband that worked all week and spend his weekends looking after the children, claiming that he would prepare dinner for them as soon as he got home because his wife was too lazy to cook for them. He was always coming up with a sob story about how nasty his wife was, and how hard he had to work to pay his bills, and so I started to feel really sorry for him.

Shape shifters move very quickly on to their victims in order to form an emotional bond. You will usually feel it within the first month if you are not already having sex with them by then, you can be quite sure you will be soon. They use seduction as a way of forming a false emotional bond with you. Every conversation you have with them is charged and intense, making you feel like you have met your soul mate. They will want to know everything about you. Often this is a ploy to gain as much information as possible so they can use this at a later to date to manipulate you. For example I had had a history of sexual abuse and a life threatening illness. It later transpired in a "fluke" conversation that Mr Dark Soul had too been sexually abused when he was a child. Now in hindsight I can look back at myself and say "what a twat I was" for believing it. But at the time their story was so very convincing.

When we are in a relationship, we never think about doing a background check or credential check on our partners least of all checking their medical records. If, however, we were going to employ someone, we would not even consider hiring that person without knowing their history and having the evidence to back it up. In relationships we take a lot of what our partners say on trust, although it usually takes time for partners to earn our trust.

During a relationship with a Dark Soul, things will start to feel very uncomfortable. You will notice that you are emotionally being drained, much like a black hole sucking everything out of you. Part of the uncomfortable feelings you get are when you start to notice that the only time he actually perks up is when your attention is focused on *him*. He will "perk up" emotionally and that's when he may treat you well emotionally. He will hook into your compassionate and loving nature. When they sense that they're losing your prime attention, that's when the cracks appear and they will do more to draw you in with sneakier tactics and a more elaborate game plan. That's when they'll transform into *whatever it takes* to keep you intrigued and involved.

The Shape Shifting Vampire

So what happens when Mr. Tender Loving Man starts to show his real colours and you realise he is actually Mr Bottomless Pit Energy Vampire. I would often notice how, whenever we would split up, even his energy field would change. He would be completely full of himself by the time he had drained my spirit dry, and then, after a couple of months of no contact, we would be back playing the game again. That's when he would perk up, drain me dry again, and then return to filling himself up.

Beware, too, of Mr Dark Soul's moods. Although I am not an expert on personality disorders, you could be dealing with a Borderline. A Borderline may appear depressed or anxious one minute, and then indifferent and vulnerable the next. They can flip between elation to mournful gloom in the blink of an eye. Hypochondria is one the things that they may use to con you. Their complaints may come and go in direct proportion to the amount of attention you are giving them. As much their physical symptoms come and go, so do their emotions. This is because they are so out of touch with their feelings, they will either have none, whatsoever, or "pretend" to have them, as a ruse to get closer to you. If you think you can "help" or "fix this man," you're certain to be disappointed. Energetically, they will snare you, hook, line, and sinker.

Being in a relationship with a Dark Soul is like being in a quagmire. You know you want to get out because you know it's dangerous, wrong, and nothing adds up, but you feel paralysed and unable to get out. Oliver reminds me of the character Glenn Quagmire, a character from the cartoon series "Family Man." Best known for his hyper-sexuality, the series features him in his wanton and deviant sexual behaviour. He's known for predatory behaviour, like drugging his dates' drinks and performing a seemingly endless chain of bizarre sexual acts.

What You See Is Not What You Get

If you imagine that the person you *think* you see in the beginning is completely *unlike* the person you are dating, this is exactly how a Shape Shifter is. If you want to see a Shape Shifter in action, watch the "Big Brother" episodes in which Nick Bateman completely cons his house mates. He starts off by giving Reiki to them and then tells them that he had lost his fiancée in a tragic car accident. He later reveals that he had done it to build up empathy between him and the contestants, although none of it was true. To try and *win the game*, he starts playing each of the victims off against each other behind their backs. When the producers realised what was going on, they asked him to leave by the back door. Ironically, before he was uncovered, he was the most popular house mate. The house mates were unaware of his duplicity and yet, outside, he received no public votes because everyone could see what he was doing!

Bateman exaggerated many of his credentials by saying that he worked as a senior broker for Lloyds of London when in fact he was only a junior at a small London firm. He also failed to point out when telling the contestants that he was a "vice president" of Fulham football ground, that he actually only possessed a vice president season ticket that was available to other fans as well.

Residents of his parents' village of Hurstborne Tarrant, Hampshire, have expressed surprise at the vilification. He was known as a thoroughly nice chap and a nice guy. He was voted "Most hated man in Britain" Upon leaving the house, he had mixed feelings and his thoughts soon turned to how much money could he make. He did a number of TV shows and then went on to write a book called *Nasty Nick: How To Be a Right Bastard.* Nick Bateman is the perfect example of putting on a different face just to get his needs met. For a man with such a big ego, I wonder how he would feel knowing his book is selling for less than 10p!

On the surface, Oliver also *appeared* to have one face and yet underneath he had quite another. He was the *family guy*, at the heart of the community, and a good father who was unhappy and just looking for some love. He also claimed to be the best salesman in his field in the country. However conversely he was more like Glenn Quagmire in Family Man, he was really a predator preying on old ladies by selling them crapmatic beds. Some of the other characteristics that the cartoon character Glenn Quagmire shared in common with Oliver were too scary to be true. He never pays for anything. He pretends to be a "deep" guy who loves women for their souls. He's done nothing to help anyone despite his liberal beliefs. He drives a Prius, giving the image of being "eco friendly." He doesn't believe in religion and thinks it's for idiots. He failed college twice, he's a failure as a father, and never sees his son. He is also a sexual pervert that likes cream pies. In fact, when I read Quagmire's biography, I nearly fell off my chair laughing. Talking about coincidence, here I was on Google one day trying to explain how I was feeling and typing in "feeling like a quagmire" and there's Family Guy!

Any kind of Shape Shifter will reinvent themselves at the drop of a hat. They may change careers and suddenly develop new found "expertise" in areas.

Sam Vaknin says

> "In general, the narcissist always prefers show-off to substance. One of the most effective methods of exposing a narcissist is by trying to delve deeper. The narcissist is shallow, a pond pretending to be an ocean. He likes to think of himself as a Renaissance man, a Jack of all trades. The narcissist never admits to ignorance in any field yet, typically,

he is ignorant of them all. It is surprisingly easy to penetrate the gloss and the veneer of the narcissist's self-proclaimed omniscience. "

This does not only apply to narcissists. Psychopaths will reinvent themselves too as will compulsive liars.

Sam Vaknin goes onto say

"Until very recently I pretended to know everything - I mean EVERYTHING, in every field of human knowledge and endeavour. I lied and invented to avoid proof of my ignorance. I pretended to know and resorted to numerous subterfuges to support my God-like omniscience (reference books hidden in my clothes, frequent visits to the restroom, cryptic notation or sudden illness, if all else failed). Where my knowledge failed me - I feigned authority, faked superiority, quoted from non-existent sources, embedded threads of truth in a canvass of falsehoods. I transformed myself into an artist of intellectual prestidigitation. As I advanced in age, this invidious quality has receded, or, rather, metamorphosed. I now claim more confined expertise. I am not ashamed to admit my ignorance and need to learn outside the fields of my self-proclaimed expertise. But this "improvement" is merely optical. Within my "territory", I am still as fiercely defensive and possessive as I have ever been. And I am still an avowed autodidact, unwilling to subject my knowledge and insights to peer scrutiny, or, for this matter, to any scrutiny. I keep re-inventing myself, adding new fields of knowledge as I go: finance, economics, psychology, philosophy, physics, politics... This crawling intellectual annexation is a round about way of reverting to my old image as the erudite "Renaissance Man".

If you want to find out what they have been doing in their careers look at their track record and check references. Do NOT assume anything or take their word as trust. Prior to meeting Oliver he was an *expert* in installation of telecommunication equipment, prior to that he had trained as a surveyor. Before that he was working in a garden centre, had worked as a bouncer, had been to horticultural college and his original choice of career was to join the army and kill people but told me he was refused on health grounds. In the short time that I knew him (a total of five years) he was first a salesman selling signs then within a few months (after getting fired) he had changed jobs to become a web designer. He ran a brief sideline business teaching people unarmed combat using martial arts. Then a brief stint as a "consultant" PA in the building industry followed shortly after. When all of these failed he went onto be an *expert* consultant in wind turbines which left him having to work as a temporary fork lift truck driver because he got fired again. Even after being caught out on for lying about working for the wind turbine company whilst he was selling beds; he continued to lie by getting himself a new *non existent* job as a manager at a national power company including a lovely new *non existent* company car, which he actually bought. When in fact he was actually still selling the delightful crapmatic beds. What was even more sinister is he used a big national company and found a person who had the same surname as him so he could clone himself to make this new *non existent* job look more authentic. So when I finally called up the last company to ask if Mr Smith worked there, they were absolutely mortified because he had never worked for them at all. What was even more creepy was he had gone to the trouble of cloning his "persona" on someone with the same surname and the company found that very worrying.

Many people who met Oliver found him either very cold and aloof and somewhat haughty whilst others I spoke to told me they found him uncomfortably "nice". Those people who had warned me off about him before the lies came out said things like "I don't want to upset you Sarah but there is something not right with Oliver, I just cant put my finger on it." The other thing that singled Oliver out, despite his outgoing persona, was his lack of emotional response and the fact that he had no friends at all.

With regards to listening to their comments and trusting my own intuition. It was through a series of interesting apparently unrelated events that led me to uncover all this lovely stuff. If I had never listened to my intuition or trusted my gut feelings and found him on the modelling site, I would have never found any of this out. Worse yet, I could have moved in with him, married him, and then found out years later. Having said that, had it not been for the fact that he was really stupid when it comes to making up lies and excuses, he would have even been a "good psychopath", if that's something to be proud of! Like most Dark Soul personalities Oliver had his good points, some of which were that he was intelligent, attractive and extremely charming but underneath a veneer of charm lay a devious liar and manipulator.

Talking of which if you want to watch an very interesting film on the Narcissistic personality at work, take a look at the film called *I,*

Psychopath starring Sam Vaknin where the commentator makes a quote on Sam Vaknin and suggests that Sam is a *wannabe Psychopath.*

The more I research Dark Souls, the more it appears that they put on one very different *persona* to the outside world and to the one that they show in their *other* lives. It appears that many live a double life. They compartmentalize (i.e. lead double lives), with completely different and unrelated sets of moral rules. In one area, they may feel entitled to do what they do to their wives, and, in another, they may go through the motions of what others expect them to do for the benefits of a relationship. That is why, when we watch news stories about serial killers on television, everyone is so shocked because the façade that they have created for themselves is so far removed from the horrible crimes they have committed.

Dark Souls are extremely charming, of a calm and collected disposition, and very plausible and persuasive. They can have a group of close friends, neighbours who consider them to be very friendly and a 'good bloke,' and will be well respected at the local pub or club. Often, they will be involved in the community, as with churches or parent groups if they have children. Friends and associates find it difficult to believe that such a person could possibly be violent towards a partner or their children. They may find it even more difficult to swallow any stories of affairs or perverted sexual behaviours outside of the "family man relationship." This "Jekyll and Hyde" personality is often referred to by professionals and by partners who have experienced the violence. That is why it is so important to keep evidence.

If his female victim threatens to leave him, he will often threaten to kill her and their children, and warns her that she will never be safe for the rest of her life. This gives him an immense hold over his female partner but eventually the situation becomes so intolerable, she finally escapes.

If they can get away with pretending to be someone else they often will. Some conmen such as Paul Bint, a UK resident who was known as the "King of the Swindlers," prey on unsuspecting victims through lonely hearts adverts. In Paul's case he pretended he was the Director of Public Prosecutions (DPP), Keir Starmer, QC. He was found guilty at Southwark Crown Court of the latest of more than 500 scams going back to his childhood, including many where he had "wormed" his way into the "hearts and homes" of women. Past convictions include cases where he had posed as other barristers, including QCs involved in the cases of Madeleine McCann, the Lockerbie bombing, and the original murder trial of Jill Dando. Bint carried off his scam by using stolen barristers' wigs, gowns, etc, and kept a copy of the legal text, *Archbold*, with bundles of documents to pull off his persona.

Often, Dark Souls will mislead their victims by exaggerating their credentials. They often lead a double life, as did my ex. On the surface, they may appear to be the perfect Mr Nice.

Neil Entwhistle, a British man, was charged with murdering his wife and daughter. At his trial he appeared to be the most unlikely defendant. He was polite, even tucking in the chair of his female lawyer every time he sat down. Despite all the evidence, his parents have always protested his innocence. Friends have quoted him as being a "lovely guy" and "couldn't have been nicer." Yet underneath this "nice" persona, Entwistle was heavily in debt and had been lying to his wife about his job prospects. He was also secretly looking for extra-marital sex and "half price" escort services on the Internet. Entwhistle joined a swingers' website and advertised to meet "American women of all ages" because he had heard they were "much better in bed than the women over the ocean." But his Internet searches just days before the murders also included methods of killing people, suicide, and bankruptcy.

Self-pitying and self-absorbed, but at the same time deeply unhappy with that self – the common verdict among experts who have studied Entwistle, suggest that he had low self-esteem, narcissism and may well have suffered been a sociopath.

During his trial Entwhistle was shown the crime scene of the murder. The photos showed the bed where Rachel Entwistle, 27, and 9-month-old Lillian Rose were found shot to death on Jan. 22, 2006 although the bodies were covered with a duvet. Having learned what I had about the cognitive dissonance that we feel when watching someone say something and react differently with body language and so I decided after watching the video that I had a distinct feeling of "uneasiness". The same feeling I had felt when Oliver had cried *crocodile tears* on telling his cancer story.

I decided to contact Steven Van Aperen for an explanation and asked if he would comment on the video and his response was:

> "One of the first things that concerned me about this tape was the fact that he was crying without any visible tears being apparent. Crocodile tears would be an apt description relating to this performance. In relation to his facial expressions I did not see anything remotely indicating grief, sorrow or sadness. Professor Paul Eckman, who compiled the Facial Action Coding System, found through his research that when we try to conceal an emotion it will often manifest itself as a facial expression within a micro second (approx. 1/25th of a second). I have dealt with many victims who have experienced

emotional pain during traumatic periods in their life and the pain is often etched across their face. This didn't appear to be the case with Entwistle. In fact his hand movements covering his face whilst viewing the tape would suggest concealing and or blocking behaviours to cover his unconvincing acting."

Despite the vast similarities I hope and pray that Oliver is not a murderer, despite his desire to kill his wife and threaten me, but he pretty much paints the same vile picture as the "nice" Mr. Entwistle. The common denominator was that both were obsessed with sex, both led a double life, and both showed signs of low self esteem, sociopathy and narcissism and both appeared to be good actors.

One thing I have learned about Dark Souls is they have a massive "self destruct" button. Call it audacity, perhaps, because they actually believe they can get away with anything. I think it is more likely stupidity and carelessness when they get caught, because their underlying belief about themselves is that they are actually worthless. As a result, they make their victims feel worthless and useless. It doesn't matter how many times they use the sympathy vote and plead for forgiveness or help: no matter how many times you think you can help them, trust me, you cannot. By enabling them, you will only get drawn back into the quagmire that is the black hole of these empty souls.

Projecting Themselves onto Their Victims

The whole relationship is like a jigsaw puzzle and the whole picture Dark Souls have portrayed of themselves is the pieces of the puzzle that do not fit. Please see my chapter on *Narcissists and Projection*. When you have dismantled the relationship and found out who they are, you will find that you are left with nothing but a pile of pieces to put back together. The puzzle doesn't fit together anymore, as though it's a few handfuls of pieces from various random boxes and all tossed into one. You are left with the feeling that nothing added up and you are never going to put all the pieces back together. This is the "projected" image they have left of themselves onto you; you, the victim, are left feeling shattered with every part of your being having been lost. You forget who you are and are left with the job of putting back the pieces of yourself back together one by one.

I always remind my clients to do an exercise when they have finished with a Dark Soul. Write down how you felt at the beginning of the relationship before you met your partner (for example, happy, sexy, empowered, full of energy, and so on). Then underneath it you write all the feelings you feel about yourself at the end of the relationship (you feel worthless, rubbish, suicidal, hate yourself, etc.). Once you have written them down, you draw a line between the two lists and at the top of the list your write YOUR name and at the bottom of the list you write their name.

The second list is their projected feelings about themselves that they have put onto you. You keep the positive list as a reminder of who you are. I would strongly suggest you write this list and place it somewhere where you can see every single day. The reason for doing this exercise is for you to see that how you felt about yourself at the end of the relationship is *not* how you genuinely feel about yourself normally, even if you had some self esteem issues in the beginning. I, for example, had never had self esteem issues about my work and yet, at the end of the relationship, I was so lacking in confidence I had to take nearly 6 months off.

The Blame Game

Most the victims of Shape Shifters will end up blaming themselves when their relationships are over. I spent many months beating myself up, thinking I was stupid and saying it must have been my fault that the relationship had gone wrong every time we split up in the beginning, and trying to make amends. When the relationship was finally over, I had to look long and hard at myself, to see where I had gone wrong and what was inside of me. I looked at my negative beliefs about myself and the ways in which I had enabled him. Of course, I had to really take ownership and responsibility for my own part in it. A Dark Soul will not take any responsibility for *anything*. It will always be someone else's fault. Blame is their way of unloading their character defects onto you and anyone else around them. Listen closely to the hateful things they say about you and their victims: they are actually talking about themselves

The blame game is one of the favourite games a Dark Soul will play with their victims. However, as victims, we end up blaming ourselves. The problem with that is that we may, in turn, end up blaming them, but then stop looking at ourselves and taking responsibility for why we were conned in the first place. Of course a Dark Soul, being a sociopath, could con anyone, but there is definitely more to being one of their victims than meets the eye.

One day I received a free tarot reading in my in box. It was a computer-based website and you randomly choose a card. The card that came up for me was the Nine of Swords: it could not have been more appropriate. The interpretation read:

"The card in the blocks position points to self-undermining tendencies, areas where you could be in denial, where you could get stuck — unless you examine **yourself** and make some corrections.

When the Nine of Swords falls in this position, it implies that there is a part of you that is experiencing some kind of break-up, disappointment, rejection or final showdown. If so, ask yourself if maintaining the relationship was worth what you had put up with in terms of humiliation and emotional burden. Why would you have invested so much of yourself for so little return?

Is it possible that you had accepted this position or unconsciously created this experience because you don't know how to give yourself the approval you desire? You must learn how to recognize your own worth, your value, and your gifts, then you can move beyond ever letting yourself be treated this way."

So in my journey toward healing, I had decided how I was going to get over this man – a man I had allowed to literally walk all over me. I let myself lose my house, lose my self-worth, and risk my own health, too. I had to look deeper. I was angry not only at Oliver but also at myself. The anger I had suppressed during my childhood for so many years finally came out like a volcano, and I had to start looking at my negative core beliefs about myself. Once I had done this, I had resolved never to let myself allow anyone to treat me this way again in my life.

I decided that if I was to get better I had better do a bit of *shape shifting* myself.

They Choose Us, We Choose Them

It takes two people to have a relationship, and a relationship between an abuser and a victim is no different. The abuser *needs* the victim as much as the victim needs the abuser. Until, of course, one of them realises that something is very wrong in the relationship and breaks away. In the case of a Dark Soul, they are not likely to ever break free from a relationship unless they discard their victims. A victim is more likely to leave them.

Whether the victim is being emotionally or physically abused, she is always left with a feeling of very little confidence. Just because you're not bruised doesn't mean you're not being emotionally battered, with scars that are far often deeper and more damaging than physical ones. Your abuser may be systematically wearing away your sense of self-worth to the point that you no longer trust your intuition or perception. Many people who have been in emotionally abusive relationships will come away with the feeling that without their abusive partner they will have nothing. They actually believe that unless they deal with their own feelings, they may continue into other relationships that mirror the previous ones. With their self esteem at a low, they may cling to the abuser. They often stay in abusive situations because they believe they have nowhere else to go. Their ultimate fear becomes being alone.

Why Pick on Me?

I spent a lot of time wondering why Oliver had chosen me as a target. I also had to look long and hard as to why I might have "chosen him back." Though I had done much soul searching and had read books on sociopaths, narcissists, and people who, like me, had been victims to them, I couldn't find any clear answers. One day, I was chatting to a very dear friend of mine who said the world is divided up into prey and predator. It was a pretty harsh statement and I recoiled at the thought that some people really did treat others like that.

Dark Souls are more likely to target people who are nurturing, trusting, kind and committed. Since sociopaths have no morals its much easier for them to con a good person than another con artist. Some experts believe that they target their victims who have high morals and integrity because of their own distinct lack of morals. They relish the challenge of destroying the moral fibres and integrity of their targets in the hope that their targets will eventually lose them too.

If you think being educated makes you immune to being conned by a sociopath. Think again. Some of the most educated people have been taken in by the charm of a predatory sociopath or narcissist. Why? Because they are so good at playing their game. They choose their targets carefully and have a knack of imitating the behaviour of others to fit in. If you do not fit into the kind, nurturing, trusting, committed, educated category you may well fall into the categories such as aspiring and successful. Perhaps you are wealthy or have your own business, the sociopath will delight in the possibility of using you as a potential victim. Why ? Because from the Dark Soul's point of view you have far more to give them.

> "Sociopaths divide the world into two groups of people: *predators and prey.* They are the predators; everyone else is prey. There are no rules of engagement. There is no compassion for the vulnerable, no sympathy for the bereaved, and no mercy for the innocent. Your weakness is their opportunity."

www.lovefraud.com

So what type of person does a Dark Soul target?

There is also one other category which the sociopath targets which is *None of the Above* and is mentioned on Lovefraud.com.

> "Perhaps you're tough enough or savvy enough to avoid the pitfalls listed above. Don't think you're immune. All kinds of people have been manipulated by sociopaths—including corrections officers and psychiatrists who know what they are dealing with. Even "honour among thieves" doesn't apply to sociopaths. Everyone is a target."

www.lovefraud.com

None of the Above

In my journey toward healing, I had read very many books about psychopaths sociopaths and narcissists how to spot them, and what makes them that way. I have read stories about their victims and as much as they all reiterate that no one is immune to their sick games I had to, for my own sanity, explore other categories. It's interesting that there is one called "none of the above." When I had stopped looking at all the other categories that I might have put myself into, including "idiot," "victim," "gullible," "target," and "silly cow," and a few *other* choice names I have called myself, I thought that certain types such as myself were more *vulnerable* to these type of predators and, if that was the case, why?

Many of the people who are reading this book right now may be thinking to themselves that they are in a relationship with a Dark Soul, i.e. a pathological person. They may have already seen so many similarities in their own cases. They may still be there, frozen with fear, and unable to leave. They may have already left their abuser or they may have been "dumped." They may, like me a few months ago, be picking up the pieces, having found themselves homeless or on the receiving end of a scam. They may have had their health threatened because their partner has put them at risk of a sexual infection. Worst of all, they may have been the victims of violence or threats, and remain so afraid they cannot leave. They may have even been the relative of a person who is the victim of a Dark Soul and want to help them.

From my own experience, meeting a Dark Soul was a wake-up call. It was a chance to investigate why had I chosen to be with an vile amplified version of my own father.

Bullies

The other thing that people find when they have been in a relationship with a Dark Soul, whether a NPD, sociopath, or psychopath, is that underneath they are nearly all *bullies*. According to *Bullyingonline.org*, Bullies tend to pick their victims or targets, usually based on these qualities, among others:

- popularity, competence, honesty, and integrity (which bullies despise)

- trustworthiness, trust, conscientiousness, loyalty, and dependability

- integrity which you're unwilling to compromise

- always willing to go that extra mile

- a sense of humour, including displays of quick-wittedness

- imagination, creativity, innovativeness, idealism, optimism, always working for improvement and betterment of self and others

- ability to master new skills

- ability to think long term and to see the bigger picture

- sensitivity and deep empathy

- helpfulness, generosity and selflessness, willing to share knowledge

- difficulty saying "no"

- diligence, industriousness

- tolerance, forgiveness, and a desire to think well of others

- low propensity to violence (i.e. you prefer to resolve conflict through dialogue rather than through violence or legal action)

- high moral standards and values which you are unwilling to compromise

- a need to feel valued

- quickness to apologise when accused, even if not guilty (this is a useful technique for defusing an aggressive customer or potential road rage incident)

- perfectionism

- higher-than-average levels of dependency, naivety and guilt

- a strong sense of fair play and a desire to always be reasonable

- high coping skills under stress, especially when the injury to health becomes apparent

- slowness to anger or a tendency to internalise anger rather than express it

I ticked most of those boxes, notably the inability to show my anger, although I realised that even when I am angry I tend to internalise it and take it out on myself, whereas Oliver had a bubbling kind of anger (which I later found out was actually rage). All the other qualities he managed to mimic perfectly, since Dark Souls have the ability to take on whatever persona they think their victims want to see. I had also been bullied as a child and would often be passive just to keep the peace. Coupled with all of the above and with my own negative beliefs that "I am powerless," "I don't know anything," and "It's all my fault," I was a perfect target. A Dark Soul will never hesitate to exploit a vulnerability," whatever that vulnerability is. In my case, it was the also the inability to see clearly that something was wrong or at least refused to accept it.

Often victims won't stand up to their abusers because they are afraid. The abuser may have disempowered you through isolation, exclusion, and manipulation, and often it's a long, slow process of enduring threatening and intimidating behaviour. Usually the target has high levels of shame, embarrassment, fear, and guilt – all stimulated by the bully, for this is how all abusers control their victims. They may feel bewildered and often still cannot believe what is happening; the target feels responsible in some way, manifested by nagging thoughts like "Why me?" and "Why did I let it happen to me?" They may start to believe that it's actually *them* that have the problem, especially if their partner is a good liar. They may even think they are imagining things. Often, when the symptoms of psychiatric injury start to appear, the bully plays the mental health card, claiming the victim "has a mental health problem."

Like me, most victims have no knowledge of sociopaths or NPD, and they have no idea how to deal with these types of people. If the victim dares to stand up to their abuser, they may find the latter quick to discredit and neutralise anyone who can talk knowledgeably about antisocial or sociopathic behaviours. They may even, in turn, pursue a vindictive vendetta against anyone who dares to hold them accountable, possibly suggesting the "victim" is the one to blame and accuse *them* of abusing, harassing, or stalking.

Most serial bullies abuse power, exhibit amoral behaviour, and lack conscience and remorse. One of the clues is to listen to how they talk about their previous relationships. They may claim that they were bullied, when *they* are, in fact, the bully. The target will very often fear that no one will believe them, and even they eventually begin questioning their situation, especially if the bully persistently (and plausibly) denies everything. The Bully relies on compulsive lying, a Jekyll & Hyde nature, deception, deviousness, evasiveness, charm, denial, counter-attack, projection, and will feign victimhood to evade accountability.

It's very easy for one to say "he picked on me" and put all the blame on the abuser, but I wondered whether there was something deeper. In addition to the negative core beliefs we hold about ourselves and with all the characteristics that an abuser looks for in a victim, is it also possible that our expectations as a partner are also based on what we had learned from our parents?

When Our Partners Are Clones of Our Parents

I wondered if we unconsciously choose our mates because they are like our parents. There is a growing body of evidence that people choose partners that mirror the characteristics of their parents. They may have similar physical traits, and they may be kind, loving and good providers. Usually women tend to choose men who look and act like their fathers whereas men will pick women who are like their mothers. Assuming that this is true and we grow up with *healthy* role models in our hard working kind, loving parents, where does this leave children of parents whose parenting skills were not so healthy? Along with research, I examined various friends and relatives and their choices of partners, and it appears that the opposite may be true as well. Some children may even choose partners that are like the opposite parent.

A man growing up with an alcoholic mother might go out of his way to not choose a woman who is an alcoholic yet you may unconsciously choose a partner with traits like his father. But what if his father is a controlling, abusive partner and he carries an underlying need to look after people? The man may end up going out with a female clone of his father, yet at the same time feel unable to refrain from his abusive behaviour. She may not be a drinker but may have developed learned habits from her mother, such as damping her feelings down. In addition, we may go out of our way to choose someone who is so initially different from our parents in looks and beliefs, only to find that later they turn into a copy of our parents, ostensibly with a different face.

When I first married my husband he was very different from my father. He never once cheated on me. If anything, he carried all the good characteristics that my father had. He was hard working and never missed a day. However, he was emotionally unavailable and I was left to look after the children most of the time on my own, much like my mother had. We often had separate holidays and he would think nothing of leaving me at home to run our business by myself.

Having mentioned earlier that I believe Oliver was an *amplified* version of my father, I wondered whether it was just me or do we really choose clones of our parents, perhaps unconsciously? Including the fact that he was married, I felt like I had turned into a copy of my mother making excuses for his lying behaviour. Somehow I felt drawn to the relationship, like a deer paralysed by a car's headlights. Many women choose married or emotionally unavailable men, so I decided to investigate this a little further. In my case, I was on a "promise" so to speak. Oliver had promised me that he was not in love with his wife and that he was going to leave her. This was a promise he made to me weekly, and yet he never fulfilled it until *she* finally asked him to leave. He would also make small promises and never keep them, from showing up on time for our meetings to making dates he could not keep. Even things like birthdays were always forgotten until the last minute or were just an afterthought. These are the kinds of things my father would do, making promises he could not keep, like saying to my mother that he would never have another affair again.

When you are in a healthy committed relationship, the first stage of any relationship is the courtship Phase and can last anywhere from 2 months to 2 years. This is when you and your partner have just met, and everything is absolutely amazing and you are learning to get to know each other.

Love is not just "a feeling," although that feeling or connection is an important aspect of a long-term relationship. Before you are able to move onto the commitment stage a couple need to spend time with each other and this includes spending time going away on holidays, going shopping and so on. When you are having an affair with a married man the honeymoon phase is extended and never really ends, it lasts throughout the whole length of the relationships. Why because we never get to first base and we are always waiting for the possibility that they might leave one day.

In the book *In Sheep's Clothing*, by George Simon, I was introduced to the "Slot Machine Syndrome." What happens is that one person invests a good deal of emotional energy and time over the years trying to make things work (much like a gambler feeds a slot machine with coins, hoping for an eventual "pay-out"). Every now and then (just like with a slot machine), there are some small rewards experienced, and this keeps the person playing. The problem is it becomes clear at some point that you're in a losing situation, but you'd still rather not walk away from your "investment."

If we have grown up with a partner who is emotionally unavailable, we may feel so comfortable with the concept that we might develop a relationship one day with a "slot machine syndrome" mentality. Basically, we keep on "investing" in the relationship like a slot machine. Even though we get small payouts from time to time, we always believe there is a jackpot at the end. We may be too afraid to leave the relationship on the "promise" that our partners are going to change because we have invested so much into the relationship. We believe a jackpot is in the offing, but in reality, and in the long term, there is none.

Chemistry versus Love

Because we are also stuck in the "feeling" that often convinces us that we are *in love*, the relationship that would have normally run its course never really ends with a married man. It continues throughout the length of the relationship, because we never get there in the first place. With hope as our motivator and Oxytocin, a powerful hormone that makes us feel like the dog's bollocks, we have a perfect simulation masquerading as love. Sandra L. Brown explains in great detail the effects of Oxytocin in her book *'Women who Love Psychopaths'*

Sandra writes :

"Oxytocin is found in men's semen which is yet another way that women have Oxytocin in their body—through his ejaculate. He is hypersexual, there is lots of sex, lots of oxytocin from her and from him!"

Interestingly enough I refused to have sex with anyone after I asked Oliver to leave. Unconsciously, I was so convinced that if I had sex with another man or allowed anyone to come inside of me I would get "bonded" with someone again and until I sorted out my own issues as to why I had attracted him in the first place the last thing I wanted was another psychopaths semen inside of me.

Oxytocin, otherwise dubbed the *trust* hormone has been used in extensive studies; one even suggested that a whiff of oxytocin made people more likely to trust someone else to look after their cash. Whether or not your partner is a psychopathic married lover, Oxytocin is also carried in a man's ejaculate so the more sex you have with him the more you bond with him and the more you trust him!

At the end of the relationship, we come to realise that the relationship with a Dark Soul, (in my case a married man) as intoxicating as it is, is often an excuse for us to have a relationship with someone who is unable to commit or is emotionally unavailable. Perhaps if we had had better role model parents, we may not have chosen partners like our parents who then turn out to be abusive, manipulative liars. It seems unfair that after having been abused as children, we so often choose abusers or emotionally unavailable partners to marry that are even worse than our own parents. It is also sad that we often pick partners that we know and feel "comfortable" with.

Of course, if you have had a good, successful role model as a parent, then it's perfect. If your father is intelligent, hard working, honest and devoted to his family, there is nothing wrong with going out with a clone of your father. There is even a good chance that your new partner and he will get on and become good friends. However, psychologists say some people settle down with someone resembling a parent they don't get along with, because they are used to that personality, however shoddy. As Pia Mellody says, it is driven by a nostalgic sense: "It feels just like I'm home again". That's a powerful pull, but if "home" was not all that good a place for us as kids, why are we drawn back to this situation if it will only serve to help recreate (or simply repeat) the experience again?

People who experienced abandonment or distancing during their childhood are magnetically attracted to the opposite kind of partners who had problems with parents or carers who smothered them. Often, they may feel very uncomfortable whenever a relationship gets too close or starts to become good. That's the point where they need to escape from it, or they may unconsciously choose partners that will abandon them or prove to be emotionally detached or abusive. Coupled with the negative attitudes that we hold about ourselves (which carry a flashing neon sign that basically says "come and get me"), partners are drawn together like magnets based on their childhood histories and unconscious beliefs. Relationship research is full of cases where eldest daughters of alcoholics marry alcoholics. Sons of controlling mothers marry controlling women. Kids who grew up in a family where there was abuse marry abusers. Adults who never experienced love from their parents will marry partners whose ability to give or receive love is blocked.

I have dated a number of men over the years and yet, in all of my years, I've only been what I can describe as "magnetically" attracted to three men in particular. Yet I believed they were all "soul mate" relationships. Interestingly enough, all three relationships had the effect of making me feel like I had met someone I was immediately *bonded* with. The other relationships did not feel the same. The three toxic ones were very sudden, the relationships moved very quickly, and I felt drawn to them instantly. In all three relationships the men were emotionally elusive, and each version of them was more controlling and abusive. In each case, I came out of the relationship wondering why I had even been with them. Unconsciously, I might have been attracting them and at the same time the universe kept "upping the volume" giving me worse versions of my father until I started to listen and realise something was really wrong.

John Nutting writes

"if you are in a relationship where there is a pre-packaged "spark," a "tingle," "chemistry," or "electricity," you are flirting with trouble. As any experienced relationship counsellor will tell you, if you do feel that exciting sensation it's probably a good idea to get out as fast as possible and hope that other person is not following you! "

Relationships as Mirrors

In a way, I believe that these people are bought into our lives as a gift. They are there to show us what we no longer need in our lives. There is a technique I teach to my clients, called the Mirror Technique, which I had learned from an inspirational American woman named Zen DeBrucke who invented the *Internal Guidance System*. It was about two years into my relationship with Oliver when I first contacted Zen. She reminded me that the reason I was still with him was because there was something in *me* that I needed to deal with.

The Mirror technique is one of the many things she uses in her work. To illustrate this, a woman is always complaining that her husband is late home from work every day. Zen suggested that there was something in this woman's life that she was doing to cause her husband to be late. The woman complained and replied "but I am never late for anything." She was told to look at ways in which she was late for someone else or had been late for herself. The same principle applies to anything in your life. If someone is not looking after you, you become angry. It could be that you are not looking after someone else or you are being angry at someone. It could also be that you are being angry at yourself. It doesn't necessarily have to be directly at the person you are "in a relationship" with. In this client's case, it turned out that she was being late for her son every day from school. Her son had complained and said he felt embarrassed because he was always the last person outside the school. When the client changed *her* behaviour towards her son, her husband suddenly started coming home on time.

Often we will find that abusive, manipulative people are bought into our lives to teach us that *we* need to change. We may not feel worthy of love or affection, or perhaps we are only used to small "payouts" every so often. We are all composed of vibrational energy, and the moment we start to change and look after ourselves, a vibrational shift occurs: the people around us start changing, too. They either start to change as well or they cannot keep up with us energetically and must make a shift. We start to see them differently, perhaps discern their true colours. The negative ones may start to reveal themselves and the more they do, the more we no longer want to be with them.

Living In the Twilight Zone

So how does it feel to be the victim of a Dark Soul? You come out feeling like you have been living in the *twilight zone.* When I first met Oliver, he presented himself as he breezed into the room with an air of grace about him. I remember looking at this dark, attractive man standing around six-feet-two, wearing a dark blue, expensive suit with the top button of his shirt slightly open. The first thing I noticed about him was his piercing eyes and thinking how gorgeous looking he was. Yet my intuitive feeling was not to touch him with a barge pole, but for some reason I did not listen to my intuition.

Oliver was also a big fan of the *Twilight* movies whereas being older I remember the old series the "Twilight Zone." Oliver had a fascination with all things to do with vampires and he was always reading "fantasy" books. I remember going to see the movie *Twilight New Moon* and he was totally mesmerised by the main character, Edward Cullen, who (to me) is somewhat asexual. Oliver was making comments and asking me if I fancied him when he actually fancied him for himself. Although I find Edward Cullen relatively attractive, whilst we were watching film Oliver kept nudging and poking me said "dont you think he's gorgeous" and yet when I looked at Oliver's body language I realised it was actually Oliver that was literally drooling over Edward.

I think the thing that upset me the most was the throat cancer story. It wasn't until three years later, when all the lies came out that I checked with my general practitioner and did some extensive research to discover that throat cancer is one of the few cancers that could not possibly be treated by alternative means that the penny finally dropped. It nearly always requires surgery at a minimum, plus a combination of radiotherapy, and so on. So when Oliver told me that he had a rare form of throat cancer and played it out for a number of months, *supposedly* going for counselling and changing his diet, etc., only to have it go into to remission a year or so later, it left a very uneasy feeling in the pit if my stomach. That feeling never quite went away because he had made it all up. I couldn't help thinking why anyone would lie about cancer. It went beyond all reason, unless, of course, to gain sympathy or get off on some sick and twisted way, knowing I was so gullible. He must have loved the way he played that story out to a tee using all of the information he had accumulated about me and my holistic background to convince me of his illness.

Oliver was always late and would act out in passive aggressive ways. It was very disarming and very insidious. It was what I can only describe as maddening behaviour. Even down to little things like saying he had turned his mobile phone off all weekend then finding that he had actually read all of his text messages and then selectively chosen to ignore them on purpose. I've found that he would create an argument that coincided perfectly with the school holidays so he wouldn't have to see me for a couple of weeks and allow what he called a "cooling off period." Oliver never wanted to end the relationship; it was always "let's have a break and see how we feel after." He was always the instigator of the argument and I was always the one that would end up suggesting the break. Yet, if I would suggest leaving him permanently, he would suddenly behave himself for a couple of weeks.

During the five years I was with Oliver, he was always procrastinating, telling me he was patient and that I was not. Because I like to do things quickly, I did everything that I said I was going to do during the time that I was with him: I bought a couple of houses and did them up. However, when I had finally started to see all the cracks and flaws, I gave him an ultimatum. I was starting to get into debt with the strain of the relationship and so I told him I was going away for a month to sort my head out. I had started to think I was the crazy one and said that if he hadn't left his wife by the time I got back, the relationship would be over. I took my kids to Thailand and a colleague offered to take me in for a week of counselling in Delhi. I flew to India and spent over 40 hours in counselling, going through my childhood and sobbing great big buckets of tears. I finally left for Thailand for another couple of weeks and then returned to England.

In November 2007 Oliver had collected the keys to one of my rental properties prior to my departure, and on my return to England, he was there to collect me from the airport. I asked him if he had left his wife and moved out as promised. The answer was... no. His excuse was that he had just been offered a brilliant new job working at £100,000 a year and that it meant for the first time ever he would have enough money to leave! However... it would require me to be a little more patient and he had promised that he would be leaving his wife by the end of the month. I had heard this story from him a hundred times before, and so, on my return from Thailand feeling confident and happy again, I decided to stick to my guns and *not* contact him. About six weeks later, I had called him up to ask how his wonderful new job was going, and asked him when he had been planning to move out. He replied "I have been thinking about it, and

I think moving to the cottage isn't such a good idea after all. It's too far from home," although it was merely twenty minutes from his house. It was back to the Twilight Zone: nothing adding up, more excuses, and nothing making any sense. He had also lost yet another job, citing his boss being too demanding.

Oliver was the master when it came to mindbogglingly creative abusive tactics such as mind warping conversations and emotional abuse. It wasn't until I actually healed that I realised how much of a manipulator he was. He was an amplified version of every other man I had had the misfortune to have a bad relationship with and yet their abuse pales into insignificance compared to the slick way that Oliver was able to deliver his game plan.

Oliver had painted himself as a man who was the perfect father, who was calm approachable, loving, kind, hard-working, and extremely organised – a man who ate healthy, looked after himself, ran every day, and kept fit (even though he was actually quite overweight). When he had moved into the cottage that I had let him stay in, I found a man that had not opened his letters in months, had piles of unpaid bills, parking tickets, and unfiled tax returns. He was lazy and ate nothing but takeaways. During the time I lived with him, I had never once seen him go for a run. I always wondered why, as a non-smoker, he never seemed bothered about me smoking, and sure enough, within weeks he was smoking again. The man who appeared to be the perfect father had not even paid his children's school fees for three or four months, even though they were about to lose their place in school.

Within two days of me asking him to finally leave he had found some new free accommodation, having been living for free at my own place for three months. He never seemed to have to pay for anything. Up until he had moved in, I had only believed what he told me. When we finally have the courage to ask these people to depart, leaving us with a feeling of deep betrayal, it's *them*, i.e. the Dark Souls, that claim to feel betrayed, not the other way round. They will tell their friends that they have been abused, that their *victim* had been the abuser and controller. When the victim has merely stopped acquiescing, that is when the Dark Soul goes into what can only be described as Rage.

This is a common tactic used by abusers. They turn the tables on their victims and make them feel paralysed. Because he was under threat he was going to do anything he could to self preserve and that included threatening the police on me when he left. All controllers will capitalize on finding that part of you that lacks self esteem. Once you become aware of your own beliefs, it will help you to protect yourself from them. I have gone into much detail in the section of this book on negative beliefs about ourselves, how I actually found the strength to leave him, and how not play into these games.

It's so easy to look back in hindsight and see all the cracks. If I could be given a gift, it would be the gift of hindsight, for the future. They say that if a man has not left his wife within a year, he will never leave. They say if someone breaks a commitment more than twice they will never stick to anything. We were together nearly five years and it was at the very end after a long break that I finally asked him to leave forever. He had returned, tail between his legs, three months beforehand saying he had never had the courage to leave, and, that with my help doing negative core belief dialogue, it had given him the courage to stand up to her. Within a week or two of him leaving, she had changed the locks. I had been married for 17 years and although the marriage wasn't brilliant and, at some point, my ex husband had become abusive, I had never felt so frightened that I would have to change the locks. In retrospect, I believe he didn't leave his wife at all. In fact, Oliver had shown me a letter that he had stolen from his wife's house. Written to her in confidence by her solicitor, it stated that she was scared of the way he had been acting towards her and the boys. For that reason, she had only wanted him to see the children with supervised access at a contact centre. That's when I started to realise that much of what he had said about her may have not been true at all.

Dark Souls , the book, really started its life a few months after speaking to John Nutting in October 2008. At the time that I was writing, Oliver was out of my life, albeit temporarily and I had already started to pick up the pieces of the mess I had created for myself by staying with him for over 4 years. My health had deteriorated, I had piled on all the weight I had lost over the last few years and my finances were a mess. It was the first time in my life when I took advice from my friends and asked for help. This included getting help from financial organisation to help with sorting out my finances and looking at ways I could heal. In addition the recession had just started and already a few months behind with my mortgage and unable to work because of my shame and guilt I took nearly six months off. During the time I spent looking after myself and doing creative things such as writing, painting and making music.

In July 2009 I had a week to pack up my large Victorian house which I had managed to sell at a reduced price. I paid off the majority of my debts but was was left losing most of my life savings. Having nowhere else to go I moved into a property I had rented out which was in negative equity which my tenants had turned into a squat. I spent my birthday, 4th July, evicting tenants with the help of two friends and a couple of police officers after they finally trashed the house with the use of hammers. The house was filthy and I spend the following six months in between working and getting up at 6am everyday decorating and making the property liveable. I also produced a music album which was to help with my healing. I called it the Phoenix.

Between July 2008 and October 2009 I had little, if any, real contact with Oliver. I was too busy collecting my thoughts and trying to sort out how I felt about all the things he had done. I also felt extremely guilt for having an affair with a married man which was one of the reasons I would always finish with him, even suggesting to him that he try and patch up his marriage with his wife on numerous occasions. I have never planned to have an affair with a married man but I felt compelled to keep on going back to him with all of the, what seemed at the time, plausible excuses that he came up with.

Apart from a brief return in October 2009 when Oliver returned tail between legs to declare his undying love and tell me he had left his wife and changed his ways and I decided to give him one very "guarded" chance, although we never slept together during that time as he became impotent. I was told later by a friend that also knew Oliver's wife that he believes Oliver used he me as a scapegoat as he already had made plans with another woman and that I was just a way of him getting some free accommodation. They said he thought that Oliver's wife knew more than just about his affairs and that Oliver has a massive self destruct button and he was about to push it as I was about to find out. As a result the rest of his life came out as an being even bigger lie. He had been fired from his previous job, had taken money from his mother to the sum of £20,000 and was lying about where he was working. When I picked up a letter that had been redirected to me he owed nearly £5,000 in unpaid school fees. Oliver's wife also stopped him from seeing the children.

I went into hospital few weeks before Xmas 2009 for a minor operation and had a massive post operative bleed and was rushed into hospital spending Xmas eve in hospital in a geriatric ward as there were no other free beds, with a lady opposite that had died hours earlier. As an empath I already knew and begged the hospital to let me go home but I was too weak. My daughter Laura cooked us all Xmas dinner as I was too weak to do anything. Oliver who had spent Xmas with his mother because his wife refused to let him see his children was asked to leave by me on New Years day 2010. He took everything that I had neatly packed up for him including a half eaten box of frosties, which I later put as a screen saver on my phone to remind me not to ever be with such a stingy man. Apart from a brief conversation with him in late January asking him to pay some bills he owed, which have still gone unpaid, I have never spoken to him or heard from him since.

And Now for Something Really Scary

"I don't think I feel things the same way you do." taken from the article "*Unburdened Mind*," by Christopher S. Putnam.

"The man sits at the table in the well-fitted attire of success – charming, witty, and instantly likeable. He is a confident, animated speaker, but he seems to be struggling with this particular point. 'It's like... at my first job,' he continues, 'I was stealing maybe a thousand bucks a month from that place. And this kid, he was new, he got wise. And he was going to turn me in, but before he got the chance I went to the manager and pinned the whole thing on him.' Now he is grinning widely. "Kid lost his job, the cops got involved, and I don't know what happened to him. And I guess something like that is supposed to make me feel bad, right? It's supposed to hurt, right? But instead, it's like there's nothing.' He smiles apologetically and shakes his head. 'Nothing.' His name is Frank, and he is a Psychopath."

A very slightly different version, "I don't feel things in the same way as you," were repeated to me over and over again during the years that I was dating Oliver. There were lots of inconsistencies in his behaviour from the day he got "sick" or rather when the sickness of his psychopathic Dark Soul personality revealed itself.

Interestingly, the way a psychopath thinks is quite different. He would most likely gather to watch an accident scene with the rest of the crowd, and even lend assistance if he perceived no threat to his own safety. But he would feel none of the panic, shock, or horror of the other onlookers. His interest would turn more to the reactions of the victims and of the crowd. He would not be repulsed by any carnage displayed, except perhaps in the same sense as serial killer Paul Bernardo, describing cutting up one of his victims' bodies as "the most disgusting thing he had ever done," referring only to the mess it had created.

On reflection of all the things that Oliver did, like talking about his wife and saying she was an abuser, controlling him, and using the silent treatment on him. He constantly spoke about how he thought she was a bad parent and a gold digger who was only interested in his inheritance. He would describe how she controlled him in bed and made him feel worthless, and then would not want to have sex with him. Oliver would say she was lazy and didn't do anything in the house. He spoke of how he didn't trust her, that she was possibly suffering from Borderline Personality Disorder, and that she would do anything to get money. He was always complaining that his wife was only concerned about his inheritance money, although I later learned that the house they had bought together had been purchased jointly, using some money that she had inherited. Oliver even went so far as to say that "She doesn't care about me, and when I had cancer she just wanted me dead so she could get all the inheritance." I realised that this was all merely projection. I believe it was an autobiographical statement about himself.

In my opinion what he did with me was a way of punishing his wife. He used his own wedding photograph on a modelling site and offering to plant his "Narcissistic Seed" on the sperm donors site. I read that many narcissists are on such sites with grandiose ideas of having more and more "clones" of themselves being born. Many of the *impregnators* are married and do not care that legally the children could come and find them when they are older. They do not think about the consequences of their actions. Often these men are banned from sites, after harassing women, and will reappear under another name within days.

Oliver also had sex with me on his wedding anniversary. By having an affair with me, I believe was his backhanded way of having a dig at his wife and family. I found out later that his own father was the patron of a big cancer research trust and I wondered how he would feel about his son lying about having it.

I watched a documentary which showed a psychopath who was wanted by the police. He wanted revenge on the police and my thoughts are that a normal person might want to get back at the police directly. Not the psychopath. His way of getting back at the police was to capture a fourteen year old girl and rape and bugger her, hiding her in an underground den for a few weeks until they eventually found him. While he had her in his clutches he spoke of her giving him "come on signals" and that she made him do it. His defence was that he wanted to *get back* at the police and he didn't "get it" that hurting an innocence child victim had nothing to do with the original crime he was trying to pay back.

I have had much discussions when I had been considering how to portray Oliver in this book whether it was fair to include stories from men who had murdered their wives because he hadn't killed anyone. I had recently watched a CSI documentary which reported on a case where a man had murdered his wife and then his children. He showed classic signs of sociopathy, yet in the family videos he *appeared* to be the perfect family man. One onlooker commented that he lacked normal emotional response and yet underneath there was a distinct underlying rage that was not easily apparent to the untrained eye.

Often these types of killers appear to be normal, yet when we see them in the paper as people having murdered people out of the blue, onlookers will say in retrospect that they either appeared so "normal", or that there were subtle clues along the way and yet no one ever took notice – until it was too late.

For many months, I was scared that Oliver would kill me. I was also more concerned that he might kill his wife, as she had no idea about his secret affair before he left or of his exploits on the Internet. I knew if she found out, like me, she would have been extremely upset and angry, but that her reaction towards him would likely not have been as gentle as mine. I tended to back down on arguments to keep the peace, whereas Oliver's friends suggested that she was not a woman to be argued with. I was concerned that if she found out what I knew all hell would let loose. My belief is that Oliver like those other killers is an accident waiting to happen.

They say a sociopath chooses not to kill because it is an *inconvenience* and that if they could get away with it, they would. One day, when I had been having a conversation with Oliver, he said to me "I have been thinking up ways in which I could get rid of my wife. I had been talking to Oliver a few weeks before he left saying I had been having vivid dreams and nightmares and then suddenly one day out of the blue he said "That's interesting, I have been having dreams about getting a sniper rifle and hiding in the grounds of our house and killing her." He said "If I could get away with killing her I would." I was shocked and said "how horrible". He laughed and said "but it was only a dream". Oliver even spoke about writing a script for a movie about a man that was living one life and then dreaming another, but that when he woke up he would actually be living his dream life. In this *dream life*, he was an ordinary guy, and in the "normal" life, his alter ego hunted people at night with a rifle. Having been in a relationship with this man for over five years, he never once had any recollection of dreaming before that day. I believed, therefore, that this was the mind of sociopath talking about his plans to kill his ex wife.

I did some further research to look at the theory of whether or not sociopaths and psychopaths actually dream or not. Dreams are our way of unconsciously processing our thoughts throughout the day. A healthy individual might dream of dying or killing someone but it is usually just a metaphor. My research led me to a few forums in which some of the victims said that their psychopathic exs never once recalled their dreams. Perhaps Psychologists should consider this for future studies?

Steven Spielberg did a film remake of the "Twilight Zone" television series. It begins with a driver (Albert Brooks) and his passenger (Dan Aykroyd) driving very late at night, singing along to Credence Clearwater Revival's cover of "Midnight Special." The pair make a game of TV theme songs, and then the conversation turns to what scares them. They pull over, and the driver of the car turns to the passenger. As they talk about horror movies, the driver says "Now for something really scary," as he slowly turns his face away from the cameras and he transforms into a demonic creature about to attack his passenger. As much as we do not want to believe that abusers are evil, beneath the mask they often are clearly insane. Of course they are not all "demons," but like the character in the *Twilight Zone* they can attack, and it's important to remember that they can do so when we least expect it.

The last thing that people question is why do these people literally get away with murder and often are never accountable for their actions. Often people who commit crimes never have any come back and unless caught can go on for years and years without any comeback. As a spiritual person I believe in Karma and therefore if I do something bad to someone I will get something bad in return. Perhaps the mere fact that someone believes in Karma means they actually create it? A Dark Soul however has no conscience and one of the reasons I believe they have no Karma is because they have no conscience. There is also an alternative view in that most people have souls and therefore when we die we reincarnate and come back, therefore we would naturally attract Karma in our lives. As Dark Souls are sometimes considered "soul less" beings one theorist believes the reason they have no Karma is because they have no soul in the first place. They suggest the only reason anything bad happens to them is because they actually are careless enough to get caught out in the first place.

The Scorpion and the Frog
Unknown Author

"One day a scorpion arrived at the bank of a river he wanted to cross, but there was no bridge. He asked a frog that was sitting nearby if he would take him across the river on his back. The frog refused and said, 'I will not, because you will sting me.'

"The scorpion replied, 'It would be foolish for me to sting you because then we would both drown.'

"The frog saw the logic in the scorpion's words, and agreed to carry the scorpion across. But when they were halfway across the river the scorpion stung the frog. The stunned frog asked, 'Why did you sting me? Now we will both die!'

"The scorpion replied, 'Because I'm a scorpion ... and that's what scorpions do.'"

10

HEALING
Game Over

The first step to recovery is to actually find out who *they* are. To do that we have to find out who *we* are. This might sound a bit strange to some readers, but for many years I had been doing a job I wasn't happy doing, and when I met Oliver, many of my childhood issues started to surface. I had gone through my moment of the "Dark Night of the Soul" a couple of years into the relationship, and had decided to change and sort my life out. Unfortunately he didn't feel the same. Although he said all the right words and made all the promises, none of his actions backed them up. There was always a dichotomy.

As a child I never wanted to be a hairdresser or a mummy or an air hostess. I actually wanted to be a spy. Talk about being careful what you wish for! I never thought I would end up becoming a spy, or in this case, more of a private detective.

From the moment I met Oliver, I used to joke with him and say I think he was playing games with me. He would deny it, to which I replied "I just have this feeling you are playing a game, and one day I will find it out." Little did I know how right my intuition was, but I did not always follow up on my intuitive feelings. I had a well-paying job, I had a nice house and I was a good mother, but I would always attract bad boy types. Having come out of a seventeen year marriage and having been single for a number of years, I was determined not to pick the wrong type of man, when Oliver came along. Although he was married, he appeared to be the perfect Mr. Right. He didn't drink like past boyfriends, he didn't smoke, and he was even a vegetarian. Although he had told me that in the past he had been "a bad boy" who smoked and took drugs at college, he appeared to be a "reformed character." He worked out regularly and appeared to be a wonderful father. He had all the qualities I would have liked to have seen in a man. Yet there was this "bad boy" part of him that I desired.

I was a fair bit older than Oliver and had had no plans to have any more children. We had decided that when he was going to leave his wife, he would split time looking after his children with her. There was no rush for us to move in together and my main concern was that his children should not be adversely affected by his marriage breakup. As much as Oliver had painted his wife in the worst of terms, I was adamant that she wasn't a bad mother and that if and when they would eventually split, he should try to do so amicably. Despite all his promises to leave, Oliver instead appeared to be getting angrier by the day. He had this underlying volcano that would erupt over little things from time to time.

During a visit to a counsellor in India I had discussed various different members of my family and a couple of different personality types came up in conversation, including the Borderline Personality. When I got home, I'd heard my mother talking about sociopaths when she had received counselling years prior. I realised I had never heard about personality disorders before, apart from things such as Bipolar and depression. I came away from India feeling like a huge weight had been lifted off my shoulders and spent two weeks back in Thailand on the beach on my own, listening daily to the Sedona method and letting any emotions and feelings go. On my return to England, feeling wonderful, suntanned, healthy, and trimmer, Oliver was there at Heathrow to collect me. Of course he had not yet left his wife and I decided not to continue to see him after he drove me home. We had had a long conversation and when he left me on the doorstep, the strangest thing happened. I don't know why, but all of a sudden I felt like he had my father's energy. He wasn't "like" my father, but he felt like my father, energetically, and I just didn't want to be around him anymore.

Six months later, after a few phone calls during which he would come up with numerous excuses as to why he still hadn't left his wife, he turned up on my birthday July 2008. It was one of the stupidest things I had ever done but, had I not done it, I may have looked back over the years wondering what I might have missed. We ended up in bed together and it felt wrong. Whereas Oliver was normally attentive, I sensed no affection. It was like making love to a robot. I came away feeling strange and I couldn't quite put my finger on it. In fact it was the last time I was to ever have sex again.

When I had found him on Google, I did some research and then contacted my counsellor friend in India, explaining that I thought Oliver to be a sociopath. I told him about the angry outbursts and my counsellor sent me an email: "Sarah it's not you it's him. Whatever you do, *do not* suggest to him that he is a sociopath." I was chomping at the bit by this time and I just kept searching for Oliver on Google. I couldn't find anything more, so I emailed the sperm donors' site where I had spotted his name. I explained that there was a married man on the site that I believed might be a problem. I gave his telephone number and name, as he had used his real name on the site. I got an immediate email back from the site owner saying she was very concerned that I had managed to find him through Google. She emailed me his information and a different email address I had never seen. She had also explained that another man had been on their site using a similar, shortened version of his name and that he had caused all kinds of problems, earning himself a permanent ban from the site. She asked if I thought this was the same man. Because the security on their website was so poor, she promptly contacted her webmaster and changed the database.

However, the universe works in strange ways! A couple of days later I checked and found that the same page took me straight into his log in page with his password pre-programmed in. In addition it allowed me to access every single person's details on the site. What an atrocious lack of security! I pressed the return button and found he had emailed about five women going back to the summer, saying he had wanted to be a sperm donor. In his emails he mentioned he would be happy to impregnate them "naturally." He had also been using the other banned name the web owner had mentioned. I immediately emailed her back and told her that the security was terrible and that the site was prone to unsuspecting women being hit on by men like this. She thanked me for drawing her attention to it and the following week the site had been secured. However, Google preserves caches of pages for up to three months. So I printed off all the evidence even though I knew Oliver was going to remove himself from the site.

What I found out in the next couple of days was enough to make me sick! I had used the beginning part of the email address the site owner had given me for Oliver, put it in Google and then 22 pages of hits of him appeared, all on sex sites. After printing page upon page of him on these websites I hadn't spoken to him since July and it was coming up to Christmas. I spent the holidays getting tested for AIDS and various STDs. I had to wait until Jan 2009 to find out if I was all clear. Fortunately, I hadn't had sex with anyone since my birthday. By this time, my self esteem was in tatters, but I decided to give him a call and confront him. I had already sent him an email and, armed with a pile of evidence, decided to meet him at the pub.

When we met, he started to get extremely angry. I looked into his eyes and suddenly the penny dropped. I said "And another thing, that cancer story you made up about your throat three years ago was a lie, too, wasn't it?" He put his head down and started mumbling about what cancer story and then finally admitted that he had made the whole thing up! With so much evidence he could do nothng but admit to it all and when I asked him why he had done all of it, his reply was simply "I don't know." Oliver was getting so angry and I was determined not to cry, so I told him if he started shouting at me in the pub I would cause a scene and tell his wife. A little voice came out of my mouth that had never been there before. This "powerless" woman suddenly looked him in the eyes and very calmly said "Get outside now" He got up walked outside and I stood in front of him. He crumbled like a big baby.

How did I manage to do it? How did I manage to find the power to stand up to a bully and finally say *no* and leave? I finally looked at my core negative beliefs about how I valued myself. Oliver gaslighting me and turning things around had been starting to make me think I was going insane. I had intuitively known something was very wrong and so I finally started listening to my intuition. That helped me find the courage to ask Oliver to leave.

There are many books that discuss sociopaths, narcissists, but few that actually give a step-by-step process to recovery nor how much they damage us spiritually. None of them look at the victims and their little red flags as to why they attracted these men in the first place. In the following chapters I discuss the ways in which I developed my own healing strategy, as well as a brief look at my dysfunctional childhood which I believe led me to have the beliefs that I had. My motivation for writing this book was to help people understand their own negative core beliefs, recognise the signs of an abusive, toxic relationship, and give them some tools they could use to help them. I also discuss how Empaths like me are more likely to be targeted and how to protect ourselves energetically. I will discuss the concept of disconnection not only from a physical, no-contact point of view, but also from an energetic point of view. Most importantly, having had such a toxic relationship, I will discuss some of the feelings that will come up as a result. It is also likely that you are going to have Post Traumatic Stress Disorder and I explain how to cope with it, understand it, along with practical ways you can look after yourself, especially if you are left financially, physically and/or emotionally damaged.

How Our Childhood Moulds Us

I always thought of my childhood as being pretty normal apart from being singled out from an early age as a gifted child and being on the plump side. But I realised my childhood was not quite as normal as I thought it was. Both Jonathan, my youngest brother, and I are gifted, yet, for some strange reason, we had both grown up thinking we were worthless. I remember having had a conversation with him a year or so ago when we had reconnected again after nearly 13 years apart. We had both had this deep feeling like nothing we ever did was ever going to be good enough. I was making music at the time, and was a reasonably successful healer and coach. My brother is one of the most gifted video animators in the industry, not to mention being one the youngest members of the magic circle working with the likes of Derren Brown. Yet, despite this, we both said that even though we were multi-talented, whenever we did things, we both always felt like we were never quite good enough.

Our family consisted of my parents, my elder brother, myself, and my younger brother. My parents stuck it out for nearly 35 years before their divorce, so I am not sure whether my mother deserved a medal for her patience or a certificate for stupidity. What I do know is that our childhood upbringing helps to mould our future. My mother was brought up in a middle class family, with a father who worked for the same firm all his life. She was a church goer and had the voice of an angel. She had been chosen to be an opera singer at a young age, but her parents could not afford to send her to Switzerland, and so she never realized her ambitions. I was told by other relatives who knew her growing up that she had been put on a pedestal when she was a child, as the perfect prodigy. She won a scholarship to one of the best schools in the country but her whole life was to be turned upside down during her teens when her own mother was struck down with multiple sclerosis. It was then that my mother had to start caring for her younger sister. My father on the other hand was a "bad boy." He came from a dysfunctional background and didn't have the "nice" background of my mother.

Interestingly, when my parents first met, my mother did not like my dad. He appeared as a teddy boy with long sideburns and persisted in asking her for a date wearing crepe soled shoes with long sideburns. When he finally turned up on the first date he had had his hair cut, and turned up wearing a suit and smoking a pipe! She was so surprised by his new persona that she never once questioned why a man would change his personality to suit her in such a short time knowing her. If I had been talking to a client, and knowing what I know now, the first thing I would think was "red flag." Why had he changed his persona so quickly?

As a child, I remember my mother as highly intelligent, extremely talented and very resourceful, and when we were small, she spent her time at home with all of us. She never had a job and was a full time mum, working hard at being a good parent, and teaching us the joys of macramé, painting, and anything else that came to mind when we were very young. She occasionally took part-time jobs to make ends meet in between looking after us. She was a patient and skilled dressmaker and had taught me how to sew at the age of seven. I could make my own clothes by the time I was a teenager. I could also run a household at eight, which included cleaning the house and looking after my baby brother. On the surface, she was a wonderful mother, but on a darker note, she suffered from ill health and severe depression. She would take to her bed for periods of a few hours to a few days. As children, we worried relentlessly over her state of health. Our home life was pretty chaotic and her moods were even more so.

Interestingly enough my mothers feeling's of depression and ill health depended on how she was feeling emotionally. When she was finally brave enough to leave her second husband I have never seen my mother healthier both physically or emotionally in all of her adult life. I believe in essence my mother is highly empathic however by staying around toxic relationships for so long sometimes we may end picking up their unowned "stuff" and becoming like our partners. Sam Vaknin says that the the narcissistic psychopath wants us to become *like them* "Victims are scarred forever, traumatized and adversely transformed." Being in a relationship with a man for 35 years and then having a further relationship with a dysfunctional person would be enough to transform anyone. However, my mother has changed for the better, and quite significantly, and I am now able to have the healthy relationship I could not always have with her when I was young. Although I am sorry to say that since the publication of the first edition of this book my mother had chosen to go back with my step father and sometimes these changes are temporary. Ss a result I am no longer having the relationship I had with her. Like I said we cannot change anyone but we can change outselves.

Because of my father, we had a pretty nomadic kind of lifestyle, moving to various different parts of the country according to where my dad would decide we would live or what adventurous idea he was going to dream up next. Would we have a new business, live in a pub, or have to move because of a family drama. I think we moved about seven times during my childhood. We found out, many years later, that the moves had often coincided with my father's multiple marital affairs. He always wanted to do different things and he had so many different businesses, that some would fail and then we would have to move again. We had lived in a pub, as well as in a wonderful house, with acres of land, and then we would be off again on a whim. That's how it was. Our house was always lively with lots of visitors. It was either clean and tidy or a total mess. Mum would spend days in bed being depressed or having a bad back, and when we would have visitors it was a panic to clean the place up so that everyone would come round and see that the house looked "normal"

I give my father the credit for being one of was the most hard working men I have ever known, along with my ex husband. He once said that if he was going to do anything at all, he would want to just give us children that which he hadn't received as a child, namely, a good education and an opportunity to do what he never could. He always remained optimistic despite being made redundant more times that most people have had hot dinners. He had worked in the car trade as a fitter and would bounce back each time he lost his job, going out and getting another job without a second thought. I think in all the years he had worked, he was only unemployed for three weeks. At the same time, my father felt intimidated by my mother because she was highly intelligent and very creative. All of us children carried her creative traits and intelligence. He would often demean himself and say he was thick or stupid.

My father never wanted to be like his own dad, with his mum always raiding his pockets when he was drunk to pay for food. Grandfather would buy presents for my dad and then take them back or pawn them because he needed the money again. Our own family finances always were a bit unstable, too. Dad would take on grand projects and then we would have to move house. I remember him telling me a story about a piano where his dad had bought him a lovely piano and then took it back a couple of weeks later. As much as he tried not to be like his own dad, my father would make promises he couldn't always keep and I hated that. My father was very charismatic, always wanting to play the part of the good guy, but, sadly, he was a compulsive womaniser. My mother would walk around with rose coloured blinkers on. I asked her as a teenager why she had stayed with my dad all these years and put up with his affairs and she would reply "Because I love him." Of course, she always took him back. I remember my mother's nervous breakdown after the birth of my youngest brother and how it had made a huge impact on our lives and still haunts us today as adults and parents. All we ever wanted was for our mother to be happy.

I knew about most of my father's relationships with other women either from his body language or the way in which he would flirt with particular women. Everyone would blame my father's behaviour on my mum's depression, and yet no one ever told my mother about his affairs. They seemed to want to collude in his infidelity. It had a terrible effect on my mother as she suffered from low self-esteem already, and it pained her not knowing which of her best friends my father was going to take to bed. The manipulation and lies wreaked havoc on my mother's health. Deep down, I think she knew all the time when he was having affairs because I always did. But when she would confront him, he would deny it, calling her crazy or depressed and suggesting she went back on antidepressants again. None of it was done in a violent way, merely very underhanded, but I knew about everything and that was half the problem. My mother used to have this romantic idea that all marriages could be like her own parents, and they had been married until the day they died. She once said to me that she had this "fairy tale" notion of marriage and that is why she had stayed so long with my father. And yet despite everything she was trying to make a horror story into a fairy tale.

Twisted Love

My parents had, in all honesty, what can only be described as a toxic love relationship or twisted love. As an adult, I was to learn all about twisted love and went onto act those stories out again and again. My parents' marriage was a sham. Through counselling, both my younger brother Jonathan and I were told that my father had a personality disorder. Labels aside, there is belief that "like attracts like." Through my own journey of discovery, I have done a lot of research and narcissistic types of personalities tend to attract similar personalities or at least narcissistic "enablers," especially when it comes to long term relationships. Enablers are types such as co-dependants or Inverted Narcissists.

I was doing a radio interview and one of the guests was a clinical psychologist. I jokingly made a fleeting comment about narcissists and how I had received perfect training in my childhood to attract the Oliver type.

A prominent psychiatrist observed recently, "Narcissists are the bread and butter of the therapeutic enterprise, not because they so often seek professional help — they are too impressed with themselves to ever think they have a problem — but because they drive so many people around them crazy." Both my brothers and I have spent time in counselling, wondering if we were mentally ill. We have all gone on to have some dysfunctional relationships throughout our adult life.

My parents "loved" each other, whatever that meant. I don't think they really knew what proper healthy love was. When a husband and wife live in denial, is this really healthy? As we were growing up my parents would play a game I call the "don't tell mum anything game." My mother spent many years on antidepressants. My father would say things like "don't tell your mum your problems because she will get upset," and so we tended to internalise everything. My eldest brother's way of coping was to "switch off." He was nicknamed "Johnny head in the air." I was just "Miss Nosey" and "Miss Do it all." I was always trying to do things to help around the house, helping my mum with my brother and being the "little mum." I also always knew something was going on when my father was cheating, and even though I would consciously listen at the top of the stairs to my parents talking, everything would be covered up. My youngest brother was the "entertainer," trying hard to get attention and feeling unloved.

We were never physically abused, and got the odd smack when we were naughty, but our emotional needs were never met. We all learned how to internalise our feelings and, as grownups, we all learned how to have dysfunctional relationships. We went on to mirror our parents' relationships with our own partners in different ways.

One time my mother did stand up to my dad's affairs. She kicked him out and said she wasn't having him back. His reaction was to try killing himself. I was probably about twelve years old. It was three AM when we got a call from the police to say that my father had "tried" unsuccessfully to commit suicide by gassing himself with the car exhaust fumes in a country lane. He had been taken into hospital, stayed there for six weeks, and then my mother had him back. I still pass the same place where he tried to kill himself and shiver goes up my spine. I asked him once why he did it and he replied "it seemed like a good idea at the time." After the incident, my eldest brother and I had spent a lot of time helping look after my little brother whilst my mum ran back and forth to the hospital.

The usual story we kids played at home was piggy in the middle. Dad didn't want to hear all about mum's stuff because as far as he was concerned, he had done nothing wrong and secondly because it was *all her imagination,* which of course it wasn't. He would encourage her to dump all her stuff on us, and have her tell us how depressed and miserable she was. My parents had split up and my father called my brother Jonathan, saying "Quick get home – your mum's suicidal and going to kill herself! You need to get home now." My brother drove home from work in a complete panic. When he had finally arrived, his reaction had been one of relief and horror as he saw her sitting there with a smile on her face, as he politely put it, "eating an egg mayonnaise sandwich." My mother has apologised for not being the grown up parent and being unable to cope when she was married to my father. She said she felt isolated and did not know who else to talk to apart from her children.

My parents had had a very unhealthy relationship and my father had an even more unhealthy relationship with women. He had an obsession with boobs. We had a shed in the garden and he collected porn magazines. In addition, he loved Page Three girls. His favourite newspaper was *The Sun* and his favourite Page Three girls were Samantha Fox and Linda Lusardi. The shed had been plastered from wall to wall with cut-out photos of girls that were younger than I was! Every single square inch was covered in photos of women with very large breasts. My mum, his sister, and his own mother all have very large breasts, and unfortunately, mine were an average size B. So I grew up with this very warped view of myself, thinking there was something wrong with me because I didn't have big boobs. Still, to this day, I feel disgusted when I look at my own breasts and think they are not normal.

My best friend once said to me that it was very strange that at eleven I was the only girl in High School that knew everything about sex. All my friends would come to me and ask me questions. My mother was very open about sex, and her reasoning was that I was inquisitive and nosey. Nobody ever questioned that she was telling me stuff that I didn't want to hear and my parents never once imagined that I had been sexually abused by someone else when I was tiny, or that I had had nightmares as a child, and that I had put on weight because I unconsciously did not want any man going near me. Instead they just stuck me on slimming pills.

When my parents finally broke up it was like the "War of the Roses." I was living away from home at the time, bringing up my own family. My father wanted to collect the car and my mum had cut his favourite leather jacket up with a razor blade and dumped it through the sunroof of his car with all his bowling trophies smashed to pieces. Even more pathetic was my father's attempts to painstakingly glue back together his favourite jacket so that my mum couldn't win.

It's interesting that when we grow up in a dysfunctional family, we have a different perception of things. Let's call it wearing different coloured glasses. I like to think that I had rose coloured glasses on or perhaps green ones. By that, I mean mine were green because I was very naïve. As we work through the book, the whole process of negative core beliefs and inner child work will be explained in full. But let's just say for example my negative core belief was that I was naïve or a little green. I might well attract situations or people in my life that would reinforce that belief, perhaps even to the extent of encountering people that would use me. I might not listen to my intuition even though it was staring me in the face and might ignore any red flags or warning signs. One of my beliefs I had only discovered after leaving Oliver was that I am powerless. The reality is I am actually very capable. I have had a successful career in banking and IT for many years. I have brought up two children. I have had a number of different successful careers. I am quite gifted and creative, and have been told I have a charismatic and Empathic quality about me which has helped me in my healing practice. If that core belief was out of balance, I might decide to do a job which was the complete opposite of that core belief, like, for example, try to run a corporation.

Having grown up in such a very dysfunctional household, neither my mother nor father were parents in the proper sense. Being the middle of three children, I often had to be a "parent" to my own parents. All of us children ended up affected to some degree, and found ourselves in dysfunctional relationships as adults, in one way or another. When you are not nurtured emotionally as children, you grow up to be high functioning on the surface. When there is sexual abuse, you often become hyper vigilant. To the outside world, you are strong and capable, but having had no boundaries set as children, we are unable to attach ourselves to normal healthy relationships as adults.

When I had left home early after a string of elusive relationships with men that would not commit to me, I married what appeared on the surface to be a hard-working, "nice" man. He was not a womaniser, but slowly as time went on he became very controlling. Although I do not think he is a abuser as such he has a strong dominant personality. He was always making sure he knew where I was because he was always jealous. One by one, during my marriage I lost all my friends or gave them up because he would criticise them or did not like them. I gave up my city job to work with him so he could make sure he was there twenty-four hours a day and ensure he knew everyone I spoke to. Over the years, my self esteem diminished so much. When we finally divorced, I ended up in hospital with Crohns Disease.

In relationships with men in general would I always start off confident in relationships and then allow my self esteem to slip over the years by letting my partners control me.

I have never really understood what love is. My ex husband told me he loved me every day in words, yet his actions said something else. No birthday presents, holidays separate from each other, sleeping in separate beds, and his whole obsession with work, money and his family didn't equate to what my understanding of real love is. It was never romantic, loving, or sexual. My daughter Laura said she had wanted to hit him one time when he gave me a cuddle and kiss because she wasn't used to parents doing that. He just never gave me any affection.

Then, I met Dan: Mr. Aloof. He hid everything from me from the moment we met, and never even let me know where he was living. He would turn up whenever he felt like it, usually once a week, get totally drunk and spend the day having sex with me. Then I wouldn't hear from him for a week, when I would receive some cryptic text messages and then the game would begin all over again. One of the games he would play was to say he was not sure what he wanted, and did not want commitment, and then accuse me of dating Oliver (as I was friends with him at the same time). He was afraid of his own shadow most of the time. He would never dare say the "love" word and said he just wanted to be free. I found out later that he, too, had cheated on me the whole time we were together; he was actually living with someone all the time, which explains why he did not want me to know his address.

Even my first boyfriend, Dave, was elusive. He was 21, when I was 13. I was his "bit on the side" and my mum colluded, in part, by allowing me to come and go as I pleased and stay out until 3 am, even though I was under aged. As a mother, she would have known his interest in me, a thirteen year old, would only have been about sex, and yet, she encouraged it. In fact her comment was "They didn't make them like that when I was your age." It wasn't until much later, when I had spoken to my counsellor, I was told, legally, it would have been considered sexual abuse of a minor. Perhaps in all fairness she was so depressed she didn't even notice what her own children were doing.

Throughout my childhood I always hid my anger. However, you cannot hide your anger forever: it will always rear its ugly head. When we start to stuff our emotions down, we compress and compound them. That's why you hear stories about so-called calm, nice people suddenly doing outrageous things or killing people, likely because of a flipped trigger rooted in their childhood. I carried the anger about my mother, father, and grandfather through my childhood, and then for another 17 years while I was married to my children's father. I appeared very outwardly passive. I carried it a few more years until I met what I thought was my one true love Oliver.

It starts in early childhood with Fairy Tales where the Prince and the Princess live happily-ever-after. It continues in movies and books in which "boy meets girl, boy loses girl, and then boy gets girl back." The music swells and the happy couple ride off into the sunset. The songs that say "I can't smile without you," "I can't live without you," and "You are my everything," describe the type of love we learned about while growing up – toxic love – an addiction with the other person as our drug of choice, as our higher power. Any time we set up another human being to be our higher power, we are going to experience failure. We will end up feeling victimized by the other person or by our self. Even when we feel victimized by the other person, we blame ourselves for the choices we had made. We are destined to fail in getting our needs met in romantic relationships because of the belief system we were taught in childhood and the messages we've received from our society while growing up: there is no goal to reach that will bring us to "happily-ever-after." We are *not* incomplete until we find our "soul mate." We are not *halves* that cannot be whole without a relationship.

My favourite music is dance music, however, if I was to choose a love song it would be '*All time love*' by Will Young and yet my favourite movie ended up being *Eternal sunshine of the spotless Mind*. After everything that happened I wanted to erase *all* memories of Oliver forever. Olivers favourite movie was *Dirty Dancing* and he had Backstreet boys '*So long as you love me*' in his car all the time. If you don't know the chorus its goes like this "*I don't care who you are, where your from, what you do, as long as you love me.*" I joked once and said to him, "I thought you liked heavy rock." He said it was his wife's CD, and he would never listen to that crap! It was only when he gave me his car and checked what remaining CD's were in the changer that he finally admitted that it was his. Even now just thinking about it makes me cringe. What an appropriate song for a Dark Soul.

Love is not supposed to be painful. There is pain involved in any relationship, but if it is painful most of the time, something is definitely not working. There is nothing wrong with wanting a relationship: it is natural and healthy. There is nothing wrong with wanting a relationship that will last forever, but expecting it to last forever is what is dysfunctional. Expectations set us up to be a victim and cause us to abandon ourselves in search of our goal. If we can start seeing relationships not as the goal but as opportunities for growth, then we can start having more functional relationships. A relationship that ends is not a failure or a punishment, it is a lesson. As long as our definition of a successful relationship is one that lasts forever, we are destined to fail. As long as we believe that we have to have the other person in our life to be happy, we are really just an addict trying to protect our supply: using another person as our drug of choice. That is not "true love," nor is it "loving." Wanting a relationship and trying to make it work, especially if the other person is dysfunctional, and setting our own needs aside in the process, is not true love.

Growing Up In a Narcissistic Family

According to *The Narcissistic Family: Diagnosis and Treatment* by Stephanie Donaldson-Pressman and Robert M. Pressman:

"The Narcissistic family often resembles the proverbial shiny red apple with a worm inside. It looks great, until you bite into and discover the worm. The rest of the apple may be just fine, but you've just lost your appetite. In the Narcissistic family, most of what happens can be 'just fine,' but the emotional underpinnings are not there."

I didn't really know who I was in my family. I felt like an extension of my parents. I felt like a dump bucket for all their unmet needs. I also knew everything that was going on in the family, we all did, and yet we weren't allowed to trust our own feelings. If we spoke up and said something was wrong, it was either all our imagination or we were making it up. My mother used to say things like "you are so naïve," when, in fact, it was a projection of her own naivety on me. Many years later, when I had asked my mother why every time I spoke up, everyone covered things up. She said everyone had colluded by covering up my father's affairs. She also admitted that she was the one that was naive and that I knew everything that was going on.

In our family our parents emotional needs were paramount. When she was depressed, we were always told not to tell her our problems because she could not cope, and so my father did whatever he wanted. As we grew older, we were able to take on more emotionally and my own father didn't want to cope with her, so we became a dumping ground for her unmet emotional needs. However we grew up thinking everything was just fine and *normal*.

Stephanie Donaldson-Pressman and Robert M. Pressman go onto to say:

"Many people who grow up in narcissistic families make statements in therapy such as 'there is no point in talking about my childhood. It was perfectly normal. Actually, I can't really remember anything about it, isn't that awful?   But it was good.'"

It wasn't until much later, when I tried to form adult bonding relationships that I realised how wrong my childhood really was.

Covertly narcissistic families are more difficult to spot. To the outsider the victims are more likely to be in denial and deny that anything has happened to them. If they grew up with a family that did not have drug or alcohol, violence or severe emotional mental problems they may not realise anything is wrong until they try to form adult bonding relationships. I had no problem forming adult relationships with workmates and friends, but I had great difficulty when it came to close relationships with men. I also avoided relationships with women, as I tended to attract needy women and would always be helping them out. Most of my non-sexual friends were men before I got married, I think partly because I had a strong bond with my brothers.

On the surface of this normal family, my dad was a very hard worker, probably the hardest working man I have ever met. My parents were very into each other when they were getting along with each other. The family photos show them lovingly looking into each others' eyes. They were quite affectionate with each other. Yet, no one saw the other side of it, where my mother would cry for days because my father had been having yet another affair, or the parties where he would sneak off for a snog with the next door neighbour. No one could see my mother's insecurities about herself when my own father put her on a pedestal and told her how wonderful she was when she sang and painted and drew, yet, in a second breath, would rip her apart for being overweight. No one could see the times when my mother would say what a hard working man our father was, and in the next moment, pull everything he did to pieces, from decorating the house to how bad he was in bed.

If we got sick my mother, was sicker. I remember my brother suffering from appendicitis and being very ill, and still my mother packed him off to school for the day, only to find him at home later with a burst appendix. When I was twelve years old, I started my periods. It was so heavy, I had to wear two tampons, a towel, and pants over my tights to stop the flow. I later learned I had severe endometriosis, which continued for most of my adult life. I came home from school one day thoroughly embarrassed because the boys at school had made fun of me. Despite all the precautions I'd mentioned, I had menstruated heavily onto the back of my skirt, and had to rush off to the toilets to clean my clothes before my next lesson, only to be humiliated in front of the whole class by the Religious Education teacher for being late. The last thing I had wanted at that moment was to be sent to bed with a hot water bottle and told that my mother had bad periods too. My mother spent most of my adult life telling me how she had bad periods. Many years later, when I was in my forties, I had to have yet another investigation and operation for my periods. My mother, in a moment of sympathy, said "You poor thing. You haven't had much luck in the period department. I am very lucky I have never had a bad period in my life." I looked at her in shock and told her that she had spent her life telling me that she'd had bad periods like mine. She looked away and remarked "Oh, I would never say such a thing. I think you have got it all wrong." My mother would often do or say one thing and then later totally deny it.

I think the most humiliating experience I had ever was going to a family party where my eldest brother was being paraded around, almost on show as he had just returned from America as the unsung hero of the family who was always put on a pedestal, through no choice of his own. My little brother was vying for attention by doing his magic tricks in the background with hardly anyone noticing him and someone came up and asked my mum about me whilst I was there. My mother then went onto explain in great detail about how I was suffering from period problems and what latest diet I was on. I wanted to ground to swallow me up whole, and wishing I had never been born.

Stephanie Donaldson-Pressman and Robert M. Pressman further write:

"Children in Narcissistic families are moving targets. Suppose that the mother in law comes for a visit. Mom has needs for praise and esteem from her family who values good parenting. So during the visit, Mum is available and cuddly to her children. So during that time, the children get their nurturing needs met and the daughter gets some free time from babysitting. The mother in law praises Mom's parenting, so mum gets her esteem needs met. Everybody is happy, temporarily. Mum met the children's needs, but only as an action coincident to getting her own needs met."

From my own experience, they may not have seen that two days before the house was a complete disaster and that we had all had to rally around as children because mum had been in bed depressed for a week or two. I had been helping out by looking after my baby brother because mum was unable to cope. Mum didn't want to put on a bad face and admit that she hadn't cleaned up the house herself, and that she had been shouting the day before. Everyone wants to make a good impression because the family are coming over and we all like to play happy families.

Most of us who grow up in a Narcissistic family feel guilty for blaming our own parents for their deficiency in parenting. We are so afraid of being angry at our own parents, it feels easier to end up blaming ourselves for every single thing that that goes wrong in our adult life: failed relationships, indecisiveness, inability to concentrate, the dinner not working out properly, our computers crashing, and even the cat peeing on the carpet.

I recently bumped into some old next door neighbours from when we were growing up. They asked about us children, and about my mother and father who have since both divorced. I told them they were doing fine. The lady asked if I was still living in my lovely house and I explained to her that I had had to sell it and move because of my relationship with Oliver and that I had messed up by meeting with an amplified version of my dad. She smiled and said "Yep, your dad. Everyone knew about him, that's why we all nicknamed him "Jack the lad, lovely man, very charming, but a complete and utter ..." Before she could finish her sentence, we both said the same word: "conman." Seeing the irony of it, we both just stood there and laughed.

The Aftermath

I guess the easiest part of ending a relationship is the leaving, or, in my case, having the courage to ask Oliver to go. Obviously, many people who are reading this book will have their own stories, and I have tried not to make this just a story about me, but more a story about how you, as a reader, can relate what I share to your own situation and take whatever you need to help you heal. Some of you will not believe in the energy aspect and be more the type of person who relates to the concepts of clinical diagnosis. Some of you may just realise that you are, or have been, in an abusive relationship or worse one with a Dark Soul!

It doesn't really matter what you call it; it's more about how *you*, as the victim, feel and how you are going to recover.

Removing Yourself from Inevitable Harm

Anyone who *really* knows me will say I am very confident and one of the more popular terms people have for me is that I am a survivor. I have had many ups and downs over the years. Sometimes I have put myself in some pretty scary situations. Some people might call me a risk taker, which, in turn, makes me very adventurous and also a very attractive target to a sociopath. I was the kind of person that would always bounce back no matter how tough things were. For example as a youngster in my teens when I left home at 17 I went off travelling around the world on my own and then went backpacking around India.

No matter what life threw at me, I would always come back fighting. I used to hate the term "survivor," because it always suggested a kind of victimhood. I might have been good at getting myself out of bad situations through hard work and strength, but whenever anyone said I was "a survivor," I would cringe. I would always cope extremely well in a crisis, then, only when the worst was over, would the realisation of what had actually happened kick in. When I had first faced the enormity of the huge mistakes I had made by not listening to my intuition, it meant looking at my own disordered self and needing to find out as much as I could about Dark Souls. I also needed to look at myself and my part in the relationship. Although I had known I would be able to remove myself from this relationship, I did not ever want to attract another version of Oliver into my life again.

Narcissists thrive on Narcissistic Supply, and someone like me who is highly empathic is like caviar to a narcissist. In the past, I had always been the person who was there for everyone, including everyone in the family. After reading *The Narcissistic Family: Diagnosis and Treatment*, I had realised a lot of the stories in the book mirrored my own childhood, and many of the children depicted went onto become co dependent. I think to some degree I had been far more co-dependent when I was married but had learned not to be by the time I had divorced. I had also been living on my own for 7 years before I met Oliver. However, I have never learned to control my empathy.

There is a theory that children of pathological parents can go one of two ways, especially if their fathers are psychopaths. The girls do not want to hate their fathers so they often become highly Empathic or co-dependent, and the boys sometimes can become like their fathers. In the book, *Just Like His Father?* the author, Dr. Liane Leedom, a board-certified psychiatrist, realized that the father of her six month old son had a personality disorder. She spent the next three years researching the scientific literature, learning how sociopathy develops, and how to prevent it.

I also realised I had to do something for my own children and didn't want them repeating my mistakes or becoming co-dependent. For starters, both children were beginning to appear highly Empathic and having difficulty coming to terms with it. I became concerned they would end up switching their Empathy off and shutting down, or that they would become co-dependent like myself and attract narcissists or sociopaths into their lives. Co-dependents are individuals who become dependent upon narcissists, alcoholics, or drug addicts. The concept of co-dependence is derived from the 'co-alcoholic' behaviour of spouses and children in chemically dependent families. Counsellors observed that family members often took on the psychological defences and survival behaviours of the alcoholic, thereby extending the disease from the individual to the entire family. Co-dependency is a condition that affects a large percentage of the adult population in varying degrees. Other terms often used for co-dependent behaviour in relation to narcissism are 'enabler,' 'covert narcissist,' or 'inverted narcissist.' Co-dependents seek security both at work and at home, so they are drawn to individuals who are, or "appear" to be, confident, positive and self-assured. Narcissists usually display these very qualities, displaying an air of superiority, grandiosity and self-importance. Co-dependents admire these qualities, and narcissists crave admiration. Although the reality is that, underneath, a narcissist feels worthless, and, as a result, will end up projecting these feelings of worthlessness onto their partner. Because Co-dependents, who have been brought up in an environment that ensures they will avoid confrontation if at all possible, are ideal fodder for the narcissist who focuses exclusively on having their needs met.

Because I had displayed symptoms of co-dependence in the past and being an overly sensitive Empath that actually picks up other people's feelings, I was often left feeling like I didn't even know who I was most of the time, especially when I was with family members or with Oliver. Yet, every time I left him, I would start to slip back into my authentic self and feel so much better.

However, the narcissist does not flourish alone. He needs a willing partner. The relationship between the Dark Soul is symbiotic. Although the narcissist inflicts mental cruelty and humiliation on his partner, the two of them support each other's neurotic behaviour. Accepting that we played a part in the dynamics of the relationship may be a hard pill for us, as targets, to swallow. The Co-dependent becomes an accommodating and understanding victim, caring for the whims and mood swings of the narcissist, eventually learning to adapt to the narcissist's world view especially if the latter is good at playing the victim role. Co-dependants love to give and narcissists love to take, and that works out nicely. The narcissist uses his partner as an anchor or a 'trusted sidekick,' and feels that the latter is an extension of him, since they lack an authentic "self" to model themselves upon in the first place. The good news, is that co-dependency is curable. With a lot of hard work, one can be free of it. However, for the narcissist, there is no real cure for them. You can spend the rest of your life hoping and wishing they will change but it's futile. As far as empathy is concerned, you can learn to switch if off.

Of course, when it comes to sociopaths, *anyone* is a potential target for sociopaths, so I was literally like prized meat. Having worked through all my issues of co-dependency long ago, I realised that being an Empath was probably one of the biggest reasons why they were so attracted to me. I didn't want to spend the rest of my life being a Dark Soul magnet. I also hated the fact that I was an Empath. However, when the co-dependent person decides to look after themselves or the Empath realises that the "stuff" they have been carrying around is not theirs, the relationship has nowhere to go anymore. It collapses in on itself like the black hole and eventually has to end.

A friend and colleague who worked with psychopaths and narcissists said that the only way to get rid of a them, was to pretend you have been defeated. Eventually they will get fed up and find a new victim or a source of new narcissistic supply. The other way is to actually think and *act* like they do. In some ways, I actually had to act like one to get rid of Oliver. I even told a few lies to keep him off my back.

Stepping Out of Denial

For me, finding all the evidence helped me to step out of denial. It became a bit of an obsession, and after realising Oliver had very narcissistic tendencies, I had decided to explore narcissism and NPD a bit further. What surprised me was that however much information I confronted Oliver with, nothing really appeared to upset him that much. First of all, I have never really stood up to anyone in my life before, so this was strange to me. When I had tried to stand up to them, they would deny everything. Oliver would just give me a blank look when I confronted him with anything as if to say "Yeah, whatever," or else he would find an excuse or feign being sorry. Failing that, he would give me the silent treatment and sulk for a couple of days or weeks. However, armed with so much evidence, he was unable to deny anything or come up with a plausible excuse any more. I also informed Oliver that I had kept all of the evidence and that if anything happened to me or anyone else I would make sure that the police would be informed immediately. The last thing a narcissist or a sociopath wants is to get caught and exposed. They will also not want to risk going to prison, mainly because it's an inconvenience, nothing more.

What my actions did do was make Oliver completely back down. He stopped bullying me and threatening me with the police for the unpaid bills I had been pursuing him for. Although he never paid the bills I decided to cut my losses. It paid off in that I was able to rid myself of him and move on, peaceful in the knowledge that he was unlikely to do anything for fear of being caught.

Some people may be asking why did I not tell his wife? Primarily a sociopath will NOT do anything if they think they will get caught. Oliver already knew I had told his mother of my concerns about him and I had also advised him that if anything suspicious were to happen to either myself, my family or his own family, I would contact the police immediately. I also do not believe it is my job to tell her and like myself she probably knows a lot more than I gave her credit for which is probably one of the reasons she has never been round to my house accusing me of stealing her husband.

One thing I would advise to anyone who is suspicious about their partner is to never confront them directly, unless you have hard evidence and even when you do you must be very meticulous about keeping it. All Dark Souls are expert liars and will deny everything even when faced with hard evidence. It's very important that you keep any evidence somewhere safe where they cannot find it. They are master *projectors* and will often accuse people of doing things that they do. For example, Oliver would go through his wife's mail and open her letters suggesting she did the same.

If you are not sure about how good they are at playing mind games and manipulating. Go back and read the section on Gaslighting. If you are in the process of divorcing a Dark Soul, make sure you are fully prepared to have a dirty fight in courts especially if children are concerned. Find yourself a good lawyer, ideally one that understands the complexities of dealing with compulsive liars.

If you are involved in an ongoing separation make sure you have witnesses. Its best you do not deal with them alone. Have a friend or relative present especially during child exchange. In cases of partner violence or child abuse, this dual personality is often clearly apparent and the plausible, manipulative personality enables them to persuade gullible court officials, lawyers, and even judges. They do this by turning the tables and saying that they are innocent of the abusive behaviours alleged by their children or the violence alleged by the former partner. The sociopath father and mother can be extremely adept at "playing victim" in court processes, accusing the other of obsessive concerns for a sick child or of actually making the child ill, or of not ensuring that the child engages in a "meaningful" relationship with them, when, in fact, the child has protested loudly that he or she does not want any contact.

I recently learned of a case where it was very clear that the child was being sexually abused by one of her parents, as she was constantly bed-wetting and playing with her genitals. However, even now, I am still unable to tell which of the parents was telling the truth. My gut feeling was the mother, who appeared to be concerned about her child's welfare and was declaring that the father was sexually abusing the little one, had a peculiar air about her. I was happy not to be putting a reference for her on paper as I didn't feel comfortable. The use of "Parental Alienation Syndrome" has proved to be a highly effective tool for sociopaths to use in disputed court proceedings regarding custody and contact with children. They can so readily engage in deception and fabrication, distortion, and embellishment of facts regarding events and actions. They are masters at attracting the sympathy of court officials and lawyers, and using them to gain what they see as their rights. Some sociopaths also appear to have infiltrated fathers' rights groups in some countries, where they have been able to influence further domination and control over females. Of course this can work both ways, as women and men are equally capable of being sociopaths.

Never suggest your partner is a sociopath or a narcissist. *Only* a professional can diagnose them and getting them to a counsellor is a whole other story. Narcissists are often able to pass a lie detector test. If you are fighting a custody battle, the legal profession will be biased and might think you are actually the pathologically ill one if you start accusing your partner of being sociopathic. Unless your partner is of the Ted Bundy serial killer variety, the legal profession will not believe you, and bringing this into the topic of conversation will go against you. It would be far more beneficial for you to focus on their bad behaviour and, more importantly, proving it with lots of evidence. I had made the mistake of calling my ex a sociopath on more than one occasion. However, his reaction was not quite what I expected. He actually showed no emotion, whatsoever, and, smirking, replied "That's not very nice."

Do your best to focus on looking after yourself and your children if you have any. Many abusers will accuse their partners of not being good parents. If you are a drinker, stop drinking and start looking out for yourself by making healthy decisions in your own life

Learn all you can about how to spot liars. Steven Van Aperen is known throughout Australia and worldwide as an expert in the fields of interviewing and detecting deception. He runs the website www.polygraph.com.au. Steven has received extensive training from the world's leading International Investigative Authorities in how and why people deceive. Referred to by the media as the 'Human Polygraph," Steven demonstrates how to detect liars by observing their verbal and non-verbal cues of behaviour. Drawing on real life examples, he demonstrates the methods in which people deceive. For example, when former US president Bill Clinton was asked if he had ever used an illegal drug he responded: "I've never violated a law of my country." Whilst this response appears to be a denial he did not answer the question. Later Clinton admitted that he had smoked marijuana whilst at Oxford University in the United Kingdom but "didn't inhale." People often lie by omission rather than commission. What people don't say is often more important than what they do say! Steven demonstrates how we use language, paralinguistic styles, past tenses, and body language to deceive others and how to recognise when people are engaging in such behaviours.

Remember that the sociopath will always play dirty. At one point I was considering taking Oliver to court over unpaid bills and rent for the brief period that he stayed in my property. However, I knew he would make outrageous accusations as he had done in the past, like accusing me of stalking him or worse. For the unpaid rent, I realised that the court proceedings would be more headache than it was worth. Sometimes it's much easier to simply offer them an incentive to walk away. If you have children, chances are they are not a very good parent and are only using their children as a way of controlling you. If you don't want to go through the courts and risk being accused of outrageous things like child abuse, sometimes you have to weigh up the pros and cons. If you believe that the money isn't worth having the abuser in your family's life, do everything in your power to figure out a way to support your children without it.

I know from my own experience, the financial cost of what I had lost (i.e. everything) was nothing compared to the benefits of getting rid of Oliver. It's something I remind myself of daily, whenever I think of how bad it could have been, had I been stupid enough to stay with him. What if I had married Oliver and taken his children on as my own? Not only would I have had to keep bailing him out financially and otherwise, but I would have spent the rest of my life at risk of catching sexually transmitted diseases not knowing where he was most days. I would never have been able to believe a single word from him. I would have probably ended up feeling suicidal and required anti depressants. I would have ended up being an even worse mother than I already had been. What's more, I would have lived the life of my mother all over again.

We owe it to our children to be strong and to remove these people from our lives. I wish my mother had left my father when we were children, or when she had first been told he was a sociopath. However my father has never once volunteered himself for counselling. I cannot possibly say whether or not my father is a sociopath or not but he lacks empathy and guilt.

Perhaps if my mother had listened and left him when we were younger, we would have had a better chance of having a better family role model and we wouldn't have attracted dysfunctional relationships as adults or copied some of our parents' negative behaviours. Unfortunately she didn't, and it wasn't until all of us had grown up and gone on to repeat our parents' mistakes that the penny finally dropped.

I've had two children and I cannot undo what I have done, but when I started seeing my own daughter going out with another Oliver clone, I had decided enough was enough. It was that which had inspired me to change, and if I must remain single to set a good example for my children, I will. I also know if I had stayed with Oliver, I would have gone down the black hole with him, taking the rest of my money and family with us, as well.

Stop Digging up Dead Corpses

Often, as adults, we feel we form an image of what perfection is in order to aspire to it. We create an image of how we *should be* in order to be accepted by everybody. We especially try to please the ones who love us, like our parents and our loved ones. Trying to be good enough for others, we create an image of perfection, be we don't fit this image. We create this image, but this image is not real. We are never going to be perfect from this point of view. Never! Not being perfect, we then reject ourselves, and the level of self rejection depends upon how effective adults were in breaking our integrity when we were children. If we had grown up in a dysfunctional household, we may be carrying shame and guilt. Humans are the only species that punish ourselves endlessly for not being what we believe we should be. We become self abusive and we use other people to abuse us as well. But no matter how much we are abused by others, *nobody* abuses us more than we do ourselves. We batter ourselves constantly with the little subconscious voice in our head: the lovely inner critic that tells us, as soon as we are alone, how stupid we are, or how bad, or unworthy we are. Our negative core beliefs kick in, but at the end of the day, nobody has abused you more than you have abused yourself, and the limit of your own self abuse is *exactly the amount* that you will tolerate from someone else! If someone abuses a little more than you abuse yourself you will probably walk away from that person. But if someone abuses you a little less than you abuse yourself, you will probably stay in the relationship and tolerate it endlessly. Staying with an abuser is like bashing yourself over the head with a big hammer daily. A better analogy might be that of "digging up a dead corpse."

I had been having a nice chat with a very dear friend of mine Angela, about why I kept on going back to Oliver when the relationship was clearly not working. She had come up with this analogy of "digging up dead corpses." She told me that I was going back to check that the relationship is okay and then finding out it's not. I would bury it again and then a couple of days, weeks, or months later I would go back and dig it up again. Why would I want to dig up a dead corpse? I dig it up, realise it's half alive and then, after a while, it's dead again and I bury it. I say to myself: "Yep, it's dead; I'll stick it back again" and so the cycle continues.

If you still cannot stop going back to the relationship and the analogy has not given you enough *visuals* to make you want to never have a relationship with them again even if they are using the "poor me" pity tactic and suggesting they might commit suicide or harm themselves. Sam Vaknin writes "Why are narcissists not prone to suicide? Simple: they died a long time ago. They are the true zombies of the world."

Finding the Motivator to Stay Away

If nothing else is going to remind us that we need to remove ourselves from inevitable harm sometimes we need to find a motivator to keep on reminding us. Often it's a *good motivator* that reminds us why we keep going back to same old destructive patterns and relationships. For example if we are stuck in a bad relationship we may keep going back because it's the little "nice" things that keep us there and we forget all the bad things. However in the case of a very toxic relationship with a Dark Soul, we need a negative motivator to get us out of a relationship, and some are not enough. Many victims continue in relationships for years.

You convince yourself even after all the negative things that you can try one more time.

When you are in this type of toxic relationship, all the negative motivators in the world will not be enough to get you out of the relationship until it finally happens. If you really want to be out of a relationship that is abusive, manipulate, controlling, and not safe ask yourself this. If you do not have any kind of motivator, remind yourself of the story above and ask yourself if you still want to be digging up dead corpses? And of course the single most important motivator of all to stay away from them is your sanity and wellbeing.

Discovering Our Negative Beliefs

As a child, I grew up with a number of really horrible beliefs about myself. I always thought of myself as fat and ugly and a bit messed up. To some degree, I was also a bit of a doormat running around after everyone and never really saying "no" when I wanted to. However, over the years, I realised as an adult that I was also an Empath. An Empath is a person who's a bit like a sponge. They soak up other people's feelings and emotions and take them on as their own. If they are not careful they end up being a gunk bucket or a dumping ground for everyone's toxic feelings and they take them on as their own. Growing up with a father who loved to project his own insecurities on to other people, one of which was being insecure and fat, I spent most of my teenage years on banned illegal slimming pills because he had a "thing" about people who were overweight. I would get marched down the doctors and always reminded I just had to lose that bit more. I grew up with body dimorphic and it took many years for me to realise that as a teenager I was actually slim and normal!

I would often feel like I was mad or messed up, but I realise this was a projection onto me as a child by my own father. As well, one of the things I was told as a small child was "it's all your imagination." When my father had had multiple affairs, it was obvious to everyone. However, because my mother was so deeply in denial, when we would tell her, he would make comments like "it's all in your head" and send my poor mother back to the doctors for antidepressants. He was the master of gaslighting and my mother spent most of her life depressed and on pills. A lot of the time, she was unable to look after us as children because she was so zonked out. One of my beliefs about myself became that "I don't know anything and it's all my imagination." I think that's why we ignore the red flags in these relationships. On a subconscious level, we know something is wrong but mine was reinforced by the fact that I really had a strong negative belief holding that in place.

One of the other strong beliefs I had had about myself was that it was "all my fault." We had grown up in a family where our emotional needs were not always met, and whenever we'd had a problem, we were told not to tell our mother because it would upset her. If any of us as children had problems at school or with relationships, we would internalise our feelings and each of us had developed our own coping mechanisms as a way of dealing with problems. I once did a radio interview and the psychologist explained that, on an emotional level, we were meeting the emotional needs of our parents and not the other way round. As a result, my choice was to blame myself and when things went wrong I often believed wrongly that it was my fault. Coupled with the feeling that "I was crazy" (when I was, in fact, not), if I would meet with people who were actually deranged, I would end up feeling that I was the one who had a problem. I would end up like my mother, going to the counsellor thinking that it was me that needed fixing rather than the other way round. These beliefs make us very vulnerable to Dark Souls and because they are so mentally unstable and tend to project their feelings onto other people, we are more likely to believe. I'd often asked counsellors if I had a personality disorder or if I was crazy. In the end, one of the counsellors actually got fed up with me and exclaimed "Sarah, there is nothing wrong with you apart from you having grown up in an unhealthy family."

I think one of the most uncomfortable yet most valuable books I've read was by Pia Mellody, entitled *Facing Co-dependence.* Pia is a Senior Clinical Advisor for The Meadows and Clinical Consultant for Mellody House in Dakota, and is known and respected as a pre-eminent authority, lecturer, and educator in the fields of addictions and relationships. Her work with co-dependence, boundaries, and the effects of childhood trauma on emotional development has profoundly influenced the treatment of addictions and issues around forming and maintaining relationships. She is the author of several extraordinary books, including *Facing Co-dependence, Facing Love Addiction*, and her latest book, *The Intimacy Factor.*

One day I was writing down all the beliefs I'd had about myself and thought there must be a way to work through them. I hadn't yet discovered everything about Oliver, but I knew something was wrong and I knew the problem I'd had about not feeling I could leave him laid with *me*. To help, I found a man in Australia by the name of John Nutting who specialised in negative core beliefs and used a process called "Voice Dialogue." It transpired that John Nutting had also trained with Pia

166

Mellody, and later on as a voice dialogue facilitator. I find his work so empowering and use it with my own clients. John created a series of worksheets originally based on his work with Dr. Hal and Dr. Sidra Stone who were the creators of the voice dialogue process, along with Dr. Nikki Nemerof.

These worksheets help us to uncover our deepest core beliefs about ourselves. Then a trained voice dialogue facilitator, like John, works with the client to process them and balance them. John maintains from his studies over the past fifteen years that it is the negative core beliefs we hold about ourselves that are most likely to cause self-sabotaging behaviour in adult life.

Unlike Neuro Linguistic Programming, which replaces an old belief with a new one, Voice Dialogue works on the principle that your beliefs never go away. They will remain with us for the rest of our lives, but once you find the opposite part of yourself that has been hiding for years you can balance them. Using voice dialogue, there are hundreds of negatives beliefs such as I am not good enough (incompetent), not good enough (unlovable), I am unwanted, I am different, I am imperfect, I am bad, I am powerless, I don't know, and so on.

John Nutting writes

"Negative Core Beliefs develop as a small child tries to work out a "because" to help them cope with something they don't understand or are troubled by in their daily life. It might be neglect, injustice, dishonest parenting, parents with addictions, abuse, or just feelings of vulnerability, fear, or shame. In a functional family environment, a child would not have needed to take on such negative beliefs. So in a way, you could describe a negative belief as 'the negative belief you needed when you shouldn't have needed a negative belief."

Of course you will always have positive beliefs about yourself but while you have powerful unbalanced negative beliefs in place, your sense of reality will be so tied up, polarised, bound, and distorted that you literally cannot see the *positive* parts within you. This is especially true if you have grown up in a dysfunctional childhood like me. What happens is that, from a target point of view, to a sociopath you are like prized meat. John Nutting goes onto explain in his book *Understanding Your Negative Core Beliefs*:

"Even when you cannot see your own negative core belief, it is sometimes so obvious to others that it is described as being like a flashing neon sign! It seems to attract the very people and events into our lives that will reinforce our negative belief so it seems more true than ever!"

My own beliefs are that I *am powerless* and *I cannot say no*. Until I had done the work on myself, I had the little red flashing neon sign above my head that lit up like a beacon. I would be "picked out" over and over again because of that sign. If you have a core belief like "I am powerless," you may work hard to compensate for your lack of power by doing a job that is the complete opposite. However, it could possibly also make you a target for people who thrive on control and can "see" your neon sign which also says "I cannot say no," and that could make you a possible target for abusers.

Although it's far more complicated than that, I will explain how it worked for me and also include a recent case history of a woman with whom I am currently working. After working through John Nutting's worksheets, I came up with a script about myself and my neon sign. It said something along the lines of *"Feel free to use me as a doormat and if you are a man, while you're at it, wipe your feet on me!"* I never thought I would be writing something so terrible about myself but my main core belief about myself was "I am powerless," powerless, that is, to say "no" to controlling men. I may not have let them physically abuse me but I certainly had difficulty in not letting them control me emotionally.

It initially started with a few phone calls to John to facilitate the process. Often it would be first thing in the morning or late at night as he was based in Australia. We had some very interesting conversations on my sofa sometimes as early as three AM. As I worked through the worksheets as fast as I could, I had a few supporting beliefs such as "it's all my fault," "I am crazy," "I am a f**k up magnet," "I am fat and ugly," and "no one listens to me," but the main belief I had was that I didn't have the power to say "no." It took me about five months to work through all of my beliefs.

I had no rules or boundaries in my house, so my children would walk all over me. Even my own bedroom was a dumping ground for everyone's stuff, complete with boxes of junk on the wardrobes. I even had the family computer in there so people could walk in and out and use my room whenever they felt like it.

The other belief I'd had about myself was that "I didn't know anything." There is a big difference between this and being stupid. Mine was more about being in denial. My own mother was very much like this so I shall explain a little further. Denial can be defined as a refusal to acknowledge reality on two levels: at the level of what is actually happening, and then at the level of what you are feeling. Say, for example, as a child you grew up with your father rarely at home because your mother told you he was working all the time. The child rationalises in her own mind that "my dad is busy" and that arouses compassion for her father rather than anger or hate towards him, because they cannot face the pain of the reality that their father is never there. This may become very confusing for the child if the father is busy womanising. She may have seen her father out with other women on the times when he was supposed to be working, but because she does not want to face the shame and anger she feels. Instead, she creates a fantasy that is easier to live with. Her mother may have also created the same fantasy. The child's denial operates on an unconscious level and remains hidden.

In a highly dysfunctional family, there is always a shared denial of reality. No matter how serious or small the problem is, the family does not become dysfunctional unless there is denial operating in the background. In addition, should any other members of the family try and break this denial up, for example, by trying to expose the truth, most of the family members will do all they can to resist that perception. Perhaps if the family is the type that argues too much, when guests come over, friends might make comments about how much the child's parents argue. When questioned as to why her parents are fighting, the child may reply "I don't know." She may do this because every time she has seen her parents argue in the past or faced them she has been met with denial, not only by them but by her whole family. The child doesn't want to feel her shame and so she will seek ways to control it, and one of the ways she does it is by denying the truth. She is left with strong feelings of anger, shame, fear, and helplessness so as a coping mechanism unable to deal with all of these emotions she may decide the only way to cope is to not actually feel at all.

From my own experience as a child I would often "see" what was going on around me, only to be told it was all my imagination. My family were experts at colluding in denial. It wasn't until all of us were in our forties that the real dysfunction of our family had actually come out. However, this was a real handicap for me when it came to forming "healthy" relationships with men, because part of me didn't want to believe what was really wrong in my relationship, and it made me a perfect target for a sociopath. I always believed it was me that was wrong and that it was all my fault.

When I first started balancing my beliefs it was difficult. My family didn't like "new Sarah" at all. I stopped speaking to my mother for a year. My daughter, at one point, became so angry with the new boundaries I was setting for myself she said "I don't like this man, John Nutting. I don't like the woman he is turning my mum into." They didn't like a mum who stood up for herself and said "no." The same applied to Oliver. This was a man who could turn up any time he wanted and make any excuse under the sun without being questioned. Although I didn't know he was sowing his oats on sex sites and planting his narcissistic seed in any lesbian couples that would believe his slick public schoolboy image, I started to realise something was very wrong. I had started to see the warning signs, and although he had done everything to cover his tracks, I was starting to get out of denial.

They say "be careful what you wish for," and it was then that my childhood fantasies about becoming a spy/private detective had become a reality. I listened to my intuition for the first time in about twenty years and started to Google search Oliver. This was the same intuition that I had ignored when I was a child every time this little voice inside my head said there was something "not quite right" and I would stuff it back down. Only this time, I wasn't stuffing it down. For five months I had worked daily on all of my negative core beliefs. One of my biggest issues was about money. My childhood abuser used to give me pocket money and had an unhealthy interest in little girls. I hated it when he visited and used to run away every time he asked me to sit on his lap. Weirdly enough, the first thing I had ever said to Oliver when we met was that I didn't want anything from him. I would always pay for everything. Oliver came from a very wealthy family and had inherited a large amount which meant he had no mortgage. I, on the other hand, had a thing about not asking for money from anyone, men in particular. I remember when my father had lent me some money once, and I had felt very uncomfortable. I went out of my way to try and pay it back as soon as I could. I would have rather resorted to borrowing money from banks at extortionate rates than ask for help. And this was one of the main reasons I lost my house.

When I found my core belief about money, it was that I was a bad person for having money. However, by this time, I had spent so much time processing all the emotions I had been feeling, and finding out about my ex and all his lies, that I had got myself into a huge amount of debt. My belief stemmed from the fact that my childhood sex abuser had given me money as a small child when he abused me to stop me from talking. It was no surprise that no matter how much money I would make, I would subconsciously want to give it all away by attracting situations into my life where I felt like I didn't deserve to keep it. Including investing in properties to set up a business with Oliver that was never going to happen.

I finally had to sell my house in 2009 and I had ended up losing all my life savings. I spent my birthday moving from my lovely large four bedroom house into a two bedroom flat that I had rented out to a friend of my daughter, only to find she had turned it into a squat. My birthday that year was spent evicting a bunch of squatters and cleaning up dog exrement, condoms, and furniture from the outbuilding where groups of youths had been having parties. Two days later, I was moving into the squat with my son and daughter and spent the next six months decorating it and making it liveable. I was still angry with Oliver and had asked him to come over and drop off some books that he had kept. I know how much they liked to keep little trophies and so I was determined he wasn't going to keep all the books he had borrowed from me. He had taken the books, promising he was going to change and sort himself out. I knew he was never going to read them. Oliver arrived on my doorstep looking very sorry for himself. He also looked very tired, had put on a lot of weight and the spark he used to have in his eyes was missing. I asked him to come upstairs. The flat was disgusting. All the ceilings were falling down and the walls had holes in where they had been punched through by the squatters. The windows were smashed and the carpet had been ripped up where the previous dog had urinated all over it. All of my possessions where packed up in boxes in the outbuilding and the yard had yet another skip load of stuff piled up ready to be collected. He had been to my old house, a beautiful Victorian property, and as I was unable to get a mortgage, I had to move to the rental property. I offered Oliver a seat and made him a coffee and suggested he take a look around the flat. He didn't want to. I said very calmly "No. No, I would like you to see. This is the culmination of four years of lies and manipulation, of lying about cancer, and keeping me sucked into a relationship with you, that you never had any intention of having. It was all about sex. I want you to see what happens to people when you make promises you cannot keep."

I told Oliver I did not blame him, but I *did* blame him for lying and keeping me tied into a relationship. He was the one that looked sorry for himself. He sat with his head slumped down, let out a half hearted sorry to which I replied, "Look at you. I am the one who should be putting my head down and feeling sorry for myself but I am not. I am strong, and I will come out of this a better person." As he left, I asked him if all the times he had told me he loved me were lies, too. He replied "Yes, they were lies as well." I thanked him and added "You can now f**k off."

Three months later I had received a call from him to say he had been working on himself, doing all the negative core belief work that I had been using on myself and my clients, and that he had finally had the courage to leave his wife. Although he had told me a very convincing story. I knew in my heart that he was lying, and I think it was more a case of his wife kicking him out and tying up loose ends. I eventually found out the rest of the lies and he was asked politely to leave on New Year's Day 2010.

I had called up John Nutting a few weeks after Oliver had finally gone and John asked me why I had taken Oliver back? I told him that I suppose with all the work I had done on myself, and knowing how powerful the changes were, I wanted to "believe" that *all* people changed. John, however, had already warned me that narcissists and psychopaths never change and that voice dialogue doesn't actually work on them.

I noticed that as a result of the changes that I had made in myself that my own family had started changing too. I now had a great relationship with my mother. My daughter was treating me like a mother, and my ex husband was starting to treat me with respect. I had even reconciled with my younger brother after fifteen years. I had noticed so many positive changes in everyone that I so wanted to believe Oliver had changed, too. But the bottom line was he was even worse than I had remembered him. I guess in essence I had wanted a miracle. I wanted to turn a horror story into a fairy tale. But since I have now grown up and done a lot of Inner Child work as well, I do not believe in fairy tales any more. I'd finally realised that if there was such a thing as a fairy tale, then Prince Charming had finally proven himself to be the Prince of Darkness.

I dropped John an email telling him how I was doing. I had had no contact with Oliver anymore and how he was now in deep trouble not only financially, but with his family and so on. I had explained how much happier I was and that I was looking after myself for the first time in years. Here is the reply from John, the latter half of which pretty much summed Oliver up:

"Dear Sarah, I know I have said it before, Sarah, but each time I read your latest e-mail I notice the way you are calming down and getting on with life in a balanced, self aware, grown-up way.

This last e-mail from you is the best of them all. Notice how some of the people around you also seem to be settling down, especially your daughter. Meanwhile, the really screwed up ones keep right on doing what they have been doing, but you ain't one of them any more so they are less inclined to contact you.

Warm hugs,
John"

Despite the fact that anyone is a target, I do believe there is a part of us Empaths that resonates with Dark Souls like a magnet. And if *we*, as people, do not change then we will always remain a target. If we come from dysfunctional childhoods and lack self esteem, they can sniff us out and we become perfect prey for them. It is very easy to blame these people for all the things that happened to us, but we are the ones that chose to be with them in the first place. We were the enablers and we are the ones that allowed them to abuse us, whether financially, emotionally, or physically. Yes, they are very clever at manipulating people, and from my own experience, even my own family were conned by Oliver's guises

One of my closest family members didn't believe me for a long time and thought I was actually making it all up. It's not until you actually show real hard evidence that anyone will believe you, and even then, the perpetrators will deny everything, given the opportunity. Many people who have come out of relationships with narcissists and/or sociopaths have an epiphany moment in which they realise that there was something in themselves that they had needed to deal with. It might be because they were lacking in self esteem or because they didn't feel worth enough to deserve anything better. Like myself, they have to look at their own issues of co-dependency and their beliefs about themselves. My own experience had taught me that not all men are bastards, and that if I were to have a relationship again, I would watch for the red flags and remove myself from inevitable harm immediately. I feel this "intuitive" discomfort now, matter how appealing the package looks on the outside. I also thank Oliver for being in my life because it has taught me what is a good man and what is not. I can now spot a Dark Soul within minutes whereas for years I didn't even know what one was. It has also taught me how to look at my own narcissistic traits I had picked up from bad parenting and how not to do them with my own children. I hope I have learned how to be a better parent as a result of my experiences.

It was at the end of May 2010 and I went with my brother to watch him do a magic show. As I sat in the audience I had the pleasure of being chatted to by two lovely men in the audience. One of them was the same star sign as my ex. He was roughly the same age as Oliver was when I first met him and he came across as friendly and nice. This man was, in fact, really a nice guy. In the past I had put my Oliver's face on every single man I met, but the last thing I wanted to do was have him "win" and leave me feeling bitter and twisted. It's a common thing with Post Traumatic Stress Disorder (PTSD) where we avoid situations and people because we don't want to relive the trauma of any events. Some women never actually date or end up going out with abusers again if they don't resolve their own issues. We all have intuition and mine, when I first met Oliver, was "do not touch him with a bargepole" and I didn't listen.

My intuition in the club when I met this guy was that he actually was a nice guy. We took each other's phone numbers and I said maybe I'd say hello next time I was in London. I sent him a text to say thank you for a nice evening and I received a lovely text back from him saying "I am glad you have taken us xxxxx's off your sh*t list." I realised how far I had come and that I was ready to start saying "yes" to love again. It might not have been him, but I was finally over Oliver, and the feeling of having been "slimed" by him did not need to apply to all men in future.

I recently worked with a woman whom I will call Jemima. She was mid forties and had been severely sexually abused as a child. Her perpetrator was a paedophile who used to masturbate over her. Often when children have early sexual experiences they start to sexualize them without understanding why they are doing it. When she told her parents what happened instead of being sympathetic her father had slapped her face for being a naughty girl. Although the police were called in, no one was prosecuted and after being examined she was taken off to the bathroom and washed by her mother and punished for being such a naughty girl. So when a few months later she was caught at seven years old masturbating on the floor her mother again chastised her telling her she was dirty and evil. As she grew up she started to have fantasies about being abused and met with men who would humiliate and abuse her. Her first relationship was highly abusive and ended up with him violently assaulting her until she finally plucked up the courage to leave him. Not realising why she was attracting these men, she went onto form another relationship with a man who beat her so badly she was left with facial disfigurement. After having left her abuser for a man she believed would look after her, Jemima realised after nearly fifteen years of marriage, she was in another controlling, abusive relationship with a man who does not love her at all, and controls everything she does. When I finally met up with her and got her to work through her belief systems, her core belief was that she was "powerless" and could not say "no." Within two weeks of doing the work with her she was sleeping in the spare bedroom not giving in to his sexual demands. They had agreed on a separation. She also managed to confront her previous sexual abusers and found the original paedophile abuser who had molested her as a seven year old posing as the "nice family man" on a social networking site. With the police involved, they are now monitoring his behaviour to ensure that he never does it again to another victim.

Usually, when you do the work, you experience a number of tests, although this is a really bad choice of words. It's just a test of your belief system which was false in the first place, because subconsciously you wanted to reinforce something that was never true anyway by re-enacting it. One of Jemima's secondary beliefs about herself was that she was "crazy" because her parents had not been sympathetic. She had started to notice that her husband was trying to play the role of the perfect husband even though he hadn't been around for years or taken any role in bringing up their son. Because they were on the verge of splitting up, it was very clear from my outsider's point of view that he was manipulating her into believing she was not a fit mother. She then started to drink more often and reinforced this "crazy" belief she had about herself. On the second visit, it happened that she had only recently started drinking and when I got her to balance her belief about herself she had realised what was happening. Although she had already made huge steps by sleeping in separate rooms and standing up to him, she realised that one of her biggest fears was leaving this man and had felt "paralysed," causing her to start drinking to cover up her feelings. I explained to her that if she was prepared to actually start going through the emotions and start stepping out of denial, this would be her ticket to freedom. She agreed to stop drinking with the support of her doctor and to work on looking after herself so that she could support her son.

One of the reasons I find the Negative core belief work so powerful is that, unlike NLP (which I have used before), it's not just a quick fix. It brings everything to our awareness and it can be used for a number of things, from negative beliefs to addictions. It helps us realise why we actually do things and then we step out of victim mode to start looking within ourselves at what we are also doing to be enablers.

From my own point of view, if I had not looked at my beliefs or gone to India for counselling as a first step, I would have never listened to that inner voice (which was screaming at me) that was telling me something was wrong in the first place. I might have carried on being in the relationships for years in denial. My own mother stayed with my father for 35 years, and every single time he'd had an affair, she would take him back, always imagining he would change. I had also believed my ex had a good heart and that eventually he would change. He said all the right things but his actions never matched up with his words. We cannot change anyone. The only person we can change is ourselves. Finding the strength to step out of victim mode and leave a Dark Soul becomes a choice when we have the proper tools to heal. Having a relationship with a pathological person is probably one of the most difficult, life-changing experiences we will ever have to come to terms with. We are left feeling that we have been dealing with someone that is nothing more than an empty shell or with a label of something out of the

DSM (Diagnostic and Statistical Manual of Mental Disorders) IV diagnostic book. We are left with a big hole in our hearts and our spiritual energy is left damaged and needing time to heal.

One of the reasons why women who come from dysfunctional families find it so easy to bond to these types of men is because they are not bought up to express a full range of wants, needs or feelings. They may be unable to discern when someone is not good for them and are often drawn to the very dangers that they so want to avoid in the first place. These types of women may have received little nurturing in their early life and therefore attract men who *appear* to be needy. They may respond to emotionally unavailable men better because they don't know anything different. If they are the type of children that have always been there for their parents they may do almost anything to keep the relationship from dissolving taking the responsibility and blame in the relationship when things go wrong because that is how they have been conditioned as a child. They may even find that "nice men" are boring.

I ran a workshop about negative beliefs and explained that if you did not resolve them then you would keep on attracting the same type of relationship over and over again. Say for example you have a little red flag over your head saying only "abusers" apply then, if a nice man were to come up to you, you wouldn't even recognise them. It would be like taking a wet fish and slapping it round your face. It would feel odd and it would smell bad. Why ? Because you had no idea what a *nice* man was.

But I realise now that boring is good and that nice is perfect and that I didn't need the excitement of a psychopath in my life any more. One of the other things that bonds dysfunctional women like me to psychopaths and narcissists is sex because they use sex as a way of forming a "false" bond with their victims. When I had first met Oliver, after a month of him saying he was madly in love with me, I became confused. I had "wanted" to believe he loved me, although his actions appeared to be only an interest in sex. So I formed a mismatch to fill in the gaps to make up for the cognitive dissonance in my heart that did not match. Of course now I realise these were just words that meant nothing.

One of my biggest beliefs about myself was that men only wanted me for sex and as a result with that little red neon flashing sign above my head, I attracted men that were literally only interested in sex and nothing else. I would highly advise anyone who has come from an abusive dysfunctional childhood to go to the *Sex and Love Addicts Anonymous* website and buy their book in addition to Sandra L. Brown's book *'Women Who Love Psychopaths'*. She explores this further in her book by discussing *The Anxiety/Sex/Bonding Cycle* ' by saying:

"The frequency of sex with the highly sexual psychopath creates bond, after bond, after bond. This is why women describe attachments and bonds with psychopaths as 'the most intense types of attachments' they have ever experienced. Repeatedly, women have stated that this attachment with the psychopath is not like attachments with non-pathological men. Misunderstanding what this intensity is, they say "I thought it meant we were right for each other and just really into each other." Or they ask, "It feels like a drug. Am I addicted to him?""

Women like Jemima and myself confuse Sex with bonding, and the psychopath is perfect at making a woman feel that she is in love with them, when all they want is sex. However once *we* are aware of what we are doing as enablers, we can stop attracting men like that, deal with our own issues, and start attracting normal healthy functional relationships.

Functional Emotional Storm Warning Radar

Psychopaths are masters at masking their authentic selves, especially from those they want to manipulate and con. Just because you have a check-list that gives you the traits of a psychopath or Dark Soul doesn't mean you will be able to spot every single one. Many a professional has been fooled by them. However, if you have no knowledge about them, the more you are able to learn about them, the more likely you'll recognise one and the less likely you will be of interest to them.

Prior to working on "Myself" I can honestly say that I was really a magnet for narcissistic persons and more than a few psychopaths. I am still the same Sarah I was before I started taking care of myself, but the little red flashing neon sign I had above my head saying "come and get me" has faded rapidly. On a positive note, I am no longer a target to sociopaths, psychopaths and narcissists and they are just not interested in me anymore. They still try it on every so often, but I can spot them as quickly as they spot me. I am no longer hit on or chatted up by Dark Souls, which is a good thing, and if they do it's only a matter of minutes before I can detect them and remove myself from inevitable harm. The "excitement" I once felt from the attraction of the "magnetic" skillfully gifted, lying Dark Soul personality has now gone and no longer attracts me. One friend and colleague even nicknamed me "narc spotter".

A few months after I had been doing the work with John Nutting, I had decided to go to the gym and lose some weight. I was very short on money and still feeling a bit "raw" around the edges. A local gym company was offering a very cheap deal on membership and so I decided to go and meet the local gym owner. It was the weirdest situation. I was met with a very unhealthy-looking, overweight looking gym owner. Immediately, I felt very uncomfortable when he refused me membership, claiming I would not be able to lose weight because I had emotional problems, that I would blame it on the gym, and that I should go and see his personal friend a counsellor. I decided to contact John and ask his opinion, so I emailed him telling him what had happened and ask him what the hell had been going on

The email I received back from my John said:

"In simple words, Sarah, your 'functional emotional storm warning radar' is starting to work really well. Congratulations. Why you knew he was *all wrong* is not important. The important thing is that you could sense it. Sure he could sense something in you that scared him and that was probably that he sensed your functional emotional storm warning radar was zeroing in on him. Last thing he would want in his little empire where he is king (with no clothes).

I imagine he and the woman therapist work together to pick out clients who are easily intimidated (using the old 'you got a big problem' scam) and then milk them dry with extra fees. You just didn't fit into his plan."

It was also very clear that I was dealing with a narcissist who is all about projecting his own insecurities about himself onto others. Hence his comments about me having emotional problems and not setting a good example to clients. The gym owner was actually talking about himself. But because I was in a vulnerable place, he picked me out by saying things to me that he knew would make me feel bad in the hope I would play into his story even though I was already having treatment. He had hoped I would take him up on his offer of going and seeing his "therapist" until he saw me fit enough to go and visit his little empire.

A few months later having lost nearly two stone in weight on my own without going to the gym I saw him outside the gym touting for business. The gym owner on the other hand, had increased in weight and looked even more angry and unhealthy than he was the last time I saw him. I was so glad my "functional emotional storm warning radar" had been working. If I had gone in there "unaware" and as vulnerable as I had been, I could have ended up in a totally different place. In the past I would not have overlooked the nasty gym owner, taken his projection personally, perhaps listened to his criticism and taken it literally because I was overweight and felt like I was crazy. I might have even possibly gone and seen his "therapist" and undone all of the work I had already done on myself and ended up feeling more insecure about myself than I did before I walked in.

Once you have balanced your beliefs, your mind will try and tell you your old beliefs are true and for a while, you will believe it. In my case, I still appeared to be attracting sociopathic type men especially when it came to dating, but the difference is that I can now spot them and I am just not interested because I know what the end result would be.

I have a very dear friend by the name of Linda who had been in an online relationship with a man overseas. They had planned to meet and he would often say he loved her and wanted to have a relationship with her. We all had mutual friends on a networking site. The man in question was called Peter, and one day, out of the blue, he got chatting on messenger and the conversation immediately turned to romance. He said he wanted to take me out on a "romantic date" and asked for my number. He explained that he was divorced and was often not available because he had two children. I was immediately suspicious but decided to "test him" because I did not want to see Linda hurt. I thought if I played along with him I would eventually find out whether he was genuine or not. When Peter called me on the telephone, I felt like he had something to hide. I started to paint a picture of Peter being a clone of my ex and refused a date with him.

Eventually, I came clean and told Linda what had happened and that he has asked me out. She said he had contacted her on Valentines day in a complete rage asking me why I had stopped speaking to him. I apologised to her, saying I really had never had any intention of going out with him, but that I believed he was a player and was trying to catch him out and protect her because I did not want to see her get hurt. A few months later I was chatting to Linda and we were talking about Oliver. She was saying how fascinating it was that I had uncovered everything about him. I said well "I just followed my intuition, the same intuition that had told me not to "touch him with a bargepole."

I asked her what had happened with Peter and if she was still in contact with him. She laughed and said "I have a confession to make." She told me that when I had first chatted with her, my intuition had told her that he had something to hide and he might possibility be a narcissist.

She went onto say "Sarah your intuition works perfectly. It is spot on! He is married with 3 children, he never was divorced, and when you refused to date him he went into complete rage and contacted me asking me why you had stopped speaking to him." She said "for three years I have been in touch with this man, sending him gifts to his home address only to find out recently that everything he ever told me about himself was a lie" She also went onto to confirm that he had been cyber dating more than five women who were her colleagues on the same networking site.

We laughed and laughed. I said "Linda, it took my mother 35 years to figure out how to spot these Dark Soul Clones and it took me only five to meet the ultimate Dark Soul. Now after doing all this work on myself, I can spot them instantly." I realised that my "emotional storm warning radar" was working perfectly. I may still attract them, but the red flashing neon sign above my head had no power over me anymore.

Looking After Our Inner Child

One of the biggest things I learned about myself whilst working with John Nutting was that I had not resolved any of my childhood traumas. As a result, along with the negative beliefs I had held about myself, it was the main driving force that got me into one dysfunctional relationship after another.

I mentioned earlier the sexual dynamic bonding process that takes place between the Dark Soul and the victim and that many of the victims find themselves pushing all of the boundaries in terms of their own moral standards. When it comes to the bedroom the Dark Soul may just as easily become a womaniser, a tease, a dominating abuser, or impotent, but it will *always always* be his unwillingness to satisfy a woman physically, emotionally or sexually. At the core of the sexual dynamics of the relationship, it is about power, control, sex and unresolved emotional issues which you can never "cure." However exciting the sexual dynamics are, the only thing you can do is cure yourself and get out as quickly as you can.

Many women like myself have come from a history of sexual abuse, and attract these types as a way of fixing up their childhood wounds. Often, as children, we become sexualised early on and having a relationship with a person who "wraps up" sex with *love* usually comes from us wanting to heal our childhood wounds, hoping they will love us, when, in fact, they have no capacity for love. We may go out with clones of our childhood abusers and if we find a connection with someone who gives us that so called "emotional feeling" or "love" through sex we are only asking for trouble.

A relationship that starts off very quickly by being loving, gentle and romantic and moves too fast can just as quickly turn around and become an abusive relationship. When I first met Oliver he was my friend and all of my childhood abuse was hidden. As a result I opened up to him. I had selectively chosen to forget the worst of it on a conscious level and yet through meeting Oliver it reared its ugly head at the age of 45 one day when I was sitting on the loo. Perhaps Oliver reminded me of him, who knows ? But the feelings and emotions (and unresolved childhood shit) I had suppressed for years came flooding to the surface one day. (Please excuse the pun). Of course I told Oliver all of this during our friendship phase, which gave him ample amunition to dream up an abuse story of his own.

What I noticed was that in the past during rights of passage such as puberty I have had odd memories about my childhood I couldn't recall. I used to have recurring nightmares about being pinned down by a dark stranger. When I reached puberty I was very body conscious and wouldn't let my father see me in my underwear. I always put it down to just being a teenager but I didn't like to be held close by him either. Then again when I had my first child Laura, I had this totally irrational fear when she was first born that my father would sexually abuse her and found it very uncomfortable watching him hold her as a small baby. Yet despite my fathers misgivings as a womaniser, my father was good with small children so I had always pushed my irrational fears to the back of my mind thinking I was crazy and that they were all in my imagination. The thought that he could have ever sexually abused me abhorred me and made me sick to the core. There had been many stories in the family over the years about abuse but none of them had anything to do with my father.

I had even had hypnotherapy in the past and started to remember something but convinced myself that the therapist was going to plant memories in my head about something that hadn't happened so I stopped going for therapy. So this "thought" or should I say an image or memory of my childhood that appeared that morning was not of my father. It was of another member of my family who was the spitting image of my father. Interestingly enough when I told Oliver about the abuse we were only friends at the time and suddenly, out of the blue, he told me he had been abused too as a child. We started to have a very strong connection as a result of our *mutual bond*, which eventually ended up in us having sex. Whether or not what Oliver told me was true I will never find out. It was shortly after that that he told me he loved me and was going to leave his wife. It is very common for abusers to tell the victims they have had the same kind of abuse by finding out things first from their victims.

I was fourteen years older than Oliver, as was his own wife by nearly ten years, and I had always believed, right from the beginning, that he had had issues around his mother. He was sent away to boarding school and it would always be a talking point about how he felt alone and unloved. He was always trying to make his mother love him and yet she appeared to remain cold and indifferent towards him, no matter what he did, and whether it was good or bad. Interestingly enough, when I had finally contacted his mother and told her about his lies, she never responded. Oliver appeared to have somewhat of an Oedipus complex, he would never say anything derogatory about his mother and yet he would discard his own father saying he hated him with a vengeance up until the age of 25. He blamed his father for all his failings. In psychoanalytic theory, the Oedipus complex is a desire for sexual involvement with the parent of the opposite sex and a sense of rivalry with the parent of the same sex. Considered a normal stage in the development of children ages three to five, it ends when the child identifies with the parent of the same sex and represses its sexual instincts. Freud believed that the process of overcoming the Oedipus complex gave rise to the superego. Yet strangely enough it turned out that Oliver was completely bi sexual. He admitted having long term affairs with men prior to meeting me and saying that he had been extremely submissive to the men he had dated even to the point of acting like a slave towards them. When he finally went for 1 session of counselling he suggested to the therapist that he had issues about feeling comfortable with his own heterosexuality and that was the reason why he felt he had treated women so badly.

His interest in sex when we first met appeared quite normal although he appeared to be very passive. He liked it when I was dominant in the bedroom and told him what to do. As time went on Oliver would often turn the tables on me and try dominating me and towards the end of the relationship and had an underlying anger that would come out in the bedroom in the form of smothering my face with his hands over my mouth and have harder sex with me. Finally at the end of the relationship he became impotent although I am not sure whether that was true or just another way of controlling me.

Interestingly, although the relationship started off with me being assertive in the bedroom I was generally passive with him both in and out of the bedroom the longer the relationship went on yet there were times when he often responded to me better when I was angry and shouting at him. He would say that his wife frequently abused him and yet he would not leave initially. We had once gone for couples counselling together long before Oliver showed his true colours. The counsellor knew the dynamics of the sexual side of our relationship, he also knew that Oliver was in a relationship with a wife that liked to verbally argue with him and refused him sex and yet in conversation he would say he hated her even though he refused to leave. The counsellor said "if you were to tell me that Oliver does not like living with his wife I would believe you, at the same time he does not like it either. Unconsciously he may well try and turn you into a clone of his wife and mother."

Passive aggressive type men prefer the company of dominant women, especially in the bedroom. When it comes to sex if they lie back and do nothing while she does all the work it puts him in a weak and dependent position. It was interesting that when I first confronted Oliver on his behaviour a year or so before I caught him out. The behaviours which were getting worst by the day he said to me "I am passive aggressive" and then spent another year making excuses.

On one level, nothing really added up and yet, on another, Oliver and I appeared to have this deep connection where we could talk about things without feeling guilty or shameful. I felt that he didn't judge me or think it was dirty or demeaning. Yet there were no real ground rules to the relationship because Oliver was still married. The only ground rules were that he was adamant that he was not sleeping with his wife any more and that I was't to date anyone else. I have always been monogamous and during the time we were together I found myself being persuaded to do things I didn't want to do. He suggested we could have a relationship that was "open" and yet he did not want me sleeping with another man. He implied it might be "nice" if I found myself another girlfriend. Oliver made a promise that he would never have sex with his wife again because he didn't even fancy her any more. In fact, he said the thought of having sex with her again made him "feel sick." I should have listened to that red flag then. He didn't want me seeing another man, and I had made a promise to myself rather than him that I would not date anyone else. Besides, why would I, our sex life was amazing and I didn't feel the need to have sex with anyone else. During the loneliest times when Oliver was away during the weekends and evenings, I would console myself that he was being a good father and that it was only short term – eventually we would have a proper relationship. He was always reminding me he would be leaving "her" soon! One of my best friends once said to me "Sarah, you are his mistress and he doesn't even treat you like a mistress. The least he could do is pay for your dinner and take you out somewhere nice."

He would always talk about *his boys* and had what I thought was an unhealthy interest in them. I talked to him about co dependence and any mention of him leaving his wife had become a battle ground. Oliver would say that it was perfectly healthy to want to spend all of your time with your children. I remember saying how I felt uncomfortable when he'd told me he still wandered around the house naked while the boys were about 5 years old. I said that wasn't normal, and he rationalised it by saying that he had gone to boarding school, where it was common for boys to walk around naked and that I was just making a big deal. As far as I was aware, according to Oliver he had been abused at his all-boys school and that he had dabbled in bisexuality. He said he had been buggered by one of the other school boys. To me it wasn't such a big deal. I, too, had had experiences with other women however, on a deeper level I knew I was heterosexual. I just thought of it as part of growing up. However I was not aware that he was a full blown bisexual until much later when I confronted him with everything.

Relationships are all about balance and it became increasingly difficult for me to become both assertive in and out of the bedroom with Oliver flipping between roles. I started to want a *normal* relationship, whatever that was. One that did not involve me either telling him what to do; whether it was in the bedroom or outside; or having him take his anger out on me in the bedroom in the next instant or worse threatening to kill me when I spoke up. For a man that appeared to be so dominant in the bedroom in the latter part of the relationship, in contrast I was so shocked to find his interests as wanting the most submissive sexually degrading done to him when I found the adverts about wanting to "eat cream pies" and "clean up sloppy seconds". It was extremely confusing.

Was he a passive type that liked to be degraded ? or was he a man that fantasised about killing and having aggressive sex ? Or perhaps he was a closet homosexual who just got off on hurting women to pay back his mother for sending him off to boarding school ?

When I had first contacted John Nutting I told him that I had been doing some things I felt uncomfortable with in particular the role play stuff that Oliver loved so much that had become completely out of hand. I knew I carried a lot of guilt and shame from my own childhood abuse and part of me enjoyed the assertive role in the bedroom but the more I wanted normal sex the more Oliver backed off. John thought that perhaps the "little girl" in me had been doing the other things as a way of unconsciously working through my sexual abuse by unconsciously playing out my childhood dramas with Oliver in the hope that I could make the horror story right that was always going to be wrong and that now I was starting to grow up. When I had finally healed the inner child in me, the grownup part of me no longer wanted any part of the relationship with Oliver any more.

John Nutting explores the inner child by suggesting that we grow up with magical muddled thinking. One of the things magical thinking does is to rob us of our ability to look after our own needs at those times when there is no one else around who can be our friend. It may even tell us that it is selfish to think about looking after ourselves, that we don't deserve this, and that we should spend our time looking after other people who are more worthy than we are.

John Nutting has created a character called the 'Little Trauma Witch'

- She doesn't understand boundaries, those energetic and physical shields that we all need to protect ourselves from the impact other people can have on us. (And our impact on other people.) Because she doesn't understand them, she usually tries to weaken them. We can try to strengthen them again but she undermines them faster than we can build them up

- Her fear of what she doesn't understand causes her to cut us off from our deep inner spirit, our soul, our sense of having a spiritual connection with our God (in whatever way we seek to know our own particular Higher Power)

- Her muddled magic undermines our sense of identity, telling us we are not who we really are but rather we are whatever others say we are. This distorts our sense of reality, our ability to see, hear, and sense what is actually happening around us. We think we are still hearing and seeing accurately when really we are missing things that are important, or hearing words that are not actually being spoken.

- Her attempts at magic distorts our self image, unbalances our self esteem, shrinks our ability to love ourselves. She may even tell us that we are being conceited, selfish, or sinful if we attempt to love ourselves or build up our self esteem!

When the Magic Trauma Witch is running the show:

- if her "magic" appears to help (even temporarily) than she becomes the preferred character responsible for dealing with more and more problems in the village, rather than handing them back to the conventional grownup part of us, once the trauma has passed.

- however, because the Little Trauma Witch does not have the maturity to handle these powers she tends to get things muddled up much of the time.

When I first started balancing my negative beliefs about myself, occasionally I would get into a real tizzy and burst into uncontrollable tears. I would be sobbing and crying for no reason, like a small child. It took me a while to realise that "Little Sarah" was the one sobbing and doing the work that the grown up bit of me should be doing. It might sound strange, but after a while, once we learn to differentiate which part of ourselves is the grownup bit and which part is the "little child" in us, doing things becomes so much easier! This is extremely useful when you have a house to sell, finances to sort out, or be an adult to your own children that had suffered as a result of your cocking up. Explaining to my own children why I had been stupid enough to fall for a Dark Soul was one of easy bits because they already knew him. Explaining how it was going to affect us for the rest of our lives financially was a whole different story.

It also took me a while to realise that much of what I had done throughout my life had been done by "little Sarah." Even though I was capable, in fact probably far more capable than some people, the little girl in me was tired and worn out. When I learned to put my inner child in a safe place and stepped into my adult energy, I actually did not feel like everything was just hard work anymore. One of the many exercises you can do when doing inner child work, is to put your inner child in a safe place (metaphorically speaking). Tell them it's okay for them to have a holiday and that the adult part of you is going to take over from now on.

John Nutting is a trained voice dialogue facilitator and as a result of my own healing journey I, too, had trained to become a facilitator. One of the processes we use is in which a facilitator introduces "the child" to a new set of parents. These are parents that we may have never had when we were young. They take on the new characteristics that may have been lacking in our own childhood.

I would highly recommend that anyone who has come out of an abusive toxic relationship who is struggling with a whole heap of financial and emotional mess or sexual abuse to clean up does some inner child work on themselves. When you have come out of these relationships you need as many tools as possible, and one of the ways in which you can help yourself is to do affirmations such as this. Sexual abusers who hurt children in particular want their victims to feel guilty and may grow up with Magical Trauma Witch running the show because they feel like they are damaged goods when in fact the person abusing them is the one who is damaged.

If you are looking for an affirmation that will help you understand what happened, especially as a broken inner child, you might find this one useful:

"Even though my thinking is damaged, it is because they were damaged goods"

Post Traumatic Stress Disorder

So you have parted ways with your abusive partner and you're on the mend. Perhaps you are picking up the pieces financially and emotionally and then all of a sudden you have a setback. You have done all the counselling and you may have even worked through your negative beliefs about yourself, but then suddenly you are wondering why everything has gone awry and you're feeling like nothing is ever going to go right. You feel stuck in a time loop, like in the movie *Ground Hog Day*, replaying events all over again, and yet this person is gone. You wonder what might be happening to you. You go to the doctor who may suggest you are depressed but you don't actually feel depressed, although you may have had depression before. You are constantly on edge and then you realise you might have something else. You realise you are suffering from a delayed reaction to trauma: Post Traumatic Stress Disorder (PTSD).

It was May 7th, 2010, a full five months since I had finally kicked Oliver out. I had done what I had considered to be all of the healing process. I had seemingly picked up all the pieces of my life but then something reared its ugly head. I could not quite figure out what was happening to me until I started to research it. About three months after our final split, I had been suffering from nightmares and not being able to sleep properly, so I promptly saw a doctor. I explained what had happened to me and said I wasn't feeling depressed, but was constantly on edge and feeling alert all the time. The doctor agreed it wasn't a good idea for me to take antidepressants although I needed to catch up on my sleep. I was prescribed a two week course of sleeping pills. The doctor although agreed I was suffering from post traumatic stress. I asked him how long it would take for me to feel better and he suggested a few months.

One evening after taking the dog for an evening walk and going for a nice relaxing bath I returned home to watch the evening news. It was May 5th, and that was the day of the general election as a result of which we had been left with a hung parliament. For anyone else in the country, it was probably just a normal election day, perhaps one of confusion and a sense of uncertainty about the future. For me, it was being left all of those feelings along with worry about whether I would ever have enough money to support myself into my retirement. There I was, being triggered again.

My last real trigger came in the guise of two faces: David Cameron, the Conservative Party leader and Nick Clegg, the Liberal Democrat leader. I realised that if you were to merge their faces, they were a clone of my ex, Oliver. As well, they were both upper class public school boys, just like him. I had even telephoned my best friend and asked her to confirm Nick Clegg's resemblance to Oliver. She replied, "Well I didn't want to say anything to upset you Sarah, but yes, absolutely, although I have to say he's a lot slimmer" and then started laughing. A week later, when both the new prime minister, David Cameron, joined forces with the Lib Dems, my brother was in the car with me. I asked him if had he heard the news about the new government and he said he didn't even know who Nick Clegg was. I had suggested he find a picture on Google. He pulled up a photo on his cell phone and said: "Oh my god, it looks like Oliver."

So what is a trigger? It's something or someone that reminds you of your ex, an abuser, a traumatic event, or something that was linked to your abuse. It could also be a smell, a feeling, or an action. Although I am not going to go into too much detail, PTSD is, in short, a cluster of symptoms as a response to trauma or repetitive traumatic events. One of the most common symptoms is flashbacks & nightmares. You find yourself reliving the event, again and again. This can happen both as a "flashback" during the day and as a nightmare while you try to sleep. These can be so realistic that it actually feels as though you are living through the experience once again. You see it in your mind, but may also feel the emotions and physical sensations of what happened, like fear, sweating, smells, sounds, and pain.

Ordinary things can trigger flashbacks. For instance, if you had had a car accident in the rain, a rainy day might start a flashback. In my case, seeing Nick Clegg's resemblance to Oliver triggered mine.

Avoidance and numbing are other coping mechanisms victims use. It can be just too upsetting to relive your experience over again, and so you distract yourself. You keep your mind busy by losing yourself in a hobby, working very hard, or spending your time absorbed in crosswords or jigsaw puzzles. Often, we will overwork or remain in denial, pretending *it* never really happened. You avoid places and people that remind you of the trauma, and try not to talk about it.

You may deal with the pain of your feelings by trying to feel nothing at all – by becoming emotionally numb. You communicate less with other people who then find it hard to live or work with you. Many victims of

Dark Souls will go on medication and take antidepressants just to avoid the feelings they have felt. From my own experience, which I discuss in this book, it's actually okay to feel and to be angry. By avoiding the feelings, you actually prolong the healing process. You may find yourself being on guard a lot of the time. You stay alert all the time, as though you are looking out for danger. This is called "hyper vigilance." You can't relax. You feel anxious and find it hard to sleep. Other people will notice that you are jumpy and irritable. Perhaps you may jump at something at which you wouldn't have before, or else be hypersensitive.

Emotional reactions to stress are often accompanied by:

- muscle aches and pains
- diarrhoea
- irregular heartbeats
- headaches
- feelings of panic and fear
- depression
- drinking too much alcohol
- using drugs (including painkillers).

There are usually three types of PTSD:

Acute: symptoms last between one and three months after the event

Chronic: symptoms last more than three months after the event

Delayed onset: symptoms don't appear until at least six months after the event

I was lucky enough not to have suffered physical abuse, although Oliver did threaten to kill me at times, and would often talk about ways in which he wanted to get rid of his wife when he finally left her. I would often lay awake at night wondering if he was stalking me or if he would do something to me when I least expected it. I had had the police involved and it became a case of "his word against mine." In the latter stages when I had finally finished with Oliver, to protect myself, I found it easier to stand up to him and not feel intimidated by his threats.

To keep him off my back, I had decided to tell Oliver that I was dating a policeman. As well, I had all the evidence I had printed of him on Internet sex sites which he certainly wouldn't have wanted his family to see. So I informed him that I had left them at the "new boyfriend's" house, and in case anything were to happen to me, he would therefore become the prime suspect. They were actually stored somewhere else that was very safe. One thing I have learned about narcissistic personalities and sociopaths, is they if you actually stand up to them, they will crumble like big babies. As long as you have all your evidence in place and your facts right, they will not harm you.

The problem with PTSD is its insidiousness. According to the website *Bullying Online*, which deals with people who have suffered physical and emotional abuse, many victims are left with deep feelings of worthlessness, rejection, and a sense of being unwanted, unlikeable, and unlovable. Some also experience a feeling of being small, insignificant, and invisible. You may be left with an overwhelming sense of betrayal, and a consequent inability and unwillingness to trust anyone, even those close to you. In contrast to the chronic fatigue, depression, etc., that accompanies PTSD, victims may have occasional false dawns with sudden bursts of energy accompanied by a feeling of "I'm better!" only to be followed by a full resurgence of symptoms a day or two later. I would often go for a couple of days where I felt wonderful only to fall flat on my face and then feel angry at myself for "being so stupid." Mostly, I would feel guilty for having fallen for Oliver in the first place.

Excessive guilt is very common with survivors of PTSD when the cause is bullying, and the guilt expresses itself in forms distinct from "survivor guilt." It can come out as an initial reluctance to take action against the perpetrator and report him, knowing that he could lose his job. Later, this reluctance gives way to a strong urge to take action against him so that others, especially your successors, don't have to suffer a similar fate. I obsessed for days about what Oliver was doing. Was he hitting on other women and scamming them, too, with his "I am in love you" stories. Was he still telling people he had cancer? When I found out he was working as a salesman ripping old ladies off and had even scammed his own mother for nearly £20,000, I ended up writing a letter to her explaining that I had been his girlfriend and that he had lied to me about having cancer. I was so angry with him I didn't want him scamming anyone else.

Many victims feel a heightened sense of unworthiness and non-entitlement (some might call this shame). Some mornings, I would wake up and not want to face my own children, especially when I didn't have any money. I felt ashamed at having lost my house because I had incurred so many debts as a result of not working. I would look in the mirror and feel like I had aged ten years in the time I had known Oliver. I always prided myself on looking younger than my years but because everything about these people is a lie and he was much younger than me, I often felt he was just using me for sex. I would tell myself things like "What planet are you on Sarah? He just wanted sex. You're fat, old, and ugly." It took me a long time to restore my confidence. I had piled on the weight and would wear baggy old clothing, believing I didn't deserve a relationship, and wrongly believing I would only attract another Dark Soul clone of Oliver.

My own feelings of deep shame came out one day when I had to go for a regular coil change. I have a UID to control my menstrual cycle, as a result of having endometriosis, which is changed every three years. Its standard practice to do a swab prior to insertion and the clinic found I had had a minor infection caused from over washing. I had started to become ultra hygiene conscience and this can cause an infection by changing the PH balance of the vagina. I normally have the UID fitted at the surgery but had been referred to the local family planning clinic because there was a long wait and they asked if I was getting my coil changed for protection against pregnancy. I replied "No, I have endometriosis, I have not had sex since 2008". The doctor looked surprised and asked why. I said well the last time I came to this hospital was to have an aids test so I haven't wanted to have sex since and then burst into tears.

It made me realise how ashamed I had felt about having sex with Oliver. If I had had sex with a normal person who loved me even though the relationship had ended I wouldn't have felt bad. I also felt the overwhelming guilt again for having had sex with a married man and the effects on his own wife if ever she were to find out. Since the psychopath does not love you, you are just there to be used as a toy or whatever else they have taken from you. Energetically you feel like you have been raped.

Many victims stay with their abusers for a long time because they feel a heightened sense of indebtedness and undue obligation. Victims of PTSD also suffer from a reluctance to earn or accept money because of their elevated sense of poverty and injustice throughout the world. When I had finally had the courage to tell anyone what really happened, outside of my close circle of friends, I was so ashamed at losing everything and I was also completely broke. Accepting money from my family was one of the hardest pills I had to swallow. While I was going through the healing process, I was finding it very difficult to work and juggle looking after the children, and so my mother had offered to help me out by lending me some money. I remember bursting into tears because I felt so ashamed. She reminded me of all the times when I had helped other family members and friends over the years. Other close friends were brilliant, too. I felt so ashamed at having to borrow money, and my pride had been so strong I would have rather borrowed money from the bank at extortionate rates. However, I wasn't in a position to borrow money to pay off my debts monthly.

Other symptoms may include an unwillingness to take ill-health retirement, incapacity, or unemployment benefits to which you are entitled because you don't want to believe you are sufficiently unwell to merit it. You may also experience a desire to help others, often overwhelming and bordering on obsession, and to be available for others at any time, regardless of the cost to yourself.

When I first found out about Oliver's double life, I had been so obsessed with it I wanted to write to his wife and make sure Oliver never hurt anyone else. Then I would flip to feeling how badly his wife would feel if she found out that her husband had been cheating on her for five years and putting himself all over the Internet. Then I would feel guilty for having had a relationship with him in the first place and beat myself up, metaphorically.

Sometimes, albeit very fleetingly, I would even consider suicide as a way out of my big financial mess. Then I would take a deep breath, think about my children, and snap myself out of it, realising that wouldn't solve anything. Then the guilt would kick in. Those people who suffer PTSD tend to think about suicide as a logical and carefully thought-out solution rather than feel hopeless because they are depressed or perhaps because their finances are in such a mess.

In addition, a person suffering from PTSD is extremely hyper-vigilant. Despite all the evidence to the contrary, the hyper-vigilant person cannot bring himself to believe that the abuser cannot, and will not, see the effect their behaviour is having; they cling naively to the mistaken belief that the bully will recognise their wrongdoing and apologise. For a long time, I really believed that Oliver would regret what he had done, but I know he is never going to be sorry.

In regards to seeing Nick Clegg as a "trigger," the fact that I am aware of triggers means they don't have any power over me anymore. I had had many triggers over the months resulting in flashbacks and nightmares. Often when we get triggered it's a sign of PTSD. Often, we will use whatever coping mechanism we can to try and get ourselves over traumatic events. I had still wanted to make things right. In the case of the man who had asked me out, I had explained briefly to him what had happened to me and that I was not ready to date again because it wouldn't have been fair to either of us. I would have been putting someone else's face on a man I knew nothing about. In the case of politicians Nick and David, I would have to remind myself of all the things they were *not*, otherwise, in the future, I would be putting Oliver's face on every man who looked, sounded, or smelled like him. If we didn't do this, we would end up thinking everyone we meet is an abuser. We would not be able to move forward, and in attempting to date again, our hyper-vigilance would make it hard for us to trust.

Often, one of the things that prevent us from moving on in the healing process is that we deeply want to believe in the good things that happened in the relationship, although it was severely flawed from the beginning. Once we accept that none of it was real and accept the pain and our feelings, we can resume healing. Sometimes we need treatments such as EMDR to help us reframe the experience. EMDR, or Eye Movement Desensitisation and Reprocessing, is a therapy used to treat phobias, post-traumatic stress disorder, trauma, and many other problems. Dr. Francine Shapiro, an American psychologist, discovered EMDR in 1987. Since then, it has been used to treat thousands of people throughout the world, including survivors of war, victims of criminal violence and child abuse, and those who have experienced disasters or trauma. During sleep, the eyes move rapidly from side to side while you dream, this is called Rapid Eye Movement (REM) Sleep. During this time, it is believed that the subconscious mind processes the day's experiences. If an event is too traumatic then the experience often goes *unprocessed* and remains "stuck," and so the traumatic experience may continue to be replayed as intrusive memories or nightmares.

One theory is that EMDR recreates this Rapid Eye Movement, which, in turn, stimulates the "sorting out" process that occurs in normal dreaming. This sorting process can be enhanced with guidance from the therapist. EMDR brings back a lot of memories, very rapidly, therefore it is rarely used on the first visit. Hypnotherapy is usually used first to ensure the patient is stable and ready for the work to come. EMDR will not cause you to forget problems or bad experiences, but the suffering associated with those memories will fade. Your life will no longer be dominated by your past and you will be able to move on.

Post-Traumatic Embitterment Disorder

Psychologist and Professor, Dr. Michael Linden, of the Research Group Psychosomatic Rehabilitation, Berlin, Germany has proposed a new disorder be added to the DSM. This disorder, termed Post-Traumatic Embitterment Disorder (PTED) is something that is difficult for victims to come to terms with. There is a fine line between getting over what had happened and becoming bitter, twisted, and never being able to trust people again.

"The essential feature of post-traumatic embitterment disorder is the development of clinically significant emotional or behavioural symptoms following a single, exceptional, though normal, negative life event. The person knows about the event and perceives it as the cause of illness. The event is experienced as unjust, as an insult, and as a humiliation. The person's response to the event must involve feelings of embitterment, rage, and helplessness. The person reacts with emotional arousal when reminded of the event. The characteristic symptoms resulting from the event are repeated intrusive memories and a persistent negative change in mental well-being. Affect modulation is unimpaired and normal affect can be observed if the person is distracted

Besides prolonged embitterment individuals may display negative mood, irritability, restlessness, and resignation. Individuals may blame themselves for the event, for not having prevented it, or for not being able to cope with it. Patients may show a variety of unspecific somatic complaints, such as loss of appetite, sleep disturbance, pain."

I remember talking to a client who had had a run-in with a Sociopath and said she felt like she could never really trust anyone again, believing that it had been the abuser's fault. She couldn't take responsibility for her own feelings, and twenty odd years later, she is still suffering from depression, displaying negative feelings, and remains unable to cope with a massive "victim" label over her head that still attracted more abusers. This led me to wonder whether she had, in turn, become a Sociopath as a way of coping with her feelings. To me, the Sociopath has won if you are left feeling like that. It means you are left with the Sociopath's feelings, and I knew I didn't want to feel like that. We are left with a choice of if we want to see the glass half empty or half full. Bitterness conjures up the image of anger, and holding on to anger is an extremely negative emotion, one that doesn't serve anyone.

According to Dr. Linden, those with PTED suffer from intrusive thoughts and memories long after the triggering event, avoiding places related to the event and are pathologically consumed by an intense desire for revenge. Furthermore, those with PTED rarely seek out psychological help. "These people don't have the feeling that they must change, but rather have the idea that the world should change or that the oppressor should change, so they don't ask for treatment," Dr. Linden points out. "They are almost treatment resistant. Revenge is not a treatment."

Dr. Linden suggests that loving, normal individuals who suddenly snap, killing their family or co-workers and then themselves, may actually be suffering from PTED. If you are feeling like you want revenge against your perpetrator, from my experience, the best "revenge" would be to heal and move on with you life. Once you step out of the denial game and start taking ownership for your feelings of anger, hurt, and pain and deal with the negative beliefs you have about yourself, taking practical steps to deal with the trauma and the recurring nightmares, then you can really start to heal. If anything, the Sociopathic personality that comes into our life is our wakeup call or reminder to be all the things they are not: to not be bitter and angry, and to not be vile and horrible. We should, instead, continue to strive to be all the things that they had found so appealing about us in the first place. At the same time, it is also a reminder that we can now spot them and all the red flags. We don't have to be doormats for the rest of our lives and we will never be conned again. In a sense, they are bought into our lives as a gift.

Dealing With Your Emotions

How to Deal With Trauma

There are a number of ways to deal with trauma, and one of the ways in which we can process it is to view it with objective eyes. When I was drawing up a healing plan for myself in the hope that it would help others, I have looked at various different types of healing like counselling and spiritual methods. One of the problems with counselling is that many people who have been harmed by a Dark Soul must relive the traumatic events over and over, and often counsellors do not understand Sociopaths or psychopaths and they have even less understanding of Narcissistic Personality Disorder. You will have already beaten yourself up time and time again if you are the type of person a Dark Soul chooses. Abusers know you would blame yourself and are highly unlikely to stand up to them. That is exactly why they picked you.

A Note on Antidepressants

It's also very easy for doctors to suggest you are depressed and prescribe antidepressants for you. Fortunately, I have a very understanding doctor who is open to alternative methods. When it was clear I wasn't suffering from depression and had explained that I had had counselling, etc., my doctor was supportive of my belief that I was suffering symptoms of PTSD. The problem with antidepressants is that although they can be great for genuine depression, they act like a mask to cover up the feelings. So often, they delay the healing process. I strongly believe it's important that you feel the emotions rather stuffing them down. Researchers agree that when depression is severe, medication can be helpful – even life saving, but antidepressants aren't a cure. Medication may treat some symptoms of depression, but can't change underlying causes of the depression in your life. Also, it takes a great deal of energy to stuff our emotions down and deny our inner pain. The more you hold in the feelings, the deeper the pain is buried, and the less likely you will be to feel happy. Antidepressants work for a while, but eventually you will have to deal with the entire Pandora's Box. You might as well take the opportunity to keep the lid off and let it all out. Remember at the bottom of every Pandora's Box is not some horrible monster, but hope, and from hope springs a whole range of infinite possibilities.

Dr Silva Hartmann a practitioner of EFT and who uses Event Psychology categorises trauma into four types of events:

- The first is deemed to be a *negative event*, and it is called a trauma.

- The second is a *positive event*, called a Guiding Star.

- The third is an event which is *so extraordinary* and unknowable that we can't say if it was good or bad, only that something did happen, and the world was never the same from that moment forth.

- The fourth is the missing event, something that *should have happened but did not*, and the search for which is causing ongoing problems until it has been experienced."

Over the years I had had negative trauma from sexual abuse and from growing up in a dysfunctional family. I had also had a guiding star in the form of a spiritual wakeup call from getting Crohns disease which showed me how important it was not to suppress and internalise our emotions. When I had looked at what happened with Oliver, I was left with the feeling that even though at the beginning I was devastated and angry, after my journey I could not say if it had been good or bad. As well, my world was absolutely never going to be the same again. On the downside, I had lost my house. As well, I had had to go through counselling but had also managed to resolve all of my childhood traumas that had haunted me for years. On a positive side, I had also rid myself of my father's "clone" and I knew that if I were ever to have a relationship again, it would be a healthy one.

Dr. Michael Millett practices Emotional Freedom Technique (EFT) which can often help along with MET's or Energy Therapy Applications. These processes are rooted in clinical psychology, psychotherapy, and traditional Chinese medicine, and are all essentially variations on the theme of Thought Field Therapy. Some are variant enough to be considered a new species.

However you deal with your emotions, it's not as important as the fact that you acknowledge them. Whether you are crying your eyes out, journalling, going for long walks to burn off excess energy, or taking a kick boxing class for the first time to release some of the anger, it is important that you are actually feeling, and then letting go, of the pain. One of the ways I had expressed my sadness at losing my beautiful house was by painting a beautiful phoenix when I moved to my tiny flat. It was brightly coloured with purples and pinks and I placed it on the wall to remind myself that this was merely an episode in my life that would transform me forever. For good measure, my mother had given me some money for my birthday and normally I would never treat myself to anything. I had decided for the first time in my life, at age 47, to get a tattoo on my back. I took the painting into the tattoo artist shop and he transferred the image onto my back. I reminded myself that everything that had happened was now in the past and, literally, behind me.

Trauma Worksheets

A good way of dealing with your emotions is to use trauma worksheets. I have modified them slightly so that you can make your own. These worksheets are based on the ones used by "The Meadows" Arizona USA and designed by Pia Melody and other Meadows therapists. We gratefully acknowledge the kind permission from The Meadows authorising Growing Awareness Pty Ltd and John Bligh Nutting to use their format and wording in these sheets.

1. What happened?	2. Who did this to you?
(Write only about specific events not overall problems. Write one or two lines only event)	(Use code name or initials only)

3. Type of trauma	4. Your age when this happened (approx.)	5. What did you feel about it when it happened?	6. What do you feel when you think about it now?
(Physical, Mental, Verbal, Emotional, Spiritual, Sexual, Secrets, Distorted Reality, Abandonment, Engulfment)		Lonely, hurt, sad, angry, fear, shame, guilt, worthless, frustration, pain, helpless, hopeless, devastated, embarrassed, annoyed	

Take a blank sheet of paper and make these private journal sheets. Divide it up into 6 columns. Divide the headings up as shown in the above diagram. It will be better if you used A4 paper turned sideways. The reason for using the trauma sheets is that it brings to your awareness what actually happened along with any feelings that accompany it.

The worksheets were originally developed for people who had experienced childhood trauma, but they work equally as well for those who have had trauma in adult life. Without going into too much detail about the *inner child* part of us, there is a part of voice dialogue work which includes working with the inner child. It's important to remember when filling out the sheets that you do it from a place of adult awareness.

Healing and recovery from past trauma and abuse can only work if it involves three essential steps: 1) self-awareness; 2) processing; and 3) validating. Incorporate these, whether you are working through the sheets as a result of adult trauma, childhood trauma, or a combination of both. You must acknowledge that:

- It really did happen to me

- It was traumatic for me (or if you prefer, "It was abuse!")

- It should not have happened to me.

- It was unfair, unjust, it was wrong ,and it has affected my life in many ways

- I did not deserve to be treated that way.

- In the case of childhood abuse, I would not do that to my child and it is okay for the *grown up* to feel angry about what they did to me.

If you are working through the sheets from a perspective of childhood trauma, you must remember to validate your feelings the same as you did with the entire list above by telling your inner child *all of the above* and that *it was not your fault!*

The reason I have included these particular worksheets is because, in most cases, being with a Dark Soul is generally *not your fault* either, even though you were an adult. When doing the exercises, keep repeating these lines over and over to yourself until you get a sense that you and your inner child have settled down. You may even breathe a deep sigh of relief. That's when you know you have processed that traumatic event. Validation helps undo some of the damage. It is particularly healing for your inner child's sense of reality when the validation comes from you, as the inner child's grownup part, but it is also healing to hear the same message again in the future from other people like therapists or members of a self-awareness group.

Do not rush into forgiveness. However, once you feel confident that you have really finished processing one particular event, you can, if you wish, *as a grown up*, choose to forgive the people responsible. Just make sure you make it clear that while the forgiveness is being given on behalf of your inner child, it is coming from your self-aware grownup side *alone* and *not from your inner child.*

A Myriad of Emotions

When you first come out of the dysfunctional relationship, after you have worked through all of your negative beliefs, you are going to feel a lot of different emotions. Many of which you may have packed down over the years. You may feel, shame, guilt, anger, sadness, grief, and so on. I know I had felt so ashamed and, not wanting to tell anyone how much of a mess I was in financially, it took me a few months before I was willing to seek help. By that time, it was too late and I was already in a position in which I had no choice but to sell my house. I had been having regular sessions dealing with reasons why I had stayed in the relationship for so long that I had been taking a lot of time off work to sort my head out.

When you are faced with an emotional crisis coupled with financial meltdown, it's sometimes difficult to juggle everything. Often I would just wake up in the morning and, faced with a pile of bills, I just didn't know where to start. Once I started seeking help with sorting out my finances, the real work started on dealing with my unresolved emotions and feelings of anger: anger at myself for being such an idiot. My anger at Oliver for three years of lies that kept me tied to a relationship which I should have walked away from earlier, had I known the truth. Coupled with the reality that I would have never found out all the other disgusting stuff if I had not stayed so long was the only positive thing that kept me moving forwards. If I had not found out there is a chance I would have had him back in my life again only to have to go through it all again years later, or would have left him for good thinking he was a "nice" guy and perhaps attracted another version on him that was even worst. I have no idea to be honest.

The first emotions you are most likely to to go through as a result of surviving any kind of abuse is guilt. Very often survivors will recall events and saying things like "I should have known...." Or "If only I hadn't done this or that...." Sometimes, it is easier to blame ourselves than to admit that the abuser was at fault. In the case of rape they may feel like they "caused the rape". If they were extremely passive as a result of being so worn down emotionally they may beat themselves up for not having fought back enough. The most likely feeling they will have is for being "stupid" enough to get into the situation in the first place. In addition they may even feel guilty for all the the feelings they have and try to cover them all up by not expressing them at all by keeping busy with work and so on and pretending they will go away.

However what I have noticed unlike *normal* relationships that end in a reasonably amicable way, the relationship with a Dark Soul is quite different. The emotions you are left with come and go in "no particular order". Until you fully heal, you are left with an unresolved pot of bubbling emotions and toxic gunk. I believe in some ways you are left feeling as discorded as the Dark Souls themselves.

When you have come out of a relationship with a Dark Soul you are most likely to suffer from Shock and Disbelief, which is discussed in more detail on the section on Post Traumatic Stress, most likely after you thought you had resolved all the other feelings you have. Sometimes the target (and yes you were a target) will have an increasingly hard time facing up to the fact that the abuse had taken place, even going so far as to make excuses for their abusers behaviour in the hope that they might be "healed" or "fixed" someday.

Most victims will feel a compete lack of control which may extend into other aspects of their lives, for varying amounts of time. As a result they may overcompensate by trying to regain control back in other areas of their life.

Fear is usually the biggest tool any kind of abuser uses to receive and maintain control. This fear is not only of bodily injury but of death as well. Many victims say that the reason they didn't fight back, or did not receive help right away because they were fearful that their abuser would injure or even kill them. Both the psychopath and the narcissist feeds off fear and as a result the victim feels powerless and ends up being afraid when they have left the relationship. They may fear their abuser returning or even fear going to sleep at night. Most victims are left with a fear of men or women in general with the irrational thoughts that someone else might hurt them. They may fear going to court. They may fear places and people that remind them of the relationship or the Dark soul. Victims are often afraid of their own anger and one of the most common symptoms is an inability to sleep properly for some time after the relationship is over often waking up and having nightmares.

Very often the victim will feel humiliated, they may feel dirty and ashamed, especially in cases where sexual abuse has taken place, or they have been coerced into doing things they felt uncomfortable with. Many things that took place during the abuse can be hard, or embarrassing to talk about to other people. Even some therapists and counsellors look distinctly uncomfortable when you explain that you have had a relationship with a psychopath. I have watched the body reactions of my own GP with a feeling of like "I don't really know what to say or do". Many victims may feel like they do not want to say anything and keep quiet. The victim also may feel paranoid that everyone around him/her can tell that they have been abused. In cases of male victims, the abuse itself is not nearly as bad as the fear of other people finding out about the abuse and that if anyone finds out they will brand them.

Anger is one of the most common feelings that develops after an attack. Anger is a healthy and common reaction for a survivor, as long as the anger is not aimed at themselves. Anger can be a helpful tool for regaining the strength and the courage needed to get back control of their life. A victim may feel angry at society or the legal system especially when dealing with a psychopath because its "their word against them" and often psychopaths will manipulate the legal system especially when it comes to divorce and so on. They may also feel angry at their significant others for not being understanding enough and more importantly they are most likely to be angry at the Abuser.

In addition to the shame and embarrassment of having to face up to the reality of having had a relationship with a psychopath. For example, if you have lost money or life savings you may have the feeling that everyone can tell, just by looking at you, that you are a victim.

With a lack of confidence and trust in their own abilities to make judgements and a distinct feeling of *powerlessness* they may often decide not to have relationships again.

However, I can tell you with complete authenticity that if you are willing to look within yourself and take control back of your life this passes with time and you do eventually start to trust again. You will move from target or victim, through to survivor to become healed. You will start to trust your own intuition, and other people eventually. And eventually you will not attract Dark Souls again. You may meet a few more along the way in your journey but you will spot them before they spot you and as a result you will learn to avoid them in the future.

Getting Angry

The first emotion you are likely to feel when you first uncover your Dark Soul's double life are shock and disbelief. The lasting impact of a major shock can either be stimulating or debilitating, depending upon one's strength of character. When overtaken by crisis, we search our hearts for inner strength with which to face the future and often we will do whatever it takes to cope. We can either go into denial or we can get angry. Anger is often a very positive emotion as long as it's not aimed directly at the perpetrator or internalised.

It does not help to send angry emails or letters to your abuser. I did that a couple of times and all it did was to make *me* upset, not him. First of all, they will just ignore them because they just don't care anyway, and, secondly, they may even use them against you. All it does is create intense negativity and gives them the much needed attention they crave.

My suggestion for releasing anger might be a controversial one, but for my own sanity I had to vent it somehow as opposed to how I used to internalise it. I have read many cases of victims of Dark Souls who remain very bitter and angry afterwards. I believe that one of the reasons we feel so angry is that, as targets, we may have not owned our own anger beforehand so it has a culminating effect. We are not only angry at them but also at ourselves. It is essential that we own our part in the dynamics of the relationship and then deal with it however best we can with whatever tools we can, whether it be counselling or healing therapy. I know I couldn't take it out on Oliver and it certainly wasn't healthy to take it out on myself, so I discovered a *controversial* way of coping with my own anger. The other thing is, because I am an Empath, I was feeling an amplified feeling of anger and it wasn't always my own; I was unconsciously picking up his rage at me for catching him. I had found a post on a support forum at *Lovefraud.com* about feeling angry and decided to respond by writing a post there and placing an advertisement as if I was in Oliver's shoes. I had decided that if I were to post it on the forum, firstly, it would be anonymous and help others understand how Dark Souls think. Secondly, I could stick it on my wall and imagine it was a lonely hearts advert for someone exactly like Oliver, and I would *never* apply to it.

It had the effect of allowing me to write about him objectively, and to see it with a bit of humour. As well, I had written it anonymously and not sent it to him. It also read in a way that I would have never wanted to apply for a relationship like that again because obviously I was dating a psychopath. If you had put what I had written in a job advert knowing who they really were, you wouldn't apply. The responses I got from the other users on the support group were interesting. One lady commented

"Dear *****, WOW! What an excellent depiction of the S you

were with. You really were able to get into his head and describe his personality, actions, wants, needs, and DISORDERED WAYS. My "wow" moment came near the end of your description of him. When I would always ask myself why? Why do they do the things they do? I like what you said...they see in us (or others) the things they know they can never be.

Your extox like so many of ours have damaged non-existent souls... they walk around empty on the inside and use us/others/anyone to fill their well hidden gaping deep dark abyss inside of them. For those of us, considering contacting or going back... you may want to reread the above post and see that you are merely applying to the above advertisement and getting involved with someone who lives their life as a total lie – and you will just be falling back into the arms of a leech disguised as a man or woman. NO CONTACT." (Lovefraud.com)

Another commented: "I would like to frame your post actually, if ever I get the compulsion to have contact."

Support Groups

Support groups such as www.lovefraud.com are excellent because they help the victim understand that they are not alone. Personally, apart from the odd post, I never really used the support forum because it kept on reminding me of Oliver. I felt I would rather avoid talking about him to other people because it kept me stuck in victim mentality. However, for some, support forums and groups are a life saver. If you stay on support forums for too long, though, you remain in victim mode and it doesn't always help you to move on. When posting any kind of comments on forums, remember also that Sociopaths are prone to be stalkers and if you are worried about your ex finding comments you have written about them, they will do one of two things: they will either delight in the fact that you are still giving them attention, especially if they have NPD as well, or else, they will use it against you, especially if you have used their real name. Never ever accuse them of doing anything unless you have evidence, and if you do write anything about them, *always* keep your posts anonymous.

I found writing my own "Do not respond" advert post very cathartic. It enabled me to move through all the other emotions I was going to feel over the following months. Most victims will feel extremely angry, but it's important that you find a way of dealing with it. Whatever you do, *do not internalise it* and, for obvious reasons, if and when you have exposed them, however tempting it is, avoid them at all costs by maintaining no contact.

Keeping Yourself to Yourself

If you are highly sensitive or empathic, I would suggest you keep off the support forums unless you are really needy. You may get sucked into other victims' stories and then feel the need to try and help them. At this point in your healing journey, you need to focus on your own emotions and recovery.

If you are on social networking sites like Facebook (which is where I found Oliver), make sure you have full privacy setting on, otherwise they will be following what you are doing and they may even try and add you as a friend under another disguise. If you can bear to be off Facebook, remove yourself or at least hide all your settings. You will need as much support as you can from family and friends especially if you have been left penniless. The last thing you want is your abuser making comments about you or finding out that you have had a bad day. Worst still, if you have moved on and are dating someone else, they may end up stalking you or try to destroy your new relationship.

There are other ways in which to process your emotions through counselling, hypnosis, EFT, EMDR, and so on. However, it's important that you actually acknowledge what you are feeling, especially if you are feeling angry. Once you have allowed the anger to pass, it may pop up again when you least expect it, perhaps when it is triggered by something. You may get angry when you get the odd bill that you know they are not going to pay, or, perhaps, if you are going through a divorce with a Dark Soul and must have contact with them. It's best if you can avoid contact with them, or at least have someone with you when it happens. It definitely speeds up the healing process, the longer you can avoid them. That includes no emails, no texts, and deleting their telephone number from your phone in case they try to call you or you are tempted to text them when you are upset.

So now that you are acknowledging your feelings and working

through all of your negative beliefs about yourself, you are empowering yourself and becoming more aware. You also become aware that being away from these toxic people is actually very healthy for you. When I talk about having **no contact**, I cannot emphasise how important it is: **no emails, no texts** and, therefore, as few triggers as possible. The other thing that is important when leaving a toxic relationship is to disconnect energetically. As an Empath, I started to be very aware, especially during the times when I was away from Oliver, how we not only connect on a physical and emotional level but on an energetic level. This was what had the most devastating effect on my health, emotional well-being, and psyche, far more than the financial effect of losing my house.

Jumping From One Frying Pan into Another

On a final note about emotions, many people who come out of a relationship want to jump from one frying pan into another. They may want to get their needs met by someone else because they feel they need to fill the void. You need time to heal when you have exchanged energies with anyone, especially if they are a Dark Soul. On a deep sexual and emotional level, you need to make sure you have disconnected from them first and don't jump in to another relationship with someone else immediately. If you do, you risk carrying all the negative energies and emotions that you took on from your ex and have not yet processed, and dumping them onto your new partner. You may also risk, if you are not properly healed, the chance of going out with another clone of your ex.

For this reason I would like you to understand that it is my belief that when you have sex, you get together with another person basically on a DNA level. It is as if you download a database of your sexual partner, a database of his life (bad and good things, healthy and unhealthy things) and this information will stay in your body and your psyche forever. So, before you get into sexual contact with someone, especially after such an abusive damaging relationship you should ask yourself serious questions. These questions are:

- Is it safe and healthy for you and your sexual partner to have sex: physically, emotionally and mentally?

- Do you really care about him and does he care about you?

- Will you and your new sexual partner gain from this sex encounter more feelings of self respect, confidence, and independence?

- Would you or your sexual partner regret this moment of sex? Would you feel guilty or hurt? Is there anyone else involved that you may hurt?

If your answers are "yes, yes, yes, and no," then you are going to have healthy sex. Both partners will exchange a positive "database." Otherwise, you are going to damage yourself and your partner and anyone else attached to them. However much you are hurting, I would advise anyone to give themselves permission to heal first. Then, when you have healed, you can start looking at having a healthy relationship again, whether it is an emotional or sexual relationship.

If you really must have a relationship again **follow your gut feelings!** We generally know when we meet someone if there is something wrong. Follow this initial feeling. If you are a person who tries to talk yourself out of an initial gut feeling, ask an *intuitive* friend to give you some insight. A neutral person can often spot the things we may purposely choose to ignore. If you still cannot trust own intuition, perhaps make a deal with one of your closest friends. Give them permission to tell you immediately, when they see any red flags that you cannot and listen to them. Do not ignore them, because having already been slimed with their energy, until you finally get your emotional radar working 100 per cent, you may well get tested along the way by bumping into more Dark Soul clones. So ask yourself this, would you really want to go digging up dead corpses again and risk being a character in *Nightmare on Elm street* all because you were stupid enough to ignore your gut ?

Do Not Take Anything Personally

When you are feeling down and depressed and have one your off days and you may have them many months after the relationship is over. I would remind you of the book I mentioned before *The Four Agreements* by Don Miguel Ruiz. One of his agreements is to never take anything anyone does or says to you personally.

I cannot stress enough how important this is when you have come out of a relationship with a Dark Soul. Often we will be asking ourselves, "Why me?" "Did I deserve it?" "Why did they hate me so much to do all of those vile things?." When I read some of the cruel heartless stories that these Dark Souls have done to some of their victims my own story seems like walk in the park compared to the way some victims have been treated. And yet all of us are left scarred and damaged in some way.

In a normal relationship we are left with some good feelings at the end of the day no matter how badly the relationship ends. Over time we can go back and remember the nice things that happened during the relationship. For example if we were married and have children, we may remember that they were a good father, or the nice times we shared together.

With Darks Souls there is little good to remember because the whole relationship is usually based on lies. Often its like a Pandora's box and the more we find out about our Dark Soul ex the more it opens up a bottomless pit of lies and deceit, and our own Pandora's box. Even little things may trigger you. For example, I was driving through a local town where I used to meet Oliver for lunch, it was five minutes away from his office. We would enjoy a lovely lunch and then when he would leave he would say "I have to go to work now". One time he left and went off in a different direction. I questioned Oliver and said "I thought your firm was that way" and he replied "well I have a meeting to go to". On driving through the same town recently I remember the dates when we had met up and had a moment of "happy nostalgia" remembering the nice lunch we had had together. He had sat there gazing into my eyes and told me how much he loved me. Then suddenly I remembered the dates; I realised that at the time we were meeting for lunch, he had actually been fired from his job. I also realised that everything else during that conversation was lies too.

As tears rolled down my face, hopefully for the very last time, I reminded myself not to take what Oliver had said or done to me personally.

Nothing that anyone does to us is because of you. It is because of themselves. If a person treats you disrespectfully, hurts or abuses you do not take it personally. At the same time as I was so poignantly reminded by my lunch meeting with Oliver when a person tells you they "love you" do not take it personally either. If someone says they "love you" its not always about you its about them. If someone is not treating you with the love and respect that you deserve its the universe's way of reminding you that you no longer need them in your life anymore. If you keep on attracting clones of these people for a while, instead of beating up on yourself and saying "Why after all this am I still attracting these same people?". Just say to yourself "Thankyou for reminding me". It takes time, but eventually you will not be sent any more of these people. It's just a test of your old belief system that was never true in the first place and the universes way of telling you you no longer need them or others like them anymore.

Do not take anything that these Dark Souls have done or said to you personally and trust that by walking away you are allowing for something better to come into your life.

Practical Advice

If you have financial problems seek help from people such as Citizens advice or a financial advisor. You would be surprised how helpful these people are when you face your situation head on and they can help you draw up a plan of action if you are left with debts after the relationship.

Get physical. Join a gym or do something you have never done before. I decided to get myself an allotment at a cost of £10 a year. Just being outside enjoying the fresh air and the feeling of accomplishment from having done something productive at the end of the day felt wonderful. I also looked forward to energetically planting new seeds. Every time I dugs up weeds I envisaged digging out the old dead weeds and putting something better in its place. If you cannot afford a gym, go for a walk instead. Don't stay couped up inside feeling sorry for yourself.

Its very cathartic to journal so write down as as often as you can and much as possible. You might even write yourself a book.

If you have children or animals start spending more time with them. They will enjoy your company. I even went out and got myself another dog from a rescue centre and the rewards we as a family got from having him were immense.

If you like flowers buy yourself them occasionally. It doesn't cost much and you don't have to wait for a man to buy them for you. Focus on the little things, like looking after yourself and try not to focus on what a bar steward your ex was. Eventually these feelings will go. If you are holding on to feeling resentful towards them just remind yourself that you are giving them energy "again" and draw it back to yourself.

If like myself you love music, start listening to it. Put on songs that make you happy NOT romantic love songs and notice what comes up on the radio. Start opening up to the message that the universe is giving you. When I was in the stages of "should I or shouldn't I" go back to him. I would ask the universe for a sign whilst listening to the radio in the car. When three tracks in a row came on with the lyrics "every time I am with you you make me want to die" along with another track "You think you are a superstar and you have such a big ego". If that wasn't enough to remind me not to go back nothing was!

When you start listening to your intuition and go with the universal flow of things you will start seeing the signs and really pay attention to those warning signs that you never listened to in the first place. The same ones that left you with an uneasy feeling or told you not to have a relationship in the first place. This is your time while you are away from these Dark Souls to focus your attention back to you and not find a single excuse to go back to them.

Every time I thought about Oliver I would envisage a big stop sign in my head and the times between thinking about him eventually diminished until I could hardly remember who he was.

In the following chapters I describe some more energetic techniques you can use on your own to disconnect energetically from your Dark Soul.

11

Spiritual Energy Healing

This section focusses on the Spiritual Energy Healing that is so essential when coming out of a relationship with a Dark Soul. Whether you believe in Energy Vampires or psychic attacks is irrelevant. It is essentially about the energy that the Dark Soul takes from their victim. Most victims are left emotional, psychically and energetically drained of their life force after leaving these relationships. And the following tools will enable the victims to disconnect from their abuser on every level. Some of them are based on spiritual techniques and some are modified and based on old shaman traditions. Whether you believe in them is not different to whether or or not you believe in a past life under hypnosis the emphasis is on how you feel after having done them.

Energy Vampires

One of the easiest words an abuser can say is "sorry." Sadly, they usually only ever say it when they are caught. Three times I exposed Dark Soul's lies and each time I confronted him. It got easier as time went on, and I eventually ran out of reasons to love him. To be in love with a person and try to change them is not real love. However, the man I was "in love" with was not the man who had presented himself in front of me. It was all an illusion.

Over the periods when I have been sorting out my issues, I had had a few interesting discussions with many "light worker" type people like myself who choose to believe that there is good in all people. Of course, it's important for us to take responsibility for our own part in the dynamics of a relationship, but, to be perfectly honest, those "fluffy bunny type" spiritual people who believe that everyone is good and kind do more harm than good. The bottom line is that some people are *evil*.

Yes, I absolutely take responsibility for being in a relationship with him and then looking at my own issues, but this man was capable of conning anyone so having everyone tell me that "I created my reality," just didn't help. Being told things like I had attracted him from a past life because of "karmic ties" and so on is not always beneficial when you are left financially broke; even when you do remember doing a past life regression and finding out he was your father who left everything to you in his will, or because I had remembered killing him with a knife in some medieval battle. Whether or not past lives exist or not is irrelevant. It may help some people to comes to terms with the abuser or it may not. Last count I shared around 5 lives with this man. Whether or not past lives are real I certainly wont be spending another lifetime with him. I would like to not have to come back after this lifetime.

Some lightworkers had even suggested that he could be "healed," and that, underneath, he was a pure energetic being full of light and I should continue to keep sending him unconditional love, despite what he had done to me. This only kept me more attached to him. I had many sessions of cord-cutting with down-to-earth light workers and spiritual healers, like myself, who pull no punches when it comes to telling you the truth, and they said that my ex's energy was vile.

As an Empath, even when I was not seeing Oliver, I would find myself waking up in the middle of the night having terrible nightmares. One time, when he had been caught in a lie, he got so angry that my son was rushed into hospital with quinsy and I felt I was under psychic attack. My son had become so sick, as a last resort I called up my ex and asked him to please stop. I reminded him of the time when I was there for him when his own son was sick with pneumonia. Interestingly enough, whether or not you believe in psychic attacks or not, within hours my son got better. He sent a text back saying "Sorry. I will not do it anymore!"

Before I describe what an energy vampire is like I would like to explain that one of the types of people that energy vampires are particularly attracted to are Empaths. In essence, an Energy Vampire is any person who sucks out more in their energy exchanges than they return to the person they are sharing with. Some people, by their very presence, seem to drain the energy of unprotected people around them. They will often associate with a victim who is highly Empathic or unable to protect themselves. Energy vampires come in all types. They have energy leaks that they need to fill and often they don't even realize they're bleeding you dry. The term "energy vampire" is also used metaphorically, to refer to people whose influence leaves a person feeling exhausted, unfocused and depressed, without ascribing the phenomenon to psychic interference. There is no medical proof that energy vampires exist and there is none that Empaths do, either, but the proof is in how you feel. The reason they take energy from people is because they're compensating to get rid of their own negative energy.

Most people only notice that they have been in the presence of an energy vampire. In extreme cases, when that person has gone, they find themselves depleted of energy and lacking the will to live, as though all their enthusiasm, excitement and joy of life had been quite literally "sucked out of them." Sometimes, people then become aware that they have been interacting with an energy vampire, someone who takes energy but doesn't give anything back, and consequently learn to avoid such people. When a person is forced to share a space with an energy vampire for any length of time, or even finds himself in a relationship with such a being, they can become quite depressed, feel very low, develop immune system problems, and may even start to feel sick or suicidal.

What is an Empath?

Having an intuitive ability can be a wonderful gift that offers healers the opportunity to better understand the pain and suffering their clients are experiencing. However, for highly sensitive individuals who are unknowingly soaking up the energy which doesn't belong to people immediately around them, even down to remotely picking up energetic information from individuals via email, it can be a veritable minefield which, if not managed properly, can literally drive an Empath insane.

From my own experience growing up, I had known very early on that something wasn't quite right and that I didn't fit into the normal category. Perhaps my own childhood was slightly unique in that I grew up in what can only be described as somewhat dysfunctional circumstances, and therefore spent much of my childhood either thinking I was completely deranged or else totally shutting my Empathy down.

If you "don't know whether to laugh or cry," it couldn't be more appropriate if you are an Empath. Hopefully, my scattered smidgens of dark humour will lighten the load of what can sometimes be a scary place for some. I have many friends and colleagues who are Empaths. Remember, "like attracts like." At one point, I had even thought Oliver was an Empath who had just "switched off." How funny that sounds now! Depending on an Empaths level of control over their ability to read emotions and feelings, some dismiss the idea they are even Empathic at all. They may go into denial, flipping between bouts of depression and being the proverbial energetic gunk sponge, soaking up every kind of negative feeling from those around. Others have their feelings firmly under control and others have been known to totally shut down altogether. Some say they are not Empathic and choose to switch it off altogether. They still appear to attract the wrong kind of relationships and then end up spending a long time working on themselves, thinking they have a problem, when, in fact, they had probably left themselves wide open to energetic attack.

Some consider it a kind of special gift or power because they can read auras and do all kinds of amazing things. They may have a psychic "mind reading" ability that puts them head and shoulders above the rest of the "normal" population. Whilst others just think that Empaths are genetic oddities, including some Empaths themselves, and they shut themselves away thinking they are unable to cope with their feelings. They think if they discuss it with anyone they will be rushed off to the nearest psychiatric hospital. Worst still, many like to stuff their feelings down by drinking alcohol and, in the worst case scenario, they take drugs like marijuana, which actually opens up even more holes in their auric field, amplifying the problem and making it ten times worse. For many years, I had hated being empathic.

Fortunately, I had stopped thinking I was insane a couple of years after I learned about Empathy. As for drinking and taking drugs, although I had dabbled in marijuana when I was younger, I do not drink alcohol at all and I am drug free, but I do smoke tobacco. I have been told by a number of people that if I stopped smoking it would protect my auric field better. I have struggled with quitting cigarettes under the stress of the last 18 months or so. So let's look at how an Empath sees things or rather how they feel things.

I was recently on an NLP course, and apparently, our brain filters out two billion bits of information every second. Out of that, we receive approximately 174. So there is a lot of information filtered out. From the NLP model, if we consider how we receive information through our sensory acuity, it is represented through either visual, kinaesthetic, auditory, or cerebral input or a combination of all four. In additional, we have other factors such as smell and taste. I know from my own experience as an Empath that I am slightly higher on the kinaesthetic scale by about 2 points but everything else is sensed at an equally high level. There wasn't a test for smell or taste but I have an extremely evolved sense of smell. Empaths appear to be bombarded with sensory information which forms an emotional picture or group of feelings in the body. Sometimes the feelings are so strong it can be difficult to differentiate where all the information is coming from.

Generally, an Empath is able to feel people's feelings. So let's examine a couple of scenarios below:

Scenario 1 Say an *unaware* Empath is taking a trip to a busy shopping centre. They go into the shop surrounded by people all busy buying presents. An Empath can usually pick up feelings when they are in close proximity to someone. Often, they can even pick up feelings remotely and there is this person surrounded by a hundred and one different feelings. They may start to feel confused, and feel a bit overwhelmed and claustrophobic. Perhaps they take a step outside and start to feel a little better reinforcing their belief they have claustrophobia, when, in fact, all they are doing is picking up energetic gunk. They muddle their way through the day. Perhaps they come home feeling totally exhausted, having bought things they probably didn't really want in the first place. They'll put off the next big shopping trip wondering why they have returned home in a bad mood or feeling totally confused. Wouldn't it have been so much easier if they had known why they were feeling that way, and if there had been steps they could have taken to not have felt that way in the first place?

Scenario 2 An *untrained* Empath wakes up in the middle of the night at 2 AM and finds herself vomiting for no apparent reason. Realising something is wrong, they have an innate feeling their partner has been sick but isn't quite sure why and cannot get hold of them. The following morning they get a call from them to say they have been out the night before, drinking and have been vomiting at exactly 2 AM the previous night. Why are they untrained because they have chosen to physically take on the other persons stuff.

Whatever you want to call it, weird, strange, telepathic, ability to mind read, or just plain odd, this is just a part of what it feels like to be an Empath, and often they are bombarded with sensory information every single day. Empaths are, by nature, because of their ability to take other peoples "stuff" on, ideal enablers. They are also experts at playing the role of the co-dependent and therefore they often act as a magnet for certain personality types that can be particularly damaging to them. In psychological terms, these personality types could be narcissists, sociopaths and borderlines, whose favourite hobby is to "project" their own feelings. Since untrained Empaths are particularly prone to believing that the feelings they sense are all their own, all the rule books regarding "perception is projection" go out of the window when it comes to them. So Empaths need to be particularly careful when it comes to dealing with energy vampires. When Empaths have a particularly strong bond with people such as family members they sometimes find it difficult to switch their Empathy off.

I had experienced what turned out to be very angry psychic attacks from Oliver. He would intentionally do it when he was angry at me or whenever I tried to finish with him. By nature I am not an angry person and these were happening out of the blue. The attacks ranged from being woken up in the middle of the night to having my children and animals targeted. The psychic attacks were aimed at finding a fear of mine and playing on it until I would feel like I was having a nervous breakdown. As an Empath, I have had to learn how to differentiate between what are my own feelings and those that have been projected onto me.

Psychic Attacks

There is a huge difference between psychic attack and post traumatic stress. From my own experience I had the misfortune of experiencing both when I left Oliver.

No one can be psychically attacked unless they have a connection with someone and they allow it. You are more likely to be psychically attacked if your energetic vibration is low and you are in a state of physical or emotional weakness. If you think about the body as energy, we have a field of energy around us which is our armour, or aura. When the body is weak, so is our aura. We make connections with people all the time – our friends, family, and so on – and a healthy connection is a bit like a cord between two energy fields. In a toxic relationship, that cord is damaged and when you try to break off a relationship with an abuser, especially one who is a narcissist, they will feel an energetic shift. They will feel like they are not getting their "fix." Even if you are not seeing them physically or having contact with them, they can still get their fix from you energetically unless you sever the link you have to them.

In my case I would disconnect frequently, and then every time I did, I received vile psychic attacks. Oliver knew all of my weaknesses, and so the attacks would come in the form of my worst fears. An attacker can only feed your fears and then, as a result, they will be amplified by *you*, the recipient of the attack. Then you will manifest it by creating whatever reality you have focussed on. For example, I have a terrible fear of moths and one of the attacks came in the form of hundreds of moths appearing in my front room one evening. How does this happen? The attacker has to know something about you, and could send the attack in the form of a conscious attack or an unconscious one because they are angry. They will project energy towards you in the form of an intention, feeling, or perhaps in a thought, and this then feeds your own worst fears.

In someone who has a healthy aura or who has no connection, such an attack will not affect them at all. It will just not resonate and you won't feel anything. However if you are weak, emotionally vulnerable, or just physically worn out, you are more prone to an attack. If you are an Empath that picks up energy, you are especially prone to being attacked. You may even pick up feelings and think they are your own, whether or not you believe in psychic attacks as a phenomenon or not. At the time when my energy was at its lowest I had just come out of hospital in December 2009 having lost a large amount of blood from a post operative bleed from what would have normally been a relatively minor operation. In addition to emotional stress, illness and general anaesthetics are one of the most frequent situations where people go through a complete or near-complete collapse of all energetic defence systems. Surgeons pay a lot of attention to physical factors of contamination but, sadly, totally disregard the energetic side

There is a well-known book by Dion Fortune, called *Psychic Self Defence*, in which she details many extreme cases of psychic attack where people have actually died. On a sombre note, my own friend and colleague Linda Callis. Linda was one the most empathic and gifted healers I have ever met in my life, she had a wonderful sense of humour and loved helping people from all backgrounds. She became the founder and creator of Neuro Muscular Transmission. I met Linda ten years ago when I first qualified as an acupuncturist and she often referred clients to me. Years later she helped me to disconnect from Oliver's energy on more than one occasion, citing his energy as vile and wanting to make her vomit.

Sadly Linda was diagnosed with cancer in 2009. It had been a treatable cancer, but she had battled over the last couple of years and so her energy and aura were extremely low. Sadly, Linda died in 2010 and at her own funeral, her husband Charles Callis had spoken of her constantly battling between the forces of light and dark. Two days before her death, she had been given the all clear to have treatment and the doctors had said she was on the mend. She was, at that point, hopeful that her cancer could be treated. At her funeral I spoke to one of her friends who said Linda had called her the previous evening to say she had been up all night having nightmares and had been plagued by psychic attacks for months on and off leading up to her death. In a weakened state, she died the following day. Lindas work continues through the centre she ran with Charles and he is hoping to publish the book that she started writing before her death called *Callis in Wonderland*.

It was a bittersweet experience knowing I had finally rid myself of Oliver but had to attend the funeral of one of the most empathic women I ever had the pleasure to meet, a few days after he left.

My Encounter into the Dark Realms of Psychic Attacks

Whether or not you believe that psychic attacks are real, I am not here to persuade you one way or another. All I can do is share my own experiences with you. So what exactly is an energy vampire and how does it feel to be with one?

I had finally sold my house. Exhausted and tired, a week later I had moved into the flat that my son had nicknamed "the s**t hole." What a hole it was, too: an old terraced house, split up into two flats with a large outbuilding that was derelict. The minute we had moved in there, it felt awful. Not only did I feel like I was being drained emotionally and physically, but psychically, too. It was very difficult to put your finger on how horrible the energy was in the flat. I had tried to remain positive and with what little money I'd had arranged to have the windows replaced and central heating installed before the winter months kicked in. I knew how to paint and decorate and woke up each morning at six AM to strip walls and get rid of skip loads of rubbish that had accumulated from a long list of difficult tenants over the past three years that I had owned it. Tenants who had left without paying bills, had been abusive, and finally the last lot who had turned it into a squat. My bedroom had been covered in dog piss and excrement, and the smell was overwhelming. It took nearly 6 weeks before it finally smelled like a normal home. We'd had to live in all the mess and clutter with the remainder of my beautiful Victorian house all packed up in boxes in the outbuilding because none of it would fit in the flat. My daughter had taken the flat downstairs as she had turned eighteen and had decided to return to college. Every single day for three months was spent living in a construction site. If it wasn't the window fitters, it was the plumbers. If it wasn't clearing up piles of old wallpaper I had stripped off the walls, it was clearing up plaster and mess that the builders had left behind that day.

I had been married to a builder for seventeen years, and we had developed a few properties over the years. It felt like déjà vu all over again, although this time I wasn't doing the property up for monetary gain; I was doing it up to make it liveable, and every single penny I was investing in the property was going down the drain because of the negative market situation. I knew from having lived in an old house before, that there was often old energy left behind in buildings from previous occupants and, as I had left with debts, the previous owners had too. In fact two days after I exchanged contracts the buyers lost their job. When I had moved to the flat, I thought I would make a new start. Perhaps I could turn the outbuilding into the music studio I had been promising myself and I kept trying to envision the house being loved and lived in rather than focussing on all the negatives, but the energy in the house felt vile. The children were having nightmares and getting woken up in the night. My dog had started to become very sick. I decided to space clear the house with the help of sage and candles envisaging white light filling the building but for some reason although it appeared to feel light, it felt like something was hiding in the flat. It was difficult to explain exactly how it made us feel.

I had always had bad periods in the past which were now under control with a contraceptive device and the minute I moved in I started bleeding every day. I had had no problems for years and yet I had been bleeding for more than a month. I had decided to contact a couple that dealt with properties that lay on weird energy lines. They said the house lay in some kind of weird lay line and that there was a presence in the house. That made sense since I had had presences in my old house and got them cleared, however this one didn't go. It was also a presence I could not feel. It felt more like a psychic attack. The dog would wake up in the middle of the night and go out to bark at nothing usually around three AM and I had been waking up to strange dreams.

The dog had become sicker and weaker. I took her to the vet and they could find nothing except a mild inflammation of her blood count. They had put her on some pills and said perhaps she had arthritis which later proved to be nothing. She had refused to move from her bed for nearly two weeks, stopped eating, and wouldn't even eliminate. The cats had started to act strangely and were constantly staring up at things in the flat. I had finally decided I could do more and, in desperation, sought the help of a professional space healer named Eileen Rawson. I had explained to her that I was expecting Oliver to drop some books off to me that he had been keeping and some other things that belonged to me. She asked me to make sure that I let Oliver come in the house before she did the space clearing and not after. She explained that she had a very uneasy feeling about him and to make sure he never came to the house after it had been cleared.

The night before I had arranged to see Oliver, Eileen had suggested he might get even angrier, and the attacks, although not affecting me, were hurting the dog to the point that she looked like she was going to keel over. My daughter came into the room and had started clapping her hands as she went off into a kind of trance like state. I was told afterwards that this is a way of clearing negative energies.

With a house full of moths that had come in the previous night while I was painting the living room, I wondered what would make anyone want to consciously attack someone. Eileen had explained that a person would do it intentionally because they were angry, or jealous or wanted to punish someone.. She too had had attacks from one man that had gone on for years. They just have to visualise their intentions. If, for example, you have a fear of moths (as I do), the attacker visualises a moon inside your home and all the moths being attracted to it. Strangely, there were actually moths everywhere. I even went into the bedroom and they were flying out of the bed sheets even though the light was off. If I hadn't believed in paranormal activity before, then changed my opinion for good.

By facing my own fears, I knew that he would not have the power to hurt me anymore. I had also decided to meet him two days before Eileen arrived. When she had finally come round to clear the house with a combination of space clearing and raising the building's vibrational energy, within about twenty minutes the dog had returned to her normal self and began wagging her tail. The following day, the house felt lighter and my uterine bleeding suddenly stopped after four months. Eileen had explained that there was an unhealthy presence in the house that had been there since we moved in, and that we had probably brought much of the energy from our old house. She stressed it was important that I didn't let Oliver into the house again afterwards. She said he would probably try to contact me within a few weeks with some sob story saying he was sick. He had indeed contacted me three months later telling me that he had left his wife, and, foolishly, I believed him.

When you detach from an energy vampire, he will feel the energetic shift and want to get their fix from you in any way that they can, hence all of the psychic attacks. It's extremely important that you do not play into this. A person can only psychically attack you if you are prepared to have an energetic connection with them. For this reason, I have explained in more detail below how to remove any ties with them by disconnecting and cord cutting. It's not just about "no contact," it's about disconnecting energetically, as well. They really do feel the shift on an energetic level and will do anything they can to regain that connection, physically or energetically.

Exercises in Disconnecting

It goes without saying that the first thing you need to do is to end contact with the Dark Soul in your life. However, some people may still have to maintain continued contact with them if they have family or business connections. I am fortunate enough to never to have to see Oliver again, but the following exercises are highly recommended whether you continue to see them or not.

How the Aura Protects Us

Whether or not you believe you have an aura doesn't matter. It is not really necessary for you to believe or not for the following exercises. If you can visualise, you can do them. However, for those of you that would like to understand a little better, your aura is powerful and sensitive and needs to be treated with the same respect as the rest of your body. The auric field is built up of layers and each layer becomes finer and finer in vibration the further away it is from your body. I won't go into too much detail about the layers of the auric field, but when we let people into our aura, we are letting them into all of us. This includes all of the layers of our energetic imprint and connection to the source. Every time we interact with a person, we take on part of their energy. If we are intimately attached to someone in the form of an emotional or sexual bond, we have formed a cord of attachment. Before doing any cord cutting, you need to make sure that you have released any feelings of anger or resentment as discussed in the emotions section.

The reason you would do a cord cutting is that you are still connected energetically and spiritually. It's a very powerful tool for when you have finished a relationship but may still feel drawn to the person, even though you're aware that the relationship is clearly unhealthy. It is also very helpful when you are feeling frightened of someone or feeling guilty even when you have left them. Relationships that have ended unhappily or unpleasantly may leave negative "strings"   attached. Negative "bonds" are extremely powerful. It is important that you understand that the reason you are cutting cords with the other person is that you are letting them go so that you can take responsibility for your own feelings and for yourself. It is not just about releasing negative emotions, but it puts the person doing the cord cutting in a place of unconditional love. That doesn't mean you have forgotten what they did to you but it moves you into a place of acceptance. The cord cutting technique I use is slightly different from other techniques you may find in other books because I have had to do energetic cord cutting from Oliver more than 100 times. Having done the exercise myself as an experienced healer and also having paid hundreds of pounds to have this done on me with the aid of spirit guides and so on, this particular technique is the only one that has truly worked.

I didn't want to spend the next ten years doing energetic cord cutting every day waking up in the middle of the night. I also remember my mother mentioning that she had nightmares for 10 years after she divorced my father and other victims taking years before they manage to sleep properly. I also mentioned earlier that I had the exercise performed on me by different energy workers and despite all my efforts to heal myself, I still felt "stuck." After doing the following exercise I could not feel Oliver in my energetic space any more.

The reason I believe that it is so difficult to disconnect from a Dark Soul is because they are prone to being energy vampires. If, like me, you are sensitive or an Empath, you'll find this technique is highly effective. It can also be used by anyone. This particular meditation is particularly good because even if the person on the other end refuses to let go of the cords, they cannot reattach because you are facilitating your own healing.

The Cord Cutting Meditation

I have been given permission to use this cord cutting meditation by Will Berlinghof of *www.willberlinghof.com*. Will Berlinghof lives in Calgary, Alberta, Canada. He is the present Interpreter or "channeller" for Cosmic Awareness.

Having used many cord cutting techniques that did not work, I've also paid hundreds of pounds for spiritual healers to cut the cords cut for me. For some reason the cords always had a way of reattaching themselves. This technique is based on a shaman ritual and the reason I find this one so powerful is because it not only takes back your power but binds the perpetrator from energetically hurting you again.

This meditation had appeared in a personal reading Will did for a friend named Vikki. When she had completed the meditation, it was so effective that she was a changed woman, literally dancing for joy because she felt so good. She has requested that the meditation be shared with others, as we all have psychic bonds with many people, both dead and alive, entities who have deliberately or inadvertently created violations, usually when the victim was young. Although not being significant at the time, the violation tied the victim and the victimizer together by the psychic cord for the rest of their lives and into past lives and into lives to come. Cruel statements by parents or relatives, bad or misguided advice that affects one's life, lack of affection by parents and loved ones, cruel and judgemental attitudes by certain entities as the child becomes a teenager, etc. Once this psychic cord is broken, these negative energies and feelings can no longer be felt by either party and as a result one's life becomes more balanced, less frustrating, buried feelings that somehow affect one's life on certain levels are instantly removed and life in the physical is immediately improved. In short, this meditation releases and ends karma that could take many lifetimes to resolve.

"Visualize yourself in a favourite place that you also associate as a very safe and healing place. It may be an actual place or an imaginary one but what is of utmost importance is that you see it as a safe place.

Once in your safe place, see yourself surrounded by a ball of pure white light. This ball of spiritual energy will both protect you and energize your efforts at cutting the cords of attachments to those individuals you wish to cut from. When you are ready, call forth the individual that you wish to cut the negative cords of attachments from.

Once you visualize the individual standing in front of you, look down and see the cord that exists between you. The cord will be attached from navel to navel and is usually dark and thick, although there can be variations on the theme. It is important to realize that you are only cutting the cords of attachment that detract or cause conflict in the relationship, not the positive ties of love and respect that exist between the individuals involved.

Next, look the person in the eye and in a Voice of Power speak the unspeakable to the person that you are doing the cord cutting with. This means that you say anything and everything that you need to say in order to clear the slate and release all pent-up energies and emotions that you have been holding inside but have been unable to express for one reason or another. It is important that you speak in a Voice of Power and Command, even if you could never do so with the person in real life. Remember you are in a safe place and are protected by the Light of Spirit.

Once you have spoken the unspeakable and there is nothing more that you wish to say, you can choose to hear the response of the other person. However, this is your choice and if you choose not to hear the other person this is perfectly alright. If you do choose to be open to a response you will only receive the inner truth of that person/soul, not the responses that you might normally expect from the person. Remember, you are not dealing with the real person but their spirit representation. They will speak only the truth to you if you are willing and able to engage. Once this stage has been completed it is time to move on to the cord cutting itself.

For this, visualize a crystal knife available to you. Take it in whichever hand feels most comfortable. Speak your intent to cut the negative cord of attachment that exists between you and the individual. Holding the cord with your free hand, bring the crystal knife blade down to the cord. Hold the knife next to the body and when ready, cut down and through the cord. If you wish you can say: 'I cut this cord of attachment with you.'

Once you have cut the cord on your side you can offer the crystal knife to the other person so that they can cut the cord on their side. The individual may or may not choose to do so.

If they do, watch the cord fall to the ground, where it is transformed into hundreds of beautiful butterflies which flutter away.

Once the cord has been cut, thank the individual and then send them on their way. If the individual does not choose to cut their side of the cord, wrap the cord around the individual and then banish them from your space. Again, use a Voice of Power to send them on their way.

You are now free to leave the space and end the meditation, or to repeat the procedure with someone else that you wish to cut cords with. You can do this exercise of release as often as you want with any individual you wish to clean up a relationship with. It is important to remember that this procedure only releases the negative attachments that drain, cripple and harm us in some way and not the positive, loving aspects of a relationship. Also if you feel the need to re-cut any cords that have become re-attached for whatever reason, you can do so at your leisure."

Retrieving Your Spiritual Energy

The following exercise is one that I have modified for my own use and I would advise you to ONLY do it when you are in a place of non emotional attachment to the other person. You must not be feeling angry and it can be done in addition to the cord cutting exercise, but wait a week or two before you do it.

This technique is based on a technique used originally when dealing with sexual trauma abuse victims and rape victims. Often we feel when we have been with these Dark Souls that we have been emotionally or spiritually raped, and that whatever we gave to the relationship was stolen from us rather than given freely. In the beginning, we would have easily given them anything but when we are with a Dark Soul, we are left with the feeling that we have been conned and that they have stolen things from us, whether it be financially or emotionally.

The following exercise is very good if you are feeling in a place where you feel like bits of you have been stolen. Unlike normal soul retrieval, you consciously retrieve back all the missing bits of energy that you gave to the other person.

So, to begin the exercise, put yourself in a relaxed place. I did mine in the comfort of a nice relaxing bath. Ensure the room is nice and relaxed, and I would suggest that you turn off the lights and light a candle.

Focus your attention inside of yourself and picture your ex in your mind. Then visualise all of the times when you gave energy to them in the form of kindness, gifts, and so on coming back to you in a stream of turquoise sparks. *Only* focus on the things that you gave to them that left you feeling like they had stolen them from you. Your unconscious mind will know what you need to focus on and what not to. As you lie there in a relaxed state, start to notice streams of light coming back towards you.

Focus on your heartbeat and relax. Imagine that your spirit or life force is a twinkling, sparkling light. You may see some colours, perhaps white, purple, or turquoise.

Now focus on the light that is trapped in the body of the Dark Soul.

Ask your unconscious mind to give you back all of the things they have taken from you in the form of energy and gifts. The following affirmation is useful. "As I lie here, I ask that everything that you stole from me be returned to its rightful place." You should not feel yourself getting emotional and will just feel like bits of your energy field are filling up.

As you lie there, imagine this light leaving their body as a ball of light, travelling back from them into your body. When you feel that you have finished and that all of the bits of you been been returned to you, thank the Dark Soul for returning them to you.

Take in a deep breath and feel your body fill up with white light until you see your whole aura filled with white light. Blow out the candle and go about your normal routine.

I did this exercise for three days running and afterwards I actually stopped thinking about Oliver. Before this meditation, he would have kept popping into my head.

Although I have modified the visualisation, I read on the original website that the energetic shift that abusers feel is very intense. They feel like something is missing from them. On a serious note, you are only taking things back from them that belong to you. You are *not* taking their energy! You absolutely do not want to be taking on any negative feelings or energy that they have, otherwise you will be creating attachments all over again! If the exercise is done properly, you will feel an energetic shift in yourself. I personally felt like my life force had literally come back. The following day I woke up feeling like my old self again. I started back on my diet, was full of energy, and have never had to do the exercise or cord cutting again. In addition all of the psychic attacks have stopped.

Rituals for Healing

Another method to use when healing from abuse is by the use of rituals. There are many rituals you can do to help you heal.

Write a Letter

One ritual you can do is to write a "letter" expressing all the things you always wanted to express to your abuser and never had the chance, courage, or such to do. Be as angry as you need to be, and say as much as you need to say. Then take the letter out to somewhere, preferably in or around nature, where you will not need to visit again. Find a place there where you can safely burn the letter and do so. Feel free to further express your anger by ripping the letter to pieces. Ensure that the pieces are small enough to burn easily. Whilst the letter is burning, release all the emotions and thoughts attached to your abuser. Feel yourself letting go of it all. After you feel as if the ritual is complete, walk away from the place and don't look back.

Also, keep reminding yourself that you are no longer with them because your emotional needs have been sold out to getting your short term needs met. Remind yourself that they are masters at pressing all of your buttons and that you no longer want to constantly service their needs. If you are feeling the need to get your "feel good" buttons pressed in the form of sex remember that a limbic bond is broken in three months, so the longer you can have no contact with them, the better. Go and buy yourself a brilliant book by The Augustine Fellowship, called *Sex and Love Addicts Anonymous*. It discusses toxic relationships and how to heal from them.

Create a Gratitude Journal

A gratitude journal is a way to consciously call attention to the things for which we are thankful each day. When we have come out of a negative relationship, especially if we have lost out financially, we can often stay focussed on the negative feelings. By focusing on gratitude, we become aware of those things and thus create a shift in our thinking for the positive.

Choose a blank notebook or journal to write in every night. Find yourself a nice spiral-bound journal that opens flat for ease in writing. Keep this notebook next to the bed with a pen readily available.

Throughout the day look for things for which you are grateful. These can include anything like "I am grateful for waking up this morning without a headache," or "I am grateful for my friend coming over today and sharing a coffee with me." Focus on everything, however small or great. You may for example write "I am grateful for seeing all the lovely flowers in bloom in the park today."

Every day write at least five things you are grateful for before you go to bed. The more you focus on positive things, the more any obstacles that come up will turn into opportunities. Use positive energy as a magnet to draw even more positive energy. Note these attractions in the gratitude journal. If you want to personalize your journal you can do so with quotes and photographs.

Letting Go

Find anything that reminds you of your abuser and get rid of it. That includes any gifts they have given you or photos you may have decided to keep of them. This just creates an energetic bond and may trigger you back into remembering the abuse, or if you are in a weakened state, remind you of all the "good times." If you have any old emails delete them, include the ones they have sent you. Delete old pictures off your phone and PC.

Oliver had given me a car before he left and I felt extremely uncomfortable driving it. If you have a *anything* that has been given to you by your abuser, sell it or give it away to someone who won't get upset by their energy or needs it more than you. Fortunately for me, the day I was going to put it on eBay, the universe intervened and wrote it off in an accident, when a hit and run driver came down the one way street where my car was parked outside my house. I was surprised when the policeman who turned up was the same policeman who had dealt with Olivers threatening behaviour and he knocked on the door and said "Hello Sarah is this your car" as I look over and saw the mangled mess of the car that had been parked a few yards along. I replied "yes I heard a bang while I was in my living room, it looks like a bit of a mess." He replied "yes it looks like a write off" "are you still having problems with Oliver only the car is licensed in his name." I explained briefly and replied "no not any more, he is gone, he came back briefly, gave me a car and I sent the log book off two days ago." When I asked who the driver was the policeman informed me that they had managed to catch him five minutes later and he had volunteered all of the information. It was just some freak accident. The insurance company paid up and I bought myself a lovely new car. I was so happy and grateful I could not believe how lucky I was firstly that I was not in the car and secondly that I did not have the inconvenience of having to sell it. I even managed to do my bathroom up with the excess money.

I realised that when you start trusting that good things do come into your life and let go of all the bad things then things really do shift.

When I had first asked Oliver to leave I had already lost my house and was living in a tiny flat. I gave away van loads of goods when I moved house because I just didn't have space and sold whatever else I could. However, faced with ever more bills I just had to trust that the money would come in somehow. Every day, I found something to be thankful for. Then, I would continue to go through all the old things I did not need any more and either gave them away to charity or sold them on eBay. The more I would "let go" of things and start appreciating what I already had, the more new things came into my life in the form of money, work, and new clients.

Despite being totally broke the moment I let go of Oliver, work picked up, my health improved, and somehow I have managed to pay all of my bills. I cannot emphasise enough how important it is to let go especially if you have things that connect you to your Dark Soul ex. By letting go of old stuff you allow something better to come in to your life.

Sometimes we hold onto "old stuff" because it makes us feel comfortable, but there is nothing more liberating than letting go of it. Emotionally and energetically, it just weighs us down. Take this opportunity, no matter how much a Dark Soul has abused you, to nurture yourself and use it as an opportunity to let go of everything that you no longer need in your life.

STOP Sign

For those of you who are highly sensitive and who have a deep connection with these Dark Souls, they find it more difficult to break away on an energetic level. I cannot emphasise how important it is NOT to think about these people on an energetic level especially if you are trying to break free from them. Many victims who have relationships with these people feel like they have an uncanny sixth sense and they almost know when the person is about to contact them by phone or text. At the same time the Dark Soul knows exactly when the time is right to contact them again, say for example when you are at your lowest or perhaps when something hasn't worked out for you. This could be by direct contact or could be on an energetic level.

Also when you have done the cord cutting the Dark Sou feels an energetic shift, like a part of them is missing, because they are not getting the energetic "fix" they are used to. They usually up "upping the volume" by trying to reconnect. If they cannot do it on a physical level they may try to do it on an energetic level in the form of a psychic attack.

So long as you stay strong this eventually passes but you must be consistent and not remain in fear. They want you to be afraid and spending the night when you are about to fall asleep wondering if and when they will onnect with you in your dreams is almost certainly likely to draw them close.

If you have managed to maintain No Contact and the Dark Soul is still persistently entering your head, by popping up in your everyday thoughts, go back to the cord cutting exercises and do it again. Then every time they enter your head, as these Dark Souls often do you should feel an energetic shift when you have done the exercises. Put up an image of a stop sign the moment you think of them. Also change what you are doing. If you are on the computer, move away. Think about something different. Just do 'anything' that is the opposite to what you have been doing to break the cycle and eventually you will stop thinking about them.

Psychic Protection

There are a number of different ways you can protect yourself and your aura. I would suggest that those who are highly sensitive do it on a daily basis. Below are just a few ways in which you can raise your vibration and prevent negative energies and thoughts from entering.

One of the easiest and most common techniques for protecting oneself is to simply imagine yourself inside a ball of white light that turns away any energy before it can touch you. When you visualize this ball of light around you, you want to make sure it appears opaque and solid in your mind's eye. This bubble should extend about a foot above your head and at least 6 inches below your feet. It doesn't have to be a perfect sphere; just make it fit around your body in whatever shape seems most comfortable or appropriate. You want to enforce the energy in the areas above and below, to be just as strong as the areas in front and behind you. Some people prefer to visualise it as flexi-glass and imagine any negative energy being thrown at them as just sliding off and unable to stick.

Any vibrations that touch it will simply pass over and around your shield like the wind moving around a mountain. In the rare circumstance that your shield comes up against someone else's, it will bend to compensate, but not break, much like two balloons pressing together. You need to hold the image of an impenetrable force field in your mind for at least a good solid minute or two, before returning to your everyday life. If you hold the image of a very strong shield such as one made of metal or try to put up a brick wall this can be good in extreme circumstances, but can also stop you from engaging with people that you might otherwise want to engage with. You may come across as appearing cold and aloof.

Practice psychic protection at least once a day until your body picks up the habit and begins to naturally reinforce your shields with energy. After a month or two you should be proficient enough that you only need to visualize your shields once a week. If you find yourself in a particularly nasty situation where you need an extra amount of protection, feel free to shield yourself again even if you had done so earlier in the day. As you become more comfortable and skilled at these techniques you will find it possible to reinforce your shield with little concentration and even while you body is in motion or otherwise distracted. If you are feeling what feels like a sudden wave of attack you can use the emergency two fingered mirror technique and if you really need to put your guard up imagine a five fingered wave. This immediately defects any negative energy back to the attacker. Just visualise holiding the mirrors up and the energy dissipates immediately.

You may also choose to wear protective crystals such as quartz, jasper, agate or turquoise. I personally use Labrodite, firstly for its beauty, and because it allows me to sleep at night and prevents nightmares. One of the other stones I used is Black Obsidian. Some people believe that Orgonite as a protective necklace. If you believe it protects you it probably will.

Smudging is excellent for removing negative energy and refers to passing yourself or an object through sacred smoke as a means of purification. When burned, certain herbs release a high vibrational energy that is used to purify unwanted, harmful forces – what most people call negative energy. Herbs like sage, cedar, sweet grass, pine, and lavender can be burned, as well as incenses such as frankincense, myrrh. Simply wave the smoking substance around you and make sure you pass through the smoke. Don't do too much. It's an energetic process, not a physical one, otherwise you might feel dizzy and faint

Sea Salt Baths have the same energetic properties as smudging and feel far nicer. Taking a sea salt bath can cleanse the physical body as well as the energy. Put two tablespoons of sea salt or more in your bath water and soak. If you cannot afford sea salt then use regular salt. Its all about intention. Imagine all the stress and harmful energy you have accumulated or taken on from others flowing into the water. Sit in the bathtub as its drains and imagine it flowing down the drain, neutralized by the salt and water. I personally take one every single day if I can.

Meditation is one of the greatest keys to psychic defence and remaining calm and focussed. Regular meditation practice leaves you clear, centred, and in a mental place where you can respond to potential threats, rather than unconsciously react to them. It doesn't matter the style or tradition of meditation. Regular practice is the key. Book yourself into a class if you have never done it before or start with a guided mediation online. You will not get the long term psychic protection benefits of meditation by doing it only once every few weeks. It must done regularly like exercise or going for a walk.

And finally the best form of psychic self-defence is to live out your true will and potential and move on with your life. What is your divine purpose? If you don't know what it is, then go and find out. Seek answers, ask for messages and you will get the answers. Start trusting your intuition. Then actually live it, breath it and do it. If you are doing what you are meant to be doing, the universe will align itself and support you and very little anyone else anyone does or says will be able to stop you including a Dark Sou. Not only is this the best form of defence but its one of the best ways of getting over a Dark Soul, however difficult the circumstances.

Promise Contract

One of the things I noticed when researching this book is that the kinds of people these Dark Souls target often are resilient and able to bounce back. They are also the type of people who will honour commitments and obligations. Personally I have always tried to keep any promises I make to myself and to others even to my own detriment. Nowadays I only make promises I know will not harm me. For example if I promise my children something I will do it. I never promise them things I cannot afford or promises I cannot keep. If I promise myself I will lose weight I always stick to it. I promised myself I would uncover Olivers lies and I did, I promised myself I would try and understand his condition, I promised myself I would write this book, I also promised myself I would be healed and well within six months of asking Oliver to leave. There are some promises I have never kept, for example I have never promised myself I could pack up smoking, why because perhaps I don't want to.

When we create a promise with ourselves it makes it much more likely to stick to it. I created a promise contract which you can modify for your own use and put up on the wall or keep someone safe. This contract is a contract between you and yourself (or higher power) and no one else. If you believe in god then its perfect - you will be more likely to not break it.

I don't know whether there is a god or not but I do believe there is evil and good and that there is something far bigger than all of us. Call it universal consciousness. Therefore if you do not believe in god. Make the promise anyway because no one else is going to make you suffer more than that authentic higher self part of you that knows everything.

Promise Contract

As of   day,   month,   year. I,   ,
resolve to never again entrust my welfare or self-esteem to someone else
who doesn't appreciate me.

By keeping this promise I have made with myself, I promise that I will no
longer put up with the humiliation, emotional, physical and psychological
burden that comes from being in a relationship with   (fill in name)
.

I promise also to never have a relationship with anyone where I will
invest so much of myself for so little in return.

I make a promise to myself to treat myself with love and respect and to
only have relationships with people who treat me equally. I also promise
to look after my health and my emotional well being and seek answers
and help where necessary.

For those Dark Souls I have the misfortune to meet in my travels I will
pay attention to my intuition and move away from the relationship
immediately them, without judgement or blame, ensuring the relationship
never starts in the first place.

I furthermore take all of the life lessons I have learned and make a
promise to myself to return to my authentic self and not allow my
experience with
              (fill in name)   , to taint any future relationships I have
with people in the future.   That also includes anyone who may be
unfortunate enough to have genuine physical or mental illnesses that need
professional help.

Signed :   Date:

Summary of Steps to Healing

1. Step out of Denial
2. Remove yourself From Inevitable Harm
3. Learn about their Pathology
4. Learn as much as you can about spotting Liars
5. Find a Motivator to Stay Away
6. Find your negative beliefs about yourself as to why you stayed with them and then DO NOT go back
7. Look after your Inner Child
8. Work through your Trauma Worksheets
9. Deal with your Emotions
10. Find A Support Group if appropriate
11. Get any help that you need
12. Deal with any Post Traumatic Stress Symptoms
13. Disconnect from your ex energetically and physically
14. Get rid of EVERYTHING that connects you to your ex
15. Deal with any residual emotions that come up
16. Create a Gratitude Journal
17. Start to Forgive
18. Move into Acceptance, and accept you will never get an apology
19. Sign yourself a Promise Contract
20. Then move on with your life

A final note on Stalking

Since the first publication of this book I decided to add this note on stalking. I changed the name of the person in the book to protect my own identity but having said that it would have been easy for Oliver to find out that I had written a book. I received a number of telephone calls a few weeks after publication during the evenings at my home from a withheld number. The caller would dial, usually around teatime, then when they would hear my voice they would hang up. After nearly two weeks of this and trying to rationalise that it was probably a sales company and that I could be paranoid, the children were starting to feel unsettled. I decided to take a gamble and wrote an email to my ex. It was firm and said that just because I chose not to take any action against him, did not mean I could not. I also explained that this would be the last time I would ask him to stop contacting me. I made it clear how much he had to lose and feigned defeat to some degree whilst at the same time making him think I "might" do something. Since psychopaths and narcissists are hihgly paranoid this is usually enough to keep them off your back. I also asked him not to email me back otherwise I risked him coming back into my life again.

No surprises when the calls immediately stopped after I send the email the following day . I am happy to say there have been none since. Having had a stalker in the past who was quite persistent I have been told by others who have been on the receiving end that sometimes these people will never give up depending on their motives. I wanted to understand why they stalked people and whether their motives for doing it were different depending on their condition. I therefore contacted Sam Vaknin who sent me some articles on stalking and how to deal with them which I have included in brief below. It is important as a potential target to remain firm and to not to become fearful and remember that unless they are a paranoid personality standing firm with these people actually works.

Abuse by proxy continues long after the relationship is officially over (at least as far as you are concerned). The majority of abusers get the message, however belatedly and reluctantly. Others – more vindictive and obsessed – continue to haunt their ex-spouses for years to come. These are the stalkers

Such stalkers come from all walks of life and cut across social, racial, gender, and cultural barriers. They usually suffer from one or more (co morbid) personality disorders. They may have anger management or emotional problems and they usually abuse drugs or alcohol. Stalkers are typically lonely, violent, and intermittently unemployed – but they are rarely full fledged criminals.

Rejected stalkers are intrusive and inordinately persistent. They recognize no boundaries – personal or legal. They honour to "contracts" and they pursue their target for years. They interpret rejection as a sign of the victim's continued interest and obsession with them. They are, therefore, impossible to get rid of. Many of them are narcissists and, thus, lack empathy, feel omnipotent and immune to the consequences of their actions.

A Typology of Stalkers

Stalkers are not made of one cloth. Some of them are psychopaths, others are schizoids, narcissists, paranoids, or an admixture of these mental health disorders. Stalkers harass their victims because they are lonely, or because it is fun (these are latent sadists), or because they can't help it (clinging or co-dependent behaviour), or for a myriad different reasons.

Clearly, coping techniques suited to one type of stalker may backfire or prove to be futile with another. The only denominator common to all bullying stalkers is their pent-up rage. The stalker is angry at his or her targets and hates them. He perceives his victims as unnecessarily and churlishly frustrating. The aim of stalking is to "educate" the victim and to punish her.

Hence the catch-22 of coping with stalkers:

The standard – and good – advice is to avoid all contact with your stalker, to ignore him, even as you take precautions. But being evaded only inflames the stalker's wrath and enhances his frustration. The more he feels sidelined and stonewalled, the more persistent he becomes, the more intrusive and the more aggressive.

It is essential, therefore, to first identify the type of abuser you are faced with.

The Erotomaniac - This kind of stalker believes that he is in love with you and that, regardless of overwhelming evidence to the contrary, the feeling is reciprocal (you are in love with him). He interprets everything you do (or refrain from doing) as coded messages confessing your eternal devotion to him and to your "relationship". Erotomaniacs are lonely, socially-inapt people. They may also be people with whom you have been involved romantically (e.g., your former spouse, a former boyfriend, a one night stand) – or otherwise (for instance, colleagues or co-workers).

Best coping strategy - Ignore the erotomaniac. Do not communicate with him or even acknowledge his existence. The erotomaniac clutches at straws and often suffers from ideas of reference. He tends to blow out of proportion every comment or gesture of his "loved one". Avoid contact – do not talk to him, return his gifts unopened, refuse to discuss him with others, delete his correspondence.

The Narcissist - Feels entitled to your time, attention, admiration, and resources. Interprets every rejection as an act of aggression which leads to a narcissistic injury. Reacts with sustained rage and vindictiveness. Can turn violent because he feels omnipotent and immune to the consequences of his actions.

Best coping strategy - Make clear that you want no further contact with him and that this decision is not personal. Be firm. Do not hesitate to inform him that you hold him responsible for his stalking, bullying, and harassment and that you will take all necessary steps to protect yourself. Narcissists are cowards and easily intimidated. Luckily, they never get emotionally attached to their prey and so can move on with ease.

The Paranoid - By far the most dangerous the lot. Lives in an inaccessible world of his own making. Cannot be reasoned with or cajoled. Thrives on threats, anxiety, and fear. Distorts every communication to feed his persecutory delusions.

Best coping strategy – Avoid at all costs. If you have to change your phone number email address or even move house then this may be the only option.

The Antisocial (Psychopath) - Though ruthless and, typically, violent, the psychopath is a calculating machine, out to maximise his gratification and personal profit. Psychopaths lack empathy and may even be sadistic – but understand well and instantly the language of carrots and sticks.

Best coping strategy - Convince your psychopath that messing with your life or with your nearest is going to cost him dearly. Do not threaten him. Simply, be unequivocal about your desire to be left in peace and your intentions to involve the Law should he stalk, harass, or threaten you. Give him a choice between being left alone and becoming the target of multiple arrests, restraining orders, and worse. Take extreme precautions at all times and meet him only in public places.

12

Acceptance

People who hurt you are only people hurting themselves. When you forgive others you release yourself from their energy and take your power back from them. When we are unable to forgive and accept, blocks build up, our personal power is given away and energetic damage can accumulate within our physical bodies, leading to more and more stress that only prolongs the healing process.

One of the best treatments for post traumatic stress is EMDR therapy. I first contacted Gill Blayney, a local EMDR practitioner who also specialises in treating people with Post Traumatic Stress Disorder. It was a few months into writing Dark Souls and every time I wrote, I would sit at the computer and get sucked back into the story. I didn't want to feel victimised any more so I thought there must be some emotion I am not processing. I had already gone through all the other feelings of shame, guilt, and anger, but I had never thought that the emotion that would come up for me during the treatment would be "acceptance."

One of the things we tend to struggle with as victims of Dark Souls is that they will change and feel remorseful for what they have done. Even a simple, genuine apology is sometimes enough to allow a victim to move on. However, a Dark Soul never feels genuinely sorry for anything unless, of course, they get caught. They will naturally feel sorry for themselves if they have narcissistic tendencies, but, in essence, a proper apology is unlikely to ever happen. Certainly don't expect to get a proper, heartfelt apology, if anything at all.

I had come out of the treatment realising I had been battling with myself in trying to accept the situation. Shortly after I had come out of hypnosis, a big smile came over my face. Gill appeared to have the same sense of humour as me and I remember thinking "The truth is there are loads of bastards out there and it could have happened to anyone." Once I had accepted the fact that, yes, he really was a bastard, and, yes, it could have happened to anyone, it was then that I had stopped beating myself up for the last time.

On the way over, I had driven past Oliver's old house, a beautiful mansion paid for by the inheritance from his family. I had seen his wife's car parked outside and guessed she had still had the gumption to stick to her guns and not have him back. I thought about all the things that had happened, all the lives he had ruined, and as I pulled out of the driveway onto the country lanes, I decided to call him up. It was the last call I was ever going to make to him. I knew in my heart he would not answer the phone. After all, what would he say?

Besides, I had made it very clear I never wanted a relationship with him again but this call was for me, not for him. I knew Oliver wouldn't answer, so I left him a voice message. I said: "I have just driven past your house, the beautiful house that you had loved so much, and I have been thinking about all the other things you loved so much as well, your children, your mum, and my kids, and seeing how much pain and misery you have caused to everyone around you, your mum, your wife, and children. You had everything, Oliver: a lovely house, a beautiful wife, a lovely girlfriend, who would have done anything for you, and yet you hurt and destroyed everyone. And for what? Because you could not keep your dick in your trousers. You lied to everyone. Now you have nothing. You have a wife that hates you, a mother that does not respect you any more, a girlfriend that doesn't want to ever see you again, and all because you couldn't be honest."

At that point I had let go and accepted whatever he was, whether he was a Dark Soul , a narcissist, a psychopath or any other label. What I did know was that he was the one who would be left feeling empty for the rest of his life, and that was punishment enough.

Many people talk about forgiving abusers. However, there is much debate as to whether we should actually forgive them or not, especially when they actually don't care whether we forgive them or not. I believe that a Dark Soul tries his best to never really allow us to forgive them properly. They will always leave us with something that stops us from forgiving them completely. We are then left with a choice as to whether we want to carry on having an energetic link with them or not. I was left with a feeling of complete indifference towards him.

It's at this point in the healing journey when I would advise anyone who has had a run-in with a Dark Soul to think of them as a normal human being and to forgive them utterly and completely. It doesn't mean ever *forgetting* what they did, but if you do not take the responsibility yourself, you will be stuck in the energy of them forever.

They cannot change the way they are. They will continue to do what they do, but you have a choice. You can choose to change. You can choose to leave them. You can choose not to be a victim anymore and, you can, as a result of no longer being with them, choose to lead a more fulfilling life.

In order to truly forgive the person who has hurt us and let go of the relationship with them, one has to live through the pain and all of the emotions. We cannot hide from the feelings of anger and hate towards that person, however intense it makes us feel. Otherwise, they will just rear their ugly head again in the future. We must truly forgive, which is why it's actually okay to be angry.

If we do not forgive them, it leads to resentment. However, when we are able to let go of this, we learn to forgive other people for what they have done to us and, more importantly, we can finally learn to forgive ourselves. This is the most important thing. We have to forgive ourselves and stop feeling guilty for getting into a relationship with them in the first place. We can stop beating ourselves up and remind ourselves that it's not our fault, and it could have happened to anyone. Forgiveness of people who have hurt us is not a sign of weakness; it simply prevents their negative impact on us from continuing to influence our lives, and this allows us to move on.

Once we have truly healed from these people we can go back to being the people we once were. But take all of the lessons learned, and move on. We are able to help others and become all of what these Dark Souls are not. Whatever they did to us, they cannot steal our souls. They are here to remind us, however much they have damaged us, that we can come back stronger and happier than we were before we met them, without that "victim" label glued to our heads.

Patti Henry, M.Ed., psychotherapist and author of *The Emotionally Unavailable Man*, talks about all of the types of men who can and cannot be healed. When speaking of sociopaths, she emphasizes that we, as the victims, spend all of our time trying to make a Dark Soul "get it," yet the minute we "get it," we become free. She goes on to say:

> "If you are living with or married to such a man, he will not be able to be emotionally available to you -- ever. He can be charming and make you feel like he's there for you, but in the next beat rip you to shreds without it disturbing his morning coffee...women involved with sociopaths spend much of their time and energy and LIVES trying to get their partner to "get it." Sadly, they can't get it...It's so against our very fiber that says we can do anything, fix anything, work harder and come up with a solution. I'm sorry. Some

things do not heal. This is one of them."

As Dr. Silvia Hartmann, founder of *Event Psychology*, suggests however you deal with your trauma, call it Dark Souls, a Guiding Star, or the events so extraordinary and unknowable that we can't say if it was good or bad, only that something did happen, and that your world will never be the same again.

All I can say in conclusion to this exploration into alternative views on psychopathic personalities and their affect on their victims, and based on my own experience, is that through extensive cord cutting, and therapy, combined with working on my negative core beliefs about myself as to why I had been attracted to Oliver in the first place, I am now healed and very happy.

Many years ago when I first trained as an acupuncturist I complained to one of my lecturers during clinical practice and asked why was I one of the only students in the clinic to attract patients with emotional problems rather than those that just had bad backs or migraines. She replied "Sarah, The universe doesn't always give us what we want but it *always* gives me what we need". She further went on to explain that acupuncture is useful for everything and if I only had training in bad backs and migraines then I would have never learnt how to treat other people. As a result of my training I have helped many people who had emotional problems and specialised in helping people overcome emotional problems and depression. Since that day I have never complained about what type of patient comes to see me and see it always as a learning experience.

With regards to why the universe felt I needed to have a relationship with Oliver , I believe I met him to teach me how to understand him, to not take it personally and I know now my future lies in having an existence free of Dark Souls however charming and lovely they appear on the outside. The most important lesson it taught me was how to love myself without condition. I may still well attract them on the odd occasion, but I can spot them before they spot me, and I no longer have anything resonating inside of myself that makes me want to enable them. I certainly wont be having a relationship with one ever again.

We all have a choice and there is a beautiful Chinese story from the Ming Dynasty. There were two brothers, whose temperaments were very different, even though they had the same parents. The elder brother was greedy and lazy, and always haggled over every detail. The young one was diligent, decent and affectionate. One day, they went out in a cart to do some business. It was raining and the road was slippery. The elder brother lost control of the halter and they fell down a cliff. They came to the netherworld. A guard, who was already waiting outside the court, took them to the King of Hell. The King of Hell said to them: "Since neither of you has done anything exceptional nor any very bad thing, both of you will be reincarnated as human again. Judge! Check whether there are families who are going to have babies."

The presiding judge studied the Roster of Life and Death carefully and said: "My King, two families, the Zhao and the Xie, are having predestined sons. The son of the Zhao will be giving aid to others when he grows up, but the Xie's son will be receiving help from others." The King of Hell said: "Such being the case, let these two brothers to be born to these two families."

Upon hearing the King's decision, the elder brother thought: If I am born to the Zhao's family, I will be working hard and giving support to others. I will be too busy running about helping others. It would be more leisurely and comfortable to receive help from others. Upon making up his mind, the elder brother knelt before the King: "My King, it will be too hard to work all my life for others. I beg your mercy to let me born to the Xie's family so I will receive help from others." The King asked: "Who will be born to the Zhao's family then?" The younger brother said: "My King, let my elder brother be born to the Xie family. I am willing to be Zhao's son and help others in need."

The two brothers were thus born to the Zhao and the Xie families, respectively. Because of his vow to help those in need, the younger brother was born to the noble and rich Zhao family. When he grew up, he was benevolent and always helped others in need. Because of the wealth of the Zhao family, he was able to help many others.

But the elder brother, whose wish was to get help from others, was born to the poor Xie family and he had to beg for the remains of meals and always received charity and sympathy from others.

As the saying goes, "To give is richer than to receive." It is most precious to have humanity. When people have kind hearts, heaven will help them.

I end my story with my most favourite quote of all times from my hero: a man by the name of Bills Hicks. His humour challenged mainstream beliefs, aiming to "enlighten people to think for themselves." His jokes included general discussions about society, religion, politics, philosophy and personal issues. Hicks' material was often deliberately controversial and a bit risqué and was steeped in dark comedy.

Unlike Oliver, who lied about having cancer, Bill Hicks died of pancreatic cancer which had spread to his liver in1994, at the age of 32. In the years after his death, his work and legacy achieved the significant admiration and acclaim of numerous comedians, writers, actors, and musicians alike. He was listed as the 19th greatest stand-up comedian of all time. Whenever I listen to his humour I always smile. I leave you with one of his most famous quotes:

"Life is like a ride in an amusement park. And when you go on it, you think it's real, because that's how powerful our minds are. And the ride goes up and down and around and around. It has thrills and chills and is very brightly coloured. And it's very loud and its fun for a while.

Some have been on the ride for a long time, and they begin to question is this real or is this just a ride? And other people have remembered and they come back to us and say 'Hey, don't worry, and don't be afraid, ever, because this is just a ride,' and we kill those people.

'Shut him up, I have a lot invested in this. Shut him up. Look at my big bank account and my family. This has to be real.'

It's just a ride.

Why do we always kill the good guys who try and tell us that? Did you ever notice that? And we let the demons run amuck. But it doesn't matter because it's just a ride. And we can change it entirely, it's all in the choice, no effort, no work, no job, no savings of money.

Just a choice right now between *fear* and **love**."

Leaving Dark Souls is not about judging them. It is not about blaming them or feeling superior to them. It is about our readiness and the capacity to change in ourselves. It is also about changing our own vibration so that we no longer attract them or feel the need to have them in our lives anymore. Dark Souls come into our lives as a gift to teach us that we can evolve into a being with higher vibrational qualities because we have chosen to leave the dead weight behind us and unravel the emotional knots that kept us bound to them in the first place. It's just a choice. Some loves come into our lives not to last forever, but rather, to teach us lessons. Try to see the relationship you had with a Dark Soul as a lesson in how NOT to have loving relationships. Then, take this as your signal to learn them - otherwise, the universe will continue to present you with the same opportunities, by upping the volume over and over again… until you do!

Once you've separated fact from fiction and found the lessons in your relationship, it's time to put all your hard work into practice and move on and get back on the amusement ride without them.

Just like Bill Hicks, I couldn't shut up and keep quiet. This is why I've told my story, so that it would help others. I hope this book has inspired you and that, whatever your life's purpose, you will remember that you cannot be kind to others unless you start being kind and loving to yourself first.

It goes without saying that being kind to yourself does not include being a Dark Soul, and that you heal with love and a great big dollop of humour.

NOTES

Numbers in boldface indicate page locations

1   "Life is like an amusement Ride" Bill Hicks

3   "I often torture myself" Sociopathworld.com

7   " you will feel an odd sensation in your solar
              plexus ...." Don Miguel Ruiz *'The Four Agreements'*
              Jan. 2001

13   "Black Hole" - Dr. Michael Millett (M. MSC) with the
              University of Metaphysics, Sedona, Arizona, USA

15   "But the point is, he just doesn't care...." - Steve Becker
              LCSW licensed clinical social worker and a writer for
              Lovefraud.com

17   *'Emptied Soul'* - Adolf Guggenbuhl-Craig

17   *The 'Mask of Sanity'* - Hervey Cleckley

17   "have a 'walk in' soul that takes over their bodies" -
              Eileen Rawson, medium and healer

25   American Psychiatric Association. Diagnostic criteria
              for 301.7: Antisocial personality disorder. *Diagnostic
              and Statistical Manual of Mental Disorders, 4th
              Edition.* American Psychiatric Association, Washington,
              DC, 1994.

32   "The Ego in healthy people" - Sam Vaknin Ph.D

32   "The Narcissist's sense of entitlement"- Sam

Women Who Love Psychopaths' - Sandra L. Brown, M.A.

68   *'Infidelity Unwrapped'* Sarah Strudwick

79   *'A theory of cognitive dissonance'* Stanford, CA: Stanford University Press Festinger, L. (1957)

79   *'Cognitive consequences of forced compliance, Journal of Abnormal and Social Psychology'*, Festinger, L. and Carlsmith, J. M. (1959)

80   "Men tend to lie by exaggeration" - *'Infidelity Unwrapped'* Sarah Strudwick

84   "Repeatedly women told me about the unusual bonding experience they had with psychopaths." - *Women Who Love Psychopaths'* - Sandra L. Brown, M.A.

89   *'Understanding the Batterer in Custody and Visitation Disputes'* - Lundy Bancroft 1998

93   *'Silent Treatment'* - Steve Becker LCSW licensed clinical social worker and a writer for *Lovefraud.com*

96   "Anyone who questions the validity of his statements" - Sam Vaknin Ph.D. *'Malignant Self Love - Narcissism Revisited'*

101   Gaslight' is a 1944 remake of a 1940 mystery-thriller film adapted from Patrick Hamilton's play starred Ingrid Bergman, Charles Boyer, directed by George Cukor

101   'Gaslighting: A marital syndrome. Journal of Contemporary Family Therapy' Gass and Nichols,Gass, Gertrude Zemon and William C. Nichols. 1988.. Journal of Contemporary Family Therapy

101   'Creepy Crawler burglaries' Victor George *'Witness To*

Evil'

Self Love – Narcissism Revisited

Sources of Help

Worldwide

Lovefraud.com Information resource site for sociopaths providing support for victims. Run by Donna Anderson.

Bullyonline.org A website for bullying both in the workplace and relationships. It also had much information on Post traumatic Stress disorder.

United Kingdom

www.ptsduk.co.uk A good information site with a 24 helpline number 01788 560800 . They are also able to refer you to a relevant specialist who deals in Post Traumatic Stress

www.samaritans.org UK: 08457 90 90 90
ROI: 1850 60 90 90

www.rapecrisis.org.uk Freephone 0808 802 9999

Recommended Reading

Understanding Your Negative Core Beliefs - John Nutting

Women Who Love Psychopaths - 2nd Edition – Sandra L. Brown

The Four Agreements - A Practical Guide to Personal Freedom, A Toltec Wisdom Book – Don Miguel Ruiz

My Journey to an Integrated Life – Melinda Sorrensen

The Zahir: A Novel of Obsession – Paulo Coelho

Psychic Self Defense – Dion Fortune

Empowered by Empathy : 25 Ways to Fly in Spirit – Rose Rosetree

Stillness Speaks - Eckhart Tolle

Malignant Self Love: Narcissism Revisited - Sam Vaknin Ph.D

Facing Co-dependency – Pia Mellody

Why does he do that? - Lundy Bancroft

Sex and Love Addicts Anonymous – A basic text for the Augustine Fellowship, Sex and Love Addicts Anonymous

The Emotionally Unavailable Man: A Blueprint for Healing - Patti Henry

The Narcissistic Family: Diagnosis and Treatment – Stephanie Donald-Pressman – Ronald M. Pressman

Living with the Passive-Aggressive Man: Coping with Hidden Aggression - From the Bedroom to the Boardroom - Scott Wetzler

The Journey: An Extraordinary Guide for Healing Your Life and Setting Yourself Free – Brandon Bays

In Sheep's Clothing - George Simon

The Sociopath Next Door – Martha Stout

The Mask of Sanity - Hervey Cleckley M.D

Without Conscience - The Disturbing World of the Psychopaths Among Us –
Robert D Hare Ph.D

Snakes in Suits – When Psychopaths go to work – Paul Babiak, Ph.D and
Robert D Hare, Ph.D D

*Remarkable Healings: A Psychiatrist Discovers Unsuspected Roots of Mental
and Physical Illness* - Dr. Shakuntala Modi

*Stop Walking on Eggshells: Taking Your Life Back When Someone You Care
About Has Borderline Personality Disorder'* - Paul T Mason, Randy Krieger

*The Gaslight Effect: How to Spot and Survive the Hidden Manipulation Others
Use to Control Your Life* – Dr Robin Stern

Why Good People Do Bad Things: How to Stop Being Your Own Worst Enemy
– Debbie Ford

*Bad Boys: Why We Love Them, How to Live with Them, and When to Leave
Them* – Dr. Carole Lieberman

Women who love too much - when you keep wishing and hoping he'll change –
Robin Norwood

Life his father - Dr Liane J. Leedom

Appendix

I wrote this poem for Oliver when he first had a lump removed on his head which he said was cancerous. Sadly he decided to tell me the cancer had returned, only this time to his throat.

The poem is called the *The Mirror* and it was supposed to help Oliver find ways to help him get over his throat cancer. Of course it never existed.

People are bought into our lives for a reason and in hindsite perhaps this poem was a poem I needed to write to myself.

This poem is my gift to all those people who have had relationships with Dark Souls and the *cancer* is an analogy for the toxic feelings we are left with if we stay with them.

The Mirror

Its another year on and our dreams are all shattered
All that we hoped for and all that had mattered
Your eyes are still sore from crying rose coloured tears
You now face your own demons as I have faced my own fears
That cancers a f***er it will keep on returning
If you don't pull out its root that lies in your heart yearning
I'm not talking about things that give you heartache and strife
I am talking about You, and what you want in your life
Its much easier to forget to just get on and do
Numbs the brain and the senses and our soul too
So I found you a mirror that was special and good
It was tucked in the cellar and carved in oak wood
Its hidden for years in a dusty old room
It holds answers to secrets and all of the things that you hide
Yet you fear looking in because of your pride
When you look in the mirror tell me what do you see
Is it you, your children, your spouse, or me
I think none of the above, because the view isn't clear
Its just smeared with anger and guilt and fear
Pull the cloth from your pocket and start to erase
All the smears on the mirror, and start clearing the haze
As you wipe away layers of dirt built over time
You will fight back the tears as you clean off the grime

Your fingers are hurting - you cant rub anymore
You'll leave it for now; there's a knock at the door
"Oh I'll deal with it later" you say to yourself
No one cares for that old mirror - so you put it back on the shelf
But you cant do that; its too special to leave
The woods starting to rot and it needs air to breath
The mirror is tarnished you must do it in time
It takes forever to polish and bring back the shine
Then you will look in the mirror it will all become clear
With each rub of the cloth you have have faced all your fear
As you look in the mirror you see only YOU
No kids, no lover, no spouse - my god what will you do?
Say hello to yourself for the first time in years
Don't mess up the mirror again with your tears
Its a special mirror that needs nurture and care as do you
If you look after it well it will be honest and true
It will reflect all your dreams your hopes and fears
But the maintenance polish is not your own tears
Its only small; not much bigger than a locket
If you keep it with you always it will fit in your pocket
Just remember to look after it as I try to do
And it will always be kind to you and let you be YOU

Sarah Strudwick 2006